"SCHOOL IN THE CLOUDS"

THE RIFT VALLEY ACADEMY STORY

Philip E. Dow

William Carey Library
Pasadena, California
www.WCLBooks.com

Published by
William Carey Library
P.O. Box 40129
Pasadena, CA 91114
(626) 720-8210

The Library of Congress has catalogued this book as follows:
Dow, Phil, 1970-
"School in the Clouds": the story of the Rift Valley Academy / Phil Dow.
p. cm.
Includes bibliographical references.
ISBN 1-87808-357-X (pbk.)
1. Rift Valley Academy (Kijabe, Kenya)—History.I.Title.
LG418.5.K54D69 2004
372.9676'27—dc22

Cover Artist: Soulfisher Design

PRINTED IN THE UNITED STATES OF AMERICA

To

THE COMMITTEE (1987 – Present)

CONTENTS

ACKNOWLEDGEMENTS

RESEARCHING AND WRITING THIS BOOK HAS BEEN deeply rewarding, perhaps because it has been a lot of hard work. I have an entirely new respect for people who seem to effortlessly turn out books that are both well written and significant. For me the process has been anything but effortless. Nevertheless, it has been a wonderful adventure; and one made all the more enjoyable by the companions I have had along the way.

Since this is my first book, there is a felt need to thank everyone who has had even the most remote influence on my life – Haile Salasse (next to whose palace I entered this world); the "rag-n-bones man" from my London childhood; Idi Amin, whose atrocities indirectly led me to Christianity; Jimmy Thomas, my second grade African-American friend in Minnesota who couldn't believe a freckled-faced white kid could be from Africa; and a host of other randomly significant people. For obvious reasons, I have narrowed my written appreciation to the following.

Thanks needs to go to the staffs at AIM Headquarters in New York, the Billy Graham Center Archives at Wheaton College and Rift Valley Academy in Kenya – all of whom allowed me access to their records and provided me with warm hospitality while I was there doing research. The title of the book was inspired by a *Washington Post* article on the school by Susan Okie in 1993.

One of my tests of friendship over the past six years has been the willingness of people to listen to me read out yet another revision of yet another page or chapter. Those who have been especially gracious in this regard include: Aaron Westlund, Mark Schaler, Rick Bransford and the rest of the Ashworth Estate, Thor Barkman, Tim Willig, my sisters Christy and Katharine; and, of course, my wife – Catherine.

Several people were willing to read and comment on significant portions of the manuscript. These include: Dr. Jay Case (Malone College), Dr. Kevin Boyle (Ohio State University), Dr. Mark Shaw (NEGST), Dr. Jonathan Bonk (OMSC), Dr. Neal Shipley (UMass-Amherst), Peter Nyoro (Oxford University Press-Nairobi), Sue Devries, my parents Stewart and Elaine Dow, members of the faculty and administration at RVA, Dick Brogden, Christy Dow Murray, "Professor" Josh Flosi; and, of course, my wife – Catherine. Any evidence of mediocrity or any errors that still remain in the book are entirely their responsibility. More seriously, the thought of this book without their corrections, comments and insights is not a pleasant one. If there are portions of this book that are praiseworthy, much of the credit belongs to them.

Others have not read portions of this book but have profoundly influenced the course of my life during the time that I was working on this book and have my deep gratitude. In no particular order they are: Professors Bruce Laurie and Milton Cantor (UMass-Amherst); Professor John Klassen (Trinity Western University); Professors Andrew Brown and Alister McGrath (CMRS, Oxford) because I realized under their brief tutelage that I was capable of producing history of value; Dr. Jason Baehr and Sara Ritchey (CMRS); Andy Barker (Umass-Amherst); Scott Dolff (Yale); the faculty and students at The Bear Creek School (Redmond, WA) and Rosslyn Academy (Nairobi, Kenya) and "The Committee" to whom this book is dedicated.

WHY THE RIFT VALLEY ACADEMY MATTERS

MY AMERICAN HISTORY CLASSES AT THE BEAR CREEK School (TBCS) were generally a mix of American and international students. I mention this only because as a teacher it was my goal that by the end of the year my students would have gained a deep understanding and appreciation of America's story; and if I was to have any chance of succeeding in this quest I had to be acutely aware of the differing concerns of my audience. Did they already see history as being important; or were they, like most teenagers, profoundly skeptical of its relevance to their lives? Bearing in mind that some of them had only lived in America for a short time I asked myself, what was their prior knowledge of American History? What emotional ties did they have to the subject matter? And how would that affect the way they approached the content?

Because my students at TBCS were divided into these two distinct audiences I saw the need to begin my course from two different but complementary angles – one directly aimed at my American student's quest for identity, both individually and nationally, and one that was directed at inspiring an intellectual thirst in the class as a whole. Towards the first aim of appealing to my American student's search for identity I developed a short exercise.

As my students got seated on their first day of school, I placed a short paragraph on the overhead that read, "You are standing on a beach in tattered clothes. You don't have any idea of who you are, where you are or why you are there. You see a ship on the horizon, and occasionally through the vegetation surrounding the beach, you see a figure or two – one of whom seems to be holding a long pointed object. What do you do?"

Once the students had written down their responses, the discussion would begin. Inevitably, the practical students looked for some form of personal identification, but none was to be found. Occasionally an adventuresome, albeit shortsighted, student would decide to swim to safety away from the island's dangerous inhabitants. Still others determined that "the best defense is a good offense" and attacked the indigenous people. After fleshing out their responses with a few clarifying questions, I would reveal the real situation. "You are on a school sponsored environmental clean up project at a nearby beach. You wisely chose to wear your tattered work clothes for the project; but you don't remember this because, toxic gases have caused you to temporarily lose your memory. And, incidentally, some of your classmates are in the bushes employing the garbage collecting devices used at amusement parks."

Having put the pieces together, the students would often burst into laughter at the ridiculous, and often tragic, responses they had to their situation. Images of themselves desperately swimming to "safety", attempting to send smoke signals or attacking one another were funny because this was simply an analogy, and there were no real consequences. Yet, this lighthearted analogy has extremely serious implications. Certainly, unless we know who we are, where we are, and how we got there – we can have little idea of how to act wisely in the present. In other words, we study our past to better understand ourselves; and in doing so are able to live more purposeful and meaningful lives.

While, in this case, the importance of historical identity is more clearly applicable to the American students, the next mini-lesson was directed towards the class as a whole. As intellectually precocious as my students were, they were not immune from an apparently universal inclination among teenagers to see history as irrelevant. Therefore, instead of trying to prove in one decisive blow that history matters, I found that it was much better to embrace the skepticism. To this end I told my students that there was one question they should bring with them to class every day – and that was, "who cares?" In other words, why should anyone give a second thought to any of this? How could what they were studying possibly have any bearing on the present, let alone their own lives? As long as the question is asked in good faith, there is simply no better or more important question to ask regarding history. In fact, it is a question that you should be asking of this introduction. Who cares? What relevance do these quaint anecdotes have to the history of the Rift Valley Academy?

In writing this book I have had in mind two distinct audiences. Like my American history class, each audience will come to this book with different but equally important concerns. The first audience is made up of those people who could be or have been directly touched by the school - either as students, faculty or parents. For thousands of these missionary families, former students and faculty the Rift Valley Academy has been a literal Godsend. The school has meant an opportunity for a quality education within a Christian community and a bridge between cultures. As a result, it has allowed missionary families to remain in Africa without forever compromising their children's chance at a healthy and successful life in their home cultures. This was certainly my experience as an alumnus of RVA. Yet my experience is but one of many. Some students have endured prolonged loneliness, others the weight of community judgment, merciless gossip or any number of personal and cross-cultural struggles. In short, not everyone has left as deeply grateful as I did. It is for these people, as much as for myself, that I write this book. For we were all dramatically impacted by the years we were a part of this community. Like generations of students before us, a significant part of our identity is wrapped up in this institution. And so, whether we come to thank or forgive the school, each of us must begin by understanding it, and understanding means starting at the beginning.

The second audience for this book is those who have not been directly touched by the school or perhaps even the missionary movement itself, but have a more general interest in either the history of Africa or Christianity. It is from this audience that I expect the question – "Who cares?" What possible significance can an isolated boarding school in the middle of Kenya have to the grand and global themes of African history, British Imperialism or the history of Christianity and Christian missions? Allow me to briefly outline what I see as compelling reasons for taking a closer look at this apparently inconsequential American institution.

For starters, whether they like it or not, anyone with an elementary knowledge of modern world history will concur that the Christian missionary movement has had a profound influence on the evolution of cultures worldwide. This is perhaps no more strikingly illustrated than in Kenya. According to David Barrett, the past century has seen the percentage of Christians in Kenya rise from less than one percent to approximately eighty percent currently. While not exclusively responsible for this remarkable development, British and American missionaries have been absolutely critical to the growth of Christianity in Kenya and elsewhere. Again, there is abundant evidence of this reality in Kenya, where the largest protestant denomination (AIC), and several other significant groups, were initiated and continue to be directly or indirectly supported by American missionaries. Thus, as the world becomes increasingly interconnected, attention to the role of these agents of globalization will only increase. Indeed, considering the significance of this development it is remarkable that historians have given so little attention to it to date.

Because a significant American missionary presence in Kenya is the present reality, many of us assume this development to have been inevitable, but this is not at all the case. Early on, the potential influence of American Christians worldwide met a significant barrier not faced by their British counterparts. Unlike the British missionaries, who could benefit from the colonial education system, the Americans did not have a way to adequately educate their children for the unique demands of life and higher education in their home country. For many would-be American missionaries, the question of educating their children was not simply a practical one, but went to the core of their Christian faith. All but the most extreme American missionary parents saw themselves as having two equally sacred callings: (1) the missionary calling; and (2) the calling to Christian parenthood. The blatant sacrifice of their children's lives to the call of missions was a price many felt God would not ask them to make. Hence, without a school able to meet the unique needs of the American missionary community it is likely that their presence in Kenya (and East Africa generally) would have been significantly curtailed.

Thus, as the story of the most successful attempt by American missionaries in Africa to educate their own children, the school's story is profoundly significant. For having apparently solved the problem of educating their children, American missionaries were freed up to invest their lives in Kenya and East Africa in a way that they did in few other regions. As the children studied at RVA, their parents were busy educating African children, translating indigenous languages, training church leaders, building schools, hospitals and churches, and sharing their Christian faith. Indeed, nearly every child at RVA throughout its history has represented a missionary couple actively involved in the spiritual, educational and political evolution of East Africa.

But the Rift Valley Academy did not simply house missionary children. Instead, it was actively and intentionally involved in producing future missionaries. As I write, there are countless examples of second, third and even fourth generation missionaries in East Africa – most all of whom were taught and molded by this school. And the impact of this phenomenon of multi-generational missionaries has been significant. While some descendents of these missionary dynasties have simply perpetuated their parent's occasionally myopic vision of American evangelicalism, others have been profoundly influenced by their African childhood. For these missionaries, their African experience translated into a deep respect and admiration for Africans and African culture. Increasingly, the result has been a missionary presence that is generally more culturally sophisticated and sensitive than that of earlier generations. Second generation missionaries have also played a significant role in the development of a relationship between the national church and the missionary community that is more explicitly egalitarian. This evolving relationship, in turn, has been at the center of the development of the uniquely African evangelicalism that now pervades the politics and culture of contemporary Kenya.

Finally, the story of the Rift Valley Academy is fascinating and important in its own right. As our world continues to shrink, RVA stands out as an ideal case study for the complex and increasingly global phenomenon of "third cultures". In this case the culture that has evolved at RVA is neither entirely Kenyan, nor American, nor British, nor any other of the myriad cultures which compose it, but something entirely unique and new. One could argue that, for this reason alone, the Rift Valley Academy is worthy of scholarly attention.

In short, while the story of the Rift Valley Academy represents only a part of the dramatic, larger narrative of the modern missionary movement in Africa, the part it does represent is significant. The school's part is significant because of its role in encouraging substantial growth in the American missionary presence in East Africa. It is significant because of its role as a greenhouse for future missionaries – missionaries who have been at the center of the development of a uniquely African evangelicalism and the growing conception of Christianity as a global religion. It is significant as an example of the modern phenomenon of "third cultures". And it is significant because of its profound influence on the lives of thousands of students, parents, staff and faculty who have been intimately tied to the school throughout its one hundred year history.

CHAPTER 1

THE RIFT VALLEY ACADEMY
IS BORN: 1896-1911

IT WAS LATE IN OCTOBER OF 1901 WHEN CHARLES Hurlburt and his small party of missionaries stepped onto the planks leading up to the transatlantic steamship that would be home for their two-month journey to British East Africa. The days before the departure of the Africa Inland Mission's (AIM) second team were filled with the bustle of last minute preparations and the anticipation of what promised to be the most meaningful adventure of their lives. Yet, as they anticipated separation from loved ones, there was also a sense of grief, not to mention a profound fear of what lay ahead. For unlike the CNN world of today, a dense fog of mystery still hung over Africa. Stories of cannibals, witchdoctors, disease and primeval greed had been circulating in Europe and America for as long as anyone could remember. It did not help matters that most of the new tales brought back by the growing fraternity of European explorers only added to the skewed stereotypes of the "Dark Continent".[1]

---

[1] Beginning with Scotsman Mungo Park in 1805 and culminating with the legendary David Livingstone in the 1870's, European explorers and pioneer missionaries of the 19th Century traced the source of the Nile, crossed the Sahara and penetrated into the very heart of Africa. An excellent collection of primary source accounts of this exploration can be found in Basil Davidson's, *African Civilization Revisited*, pgs.319, and 347-353.

Imagine the intensity of the farewells in the New York Harbor that October morning. Goodbye could very well mean forever, and everyone involved understood this. Of the first group of AIM missionaries who went out just six years previously only one had remained on the field. Three of the group had returned home gravely ill and three others, including Peter Cameron Scott - the mission's Scottish founder, had died in Africa.[2] Even for those fortunate enough to remain healthy and safe, letters home took anywhere from six months to a year to arrive – if they arrived at all. This was not the separation of summer revival camps or college terms. This separation felt like death. Death to intimate friendships. Death to cherished places. Death to life as they had known it.

Hurlburt's tiny band of pioneer missionaries knew the potential costs of the task ahead of them, but they boarded the ocean-liner anyway. Why? Historians have been at loggerheads in an attempt to explain how otherwise normal people could have taken a risk of this magnitude. Some have concluded that groups like Hurlburt's were both conscious and unconscious agents of nationalistic imperialism and industrial capitalism. Others have suggested that guilt-driven humanitarianism or religious fanaticism were primarily responsible for this odd behavior. The truth is that in some cases each of these motivations might have been present. Yet admitting that a host of motives were involved in the missionary movement at large doesn't answer the more pointed question we are confronted with. Why did this particular band of nondescript AIM pioneers step onto that ship that cold October morning?

Aristotle put forth what seems to be a prudent rule of thumb when attempting to understand why people do what they do. Ignore speculation and hypothesizing altogether – judge people by their words and actions. With this in mind, let's examine Hurlburt's band of missionaries. What did they say and what did they do?

The African Inland Mission was extremely clear about their intentions to spread the Christian message in Africa. In the very first issue of their newsletter *Hearing and Doing* (January 1896) the goals of AIM were spelled out as follows:

> The purpose of the African Inland Mission is easily stated... In the Soudan region are sixty million human beings who have never heard

---

[2] Tignor, Robert. *The Colonial Transformation of Kenya*, 117, & *A Short History of AIM*, p.9. Published in 1903, a copy remains at AIM's headquarters in Pearl River, NY.

the name of Christ in praise, prayer, or promise. Six thousand a day are going down unwarned, ungospeled to eternal death. This vast host is today practically untouched by the message of Christ...(We) purpose to enter and do all that faith, and zeal, and love can do to aid in evangelizing (Africa).[3]

It is significant to note that AIM's claim of a "practically" non-Christian East Africa in 1896 was entirely accurate. In 1900 the number of Christian Africans in British East Africa was no more than five thousand, less than .2% of the population.[4] And even these converts were relatively new, having come into contact with Christianity through the tiny number of Catholic and Anglican missionaries who had begun to trickle into the region after 1850. If AIM's goal was, as they said it was, to spread the message of Christianity to those who had yet to hear of it, they were certainly going to the right place.

Thus whether one approves or disapproves of AIM's evangelistic intentions, there is no ambiguity in their stated motives. But what of their deeds? As the next several chapters will attest, the actions of AIM are consistent with their spoken intent. In short, they meant what they said and said what they meant.

AS WE WILL see material or political ambition was not the driving force behind AIM. However, the birth of the missionary movement did coincide with the Second Industrial Revolution and increasing European nationalism. And it is clear that at times Hurlburt and his band of missionaries benefited directly from imperialistically driven projects. One such project was the railroad from Mombasa to Uganda. Dubbed by one London magazine the "Lunatic Express", the stalled railroad sat only partially complete upon the AIM team's arrival.[5] Progress had been slowed due to the now infamous man-eating lions of Tsavo. As a result, terrified Indian workers brought to British East Africa for the purpose of building the railroad had on several occasions refused to work. Even when they did work, malaria, dysentery and ubiquitous termites slowed progress to a snail's pace. By the time the railroad reached its final

---

[3] *Hearing and Doing*, "The Work", January 1896, pgs. 3-4.
[4] Barrett, David. *The Encyclopedia of World Christianity*, "Kenya". Oxford University Press, Nairobi: 1982. By the turn of the millennium approximately 80% of the Kenyan population counted themselves Christian.
[5] McFerrin, Linda, "Rail Tales" printed in the Travel Section of the Nov. 9, 1997 Seattle Times.

destination of Uganda, over 2,400 Indians had died and over five million British Pounds had been spent.[6]

By the time Hurlburt's party arrived in 1901, the "Lunatic Express" could only provide a two hundred and fifty mile train ride on a Toonerville Trolley. The train averaged a lethargic ten miles per hour and at times slowed to such a pace that Mr. Hurlburt joined the conductor as he walked alongside the train to take aim at the plentiful and unsuspecting game.[7] Writing home, Hurlburt expressed his first reaction to his new home:

> For twenty five miles inland the country presents an attractive appearance, large and beautiful mango trees, tall coconut palms, banana plantations and various tropical fruits, but it gradually loses it, becoming more and more barren, the trees assuming a gnarled and twisted shape, as though they had come forth reluctantly.[8]

When the missionaries exhausted the available train tracks one hundred miles short of Nairobi, they were forced to rely on ox carts and foot power to see them to their immediate journey's end.

The second example of imperialism's small but growing presence in East Africa at the time was, of course, Nairobi. What the AIM party found sitting on the site of today's bustling modern city was an insignificant and fragile colonial outpost comprised of a few simple shops, some humble homes and an administrative post, all inhabited by an eclectic collection of colorful personalities. In a sense early Nairobi was Old Britannia's Dodge City. Indeed, events surrounding the young outpost were in some respects analogous to the American West. Although virtually ignored in many texts on Kenyan history, during this period a small British force and their native auxiliaries were fighting various tribes who had allied themselves against the newly arrived Europeans. At least twenty-five pitched battles took place between 1898 and 1903 in which upwards of 6,000 Africans were killed.

By the time the AIM missionaries arrived most of the African combatants were fighting either to protect their lands or were using the British to enlarge their own lands. There were simply too few Europeans to create the tension that was to come later. However, while at this point

---

[6] Edgerton, Robert B. *Mau Mau: An African Crucible*, 1.
[7] The story of Charles Hurlburt can be found at the AIM headquarters in Pearl River, NY. It is unpublished and untitled save "C. Hurlburt" written in pen, 7.
[8] Ibid, pgs. 7-8.

only 1% of African land was taken, there is some evidence that the Kikuyu in particular were beginning to harbor deep-seated resentment against the European newcomers.[9] In 1902 an entire village killed one new settler. The method was especially disturbing. While the European man was pegged to the ground with spears, a stick was thrust into his mouth to keep it pried open. This done, the entire village took turns urinating into his mouth until he died of drowning.[10]

However, this graphic example stands out in stark contrast to the general atmosphere in early colonial Kenya. Hurlburt and his group were not walking into a land full of bloodthirsty tribes. Writing just a year later from AIM's new mission station at Kijabe, John Stauffacher wrote (perhaps somewhat naively), "How everything surprises me here. There are none of the dangers I dreamt about... The people here are perfectly safe have none of those peculiar customs you hear about."[11]

The choice of Kijabe as the center for AIM's activities also reflected the political and material objectives of the colonial government. There had been at least two temporary headquarters for AIM prior to the move to Kijabe. Machakos, the most recent, was ultimately rejected because of its fifteen mile distance from the railroad – what amounted to a long day by ox-cart. With proximity to the railroad a primary concern, Hurlburt took a trip up and down the Lunatic Express in search of the ideal location for a permanent mission home. It was among the green grasses and acacia-lined shores of Lake Naivasha that Hurlburt stepped off the train convinced he had found the proper spot. By the time he arrived at Naivasha and met with the colonial administrator it was late in the afternoon; and while his request for a land grant was met with approval by the colonial officer, because of the late hour, it was decided that the 99-year lease would be formalized in the morning.[12]

---

[9] Oliver, Roland & F.D. Fage. *A Short History of Africa*, 176.

[10] Edgerton, Robert B. *Mau Mau: An African Crucible*, 5.

[11] This letter from John Stauffacher to his future wife Florence Minch on Feb. 22, 1903 can be found in the Billy Graham Center Archives at Wheaton College under "F-1; Box 2; CN281".

[12] Taken from a speech given by longtime AIM missionary and author Shelley Arenson to the faculty and students of RVA upon the commencement of the Stanley and Livingstone Games during the 1996-97 school year. A note on the railroad: without the railroad access of missionaries and other colonists to Kenya's interior would have been limited and it is quite possible the numbers of both groups (especially the colonists) would have been radically curtailed. This rightly assumed, the entire history of the region would have been different.

Fresh from what must have been a night of optimistic planning, Hurlburt returned early the next morning to the news that during the night the land had been given to someone else. Unbeknownst to Hurlburt, the newly arrived Lord Delamere was also at Naivasha and had joined the colonial administrator for several drinks later that evening. When told that the Naivasha land was going to go to the missionaries, Delamere was indignant. He believed an excellent piece of farmland like that should not be wasted on missionaries. Instead he proposed that he should be given the land and with that the long standing Delamere Dairy at Naivasha was established.[13]

Hurlburt was forced to settle for a second choice, a flat clearing half way up the escarpment known as Olikijabe or Kijabe. The sparse villages surrounding this land were inhabited primarily by the Kikuyu, who themselves were relative newcomers to the area. Late in the 19th Century, the Kikuyu began moving down from Mt. Kenya in the hopes of finding more land. When they arrived, the primarily hunting and gathering Dorobo people inhabited the Kijabe area. Central to the diet and culture of the Dorobo was honey and, prior to the arrival of the Kikuyu, the task of finding and extracting honey from the natural beehives had been a long and potentially painful process. Much to the delight of the Dorobo, the Kikuyu brought with them their own manufactured beehives. As local folklore has it, with land to spare, the Dorobo began buying the Kikuyu hives at approximately 1 for every ten acres of land. When most Kikuyu families sought between 30 and 40 acres, the price of 3-4 beehives was standard. As more and more Kikuyu moved into the area, the Dorobo either moved on or intermarried into the Kikuyu. Many Kikuyu in the area still trace part of their family line to a Dorobo grandparent or great grandparent.[14]

While a second choice, Kijabe had all of those elements that were most important to Hurlburt – proximity to the railroad, a central location and a healthy climate.[15] At 7,200 ft., Kijabe was above the malaria belt and remained moderately cool in contrast to the suffocating heat regularly experienced in the valley below. Yet, the choice of Kijabe was not without its naysayers. Beyond the wild animals that posed a regular

---

[13] Ibid. The various exploits of Lord Delamere are infamous in Kenyan colonial lore. Countless stories abound of drunken dances across tables, sexual trysts and so on. Nevertheless, Delamere was respected in many ways for being (when sober) a kind and honorable man.

[14] Ibid.

[15] Ibid. The name Kijabe, or "Olikijabe" as the Masai called it, means, "hill of the cold wind".

safety concern anywhere in Kenya, it was believed that the high elevation of Kijabe would leave the missionaries susceptible to "Kenya nerves" -- a mythical neurological disorder that led to acute anxiety and other psychologically linked ailments.

Proximity to the sun was another concern for many. It was said that the sun's "actinic" rays caused a whole host of conditions from a loss of memory and high blood pressure to various female disorders and sterility. Winston Churchill, when visiting Kenya as a young man, was encouraged to wear a hat both in and out of doors as the tin roofs were considered insufficient to keep out the sun's deadly rays.[16] This fear was to linger well into the 1930's when hats and pith helmets were required for the young scholars at RVA.[17] Nevertheless, in 1902 Hurlburt and the fledgling AIM missionaries began to construct the rudimentary structures that would serve as their homes and the beginning of what was to become the largest mission station in Africa.

EVEN THOUGH FEW, if any, missionaries publicly expressed it, the unavoidable concern of educating their children was constantly beneath the surface. Hurlburt himself had five children; and by 1906 at least one other family at Kijabe, and several families at other mission stations around Kenya, had children of school age. While the mission acknowledged the need for education, the policy was that education was the responsibility of each family and not the mission.[18] This put the missionaries in an awkward position. To AIM, its supporters, and of course the missionaries themselves, the all-consuming vision was the work of winning souls. More than any other mission in East Africa, AIM was unswervingly evangelistic. D.L. Moody voiced the AIM perspective stating, "(there must be) subordination of all other concerns... to soul-saving and practical Christianity".[19] This is the sacred task they had been called to. Yet, as Christian parents they also had the sacred task of raising their children; and in the modern world ignoring the education of their children was tantamount to abandonment. If there was no school, who then would teach their children? When no options were forthcoming the missionary families faced a choice. Either

---

[16] Edgerton, Robert. *Mau Mau: An African Crucible*, 12-13.

[17] A list of necessary school supplies for the scholars at RVA during the 1930's can be found at the Rift Valley Academy, Kijabe, Kenya.

[18] This interview of longtime RVA principal Herb Downing by Robert Shuster (June 14, 1983) can be found at the BGC Archives under "T1 CN251".

[19] Marsden, George. *Fundamentalism and American Culture*, 43.

return to America and forsake their missionary calling or stay and apparently compromise their parental calling.

Despite the Home Council's position that the mission bore no responsibility for the education of missionary children, Hurlburt quickly recognized that a school was essential to the future of the mission. Accordingly he began to take practical steps to turn this vision into a reality. In 1906, on the return passage from a furlough in America, Hurlburt approached a new AIM missionary, Miss Josephine Hope, with a strange request.[20] Knowing that she had had extensive experience teaching in Montessori schools, Hurlburt asked if she would be willing to teach the children of their missionaries.[21] Although Miss Hope had intended to use her experience in African education, she accepted the request and began to prepare for the task of starting a new school.

The first classroom was in a mission house at Kijabe. The basic room consisted of a 10-ft. square tempered earth floor and no desks or educational equipment. Canvas covered the rough unfinished walls and a sagging ceiling of unbleached muslin kept insects, straw and twigs from falling from the thatched roof above.[22] Even though the first four students progressed surprisingly well in their studies, it was clear to the school's founders that the school could not succeed for long as it was. When the chapel building was finished six months later the school was moved there. [23]

By 1907 the chapel was broken up into four rooms where Miss Hope taught both white and African students. Despite the common roof, the two groups were seen as distinct both in terms of educational goals and privileges. Of the four rooms in the chapel, two at one end were devoted to the larger African school. At the opposite end of the chapel was one room devoted to the "white" school. Separating the two schools was a room used by Miss Hope and the irregular set of missionaries who offered temporary, and often times begrudging, assistance at the schools.[24]

This physical division between the white and African schools was extended to the curriculum. It was the opinion of AIM that the purpose

---

[20] Anderson, Dick. *We Felt Like Grasshoppers*, 205.

[21] This unpublished article by RVA's first teacher Miss Josephine Hope can be found within a number of documents, most notably the unpublished story of the Downing family by the eldest daughter of Lee Downing entitled, "Our Roots". This can be found at the BGC Archives in the AIM collection.

[22] Ibid, & Anderson, *We Felt Like Grasshoppers*, 205.

[23] "Our Roots", 36.

[24] Anderson, *We Felt Like Grasshoppers*, 207.

of African education was first to achieve the literacy needed to read and understand the Bible and second to provide the limited skills needed to succeed in the largely agricultural Kenyan economy. Because of this perceived need, a rigorous college preparatory education was not seen as necessary. The African students, therefore, were taught in the morning and then given leave to return home in the afternoons to help with the family livestock or farms. The white children, whose goal was Bible College or university, continued in their studies until mid-afternoon.[25]

Even before Miss Hope agreed to become the first teacher at RVA, Hurlburt's vision for a school had received a major boost. During Hurlburt's furlough in 1905 a wealthy friend had asked him what the most pressing needs of the mission were. Among other things, Hurlburt had mentioned a school for the children of AIM missionaries. Nothing more was said, but sometime in 1908 that gentleman donated a large sum of money in the name of his stepmother, Mrs. Butterworth, to be used in the building of a school for missionary children.[26]

Shortly after the Butterworth funds had been donated, Hurlburt and Miss Hope began making plans for a new school building. While the plans were a group effort, Hurlburt took charge of finding the ideal location for the school and Miss Hope worked on the layout of the school's interior.[27] The site eventually decided upon was a plot of scrub brush and small trees at the north end of the mission station known to the local Kikuyu as Kiambogo, "place of the Buffalo", because of the regularity with which these temperamental beasts visited the area.

Prior to the Butterworth funds, RVA was capable of serving a student body of ten students – a size barely sufficient to meet the needs of the small number of missionary families in Kenya already, and certainly not enough to allow for growth of that movement. Although the current numbers did not suggest the need for a larger facility, Hurlburt and Hope believed that a larger school would allow for an increase in the quality and quantity of American protestant missionaries to East Africa. Therefore, the ambitious plans developed by Miss Hope included the necessary classroom and dormitory facilities to house at

---

[25] Stumpf, Hulda J., "Rift Valley Academy" Inland Africa. April 1919, 7&13. A periodical has been published by AIM regularly from 1896 to the present. It was called "Hearing and Doing" until 1916 when its name was changed to "Inland Africa". Copies of every edition are bound in both the BGC Archives at Wheaton and AIM's archives at Pearl River.

[26] Interview with "Doc" Propst by Rich Dilworth, Aug. 9, 1997. This will soon be available at the BGC Archives in Wheaton.

[27] Stumpf, Hulda J., "The Rift Valley Academy" *Inland Africa*. April 1919, 6-7.

least forty students comfortably. There were to be classrooms, a kitchen, a dining commons and a library on the first floor. On the second floor was the dorm parent's quarters sandwiched between the girl's and boy's dormitories. Beneath the building were a couple of storage rooms and a set of catacombs which were destined to be the home of countless adventures for generations of students to come.[28]

Actual construction began in 1909. Three kilns were made and trained Indian masons, in Kenya because of the railroad, were hired to fire the bricks called for in the building's plans. Unfortunately, the difficulties and dangers of the railroad followed the Indian workers and within a short time the largest kiln burst into flames and was destroyed.[29] Convinced that producing bricks was too dangerous; some of the workers left the site for good. Evidently Hurlburt agreed, because a search was begun for a local stone with enough substance to build.

It was another, primeval, kiln which produced the material eventually chosen as the most suitable rock for construction. Several kilometers from the site of the mission station, a substantial semi-volcanic rock was found. With this discovery the most arduous and tedious part of the labor became the chiseling and transportation of Mt. Logonot's ancient offspring to the mission compound. This intensely physical work was carried on by almost 200 African workers.[30] Thus, from the lava and ash of Africa's womb came forth the cornerstone of the Rift Valley Academy – the Kiambogo building.

HURLBURT'S 1905 FURLOUGH led to another significant milestone in RVA's history. As a community pillar and former leader of the YMCA in Philadelphia, Hurlburt's decision to go to Africa as a pioneer missionary had received considerable notice. Visions of a wild and untouched Africa continued to fire the adventuresome imaginations of many in America, not the least of which was then President Theodore Roosevelt. The ultimate adventurer, Roosevelt was already beginning to plan a hunting safari to Africa with his son Kermit when he heard that Hurlburt was in America. Always a man of action, Roosevelt promptly sent Hurlburt an invitation to meet with him at the White House. The meeting itself lasted several hours and left both men with a high regard for the other. In fact, years later Roosevelt remembered Hurlburt as, "the

---

[28] Ibid.
[29] Entwistle, Roy. "The Rift Valley Academy, Kijabe, Kenya From 1946-1966: Problems and Progress". Unpublished MA Thesis at Seattle Pacific College, 1968, p5.
[30] Ibid.

greatest man he had met in Africa".[31]   In return for Hurlburt's advice Roosevelt promised to help AIM gain entry into the Belgian Congo – a miraculous story in its own right – and accepted an invitation to visit the mission station at Kijabe when he arrived in Africa.[32]

In 1909 shortly after leaving office Roosevelt came to East Africa. The first of Roosevelt's three trips to Kijabe came in June of that year. In his diary, later published as *African Game Trails*, Roosevelt remarked that, "At Kijabe I spent several exceedingly interesting hours."[33]   It was during this first stopover that Roosevelt was asked to return in August to lay the cornerstone for Kiambogo, which he did on August 4, 1909.

The event was not only momentous for AIM, but for the fledgling missionary and settler community in British East Africa.   When the fourth of August came around, Kijabe found itself the sudden (and temporary) center of colonial life.   British and Dutch farmers, government officials and other missionaries converged on the mission station – some coming on foot from as far away as forty miles.[34] Roosevelt understood the importance of the occasion to the community gathered at Kijabe, as well as to the larger humanitarian movement many of these men and women represented.   Thus he began his remarks saying:

> Mr. Hurlburt, I think I need hardly say that it is a real and great pleasure to me to be here today, and to take my part at the laying of the cornerstone of the building, which I believe will be associated with real and permanent good to the people of East Africa, and which will be associated with an amount of good which we cannot at present foretell.[35]

Understanding that the school was to act as a vital support for the humanitarian and economic development envisioned for the region, Roosevelt spent considerable time addressing the big picture before

---

[31] As quoted in Stephen Morad's unpublished Ph.D. dissertation at the University of Edinburgh entitled, "The Founding Principles of the African Inland Mission and Their Interaction with the African Context in Kenya From 1895 to 1939: the Study of a Faith Mission", 1997, p. 145.

[32] Downing, Lucile (?). "Our Roots", 38 & "C. Hurlburt", 47. For more information see #'s 9 & 24.

[33] Ibid.

[34] Anderson, Dick. *We Felt Like Grasshoppers*, 206.

[35] Banks, Howard (ed.). "Mr. Roosevelt at Kijabe", *Hearing and Doing*, Sept. 1909, p. 8.

focusing in on the future of the school itself. It is interesting to note that in his comments on the larger goals of the group assembled at Kijabe, Roosevelt reflected, to some degree, their complex and at times contradictory sentiments. For instance, his comments early on reflect a vision for an independent and self-governing Africa. He stated:

> I am so pleased that your effort be so largely to teach the teachers and train the trainers among these tribes; that you are trying to turn out people who shall go back and live among their own fellow-tribesmen and raise them, not to become make-believe or imitation whites, but by going back to their own people and helping to train them along lines which will prevent the reproach, that after all this is only a white man's affair... You turn out leaders who are to take the lead in the uplifting of their own race.[36]

Even so, it is clear that Roosevelt held that the African people were yet so primitive that the task of their advancement remained largely in the hands of the superior white civilization. To this effect he remarked, "It is our plain duty, Mr. Hurlburt, I mean that it is the duty of all white men who occupy positions in the tropics, whether it is in the Philippines or British East Africa or any place else, to try to help the backward race...".[37]

Concerning the school itself, Roosevelt commented, " When I was traveling through the country, I was interested in coming to two or three houses where they spoke of this school as the only possible place for having their children trained... Much can be done through this school, and I am happy to say that it is evident... it will be a particular pleasure to me when I go back to my own country, to report what is being accomplished by this interdenominational mission."[38]   With that Teddy

---

[36] Ibid. 6.

[37] Ibid. 7. One of the many transcripts of this speech even quotes Roosevelt, shouting above the wind after the formal speech had finished that, "If you give me a chance in London or anywhere else, I will talk just as straight as I can... that this is destined to be a white man's land". What is significant about this transcript is that it was excluded from AIM's official transcript of the speech. Why does that matter? If it was in fact said, it is significant because it implies that AIM and the editor of *Hearing and Doing* were opposed to (or at very least uncomfortable with) the racially charged colonizing project from an early date.

[38] Banks, Howard (ed.) "Mr. Roosevelt at Kijabe", *Hearing and Doing*, Sept. 1909, p. 6-8.

Roosevelt returned to America, leaving behind a cornerstone with the words inscribed, "Laid by Hon. T. Roosevelt Aug. 4, 1909".[39]

MEANWHILE AS THE building began to take shape, Miss Hope continued teaching with only the most basic of resources and a haphazard staff. Every missionary with AIM was in Africa primarily to evangelize the pagan African. As a result, most were highly reluctant to teach in a school of mostly Christian white children.[40] That was the work of pretenders, not the lofty stuff of the Livingstones, Moffats and Careys. This attitude became even more pronounced when Miss Hope left in 1910 to secure better educational resources for RVA in America. During this period the students were forced to learn under an assortment of sulking and ill-prepared teachers. In this way the children of missionaries often became the victims of a sort of reverse discrimination. A pattern began at this time which was to last well into the 1940's. When a missionary was specifically "called" to teach at RVA, the school made significant strides forward. In contrast, when missionaries were forced to teach at RVA due to illness or a temporary lack of teachers, the school and its students struggled. Lucile Downing, who was a student at RVA during these first years, recalls this pattern:

> (I have) beautiful memories of some of my teachers who were gifted and dedicated… then I have memories of others! Occasionally the Field Council had to force people to teach a term or two at RVA. Many felt that teaching white kids was not mission work – they had come to Africa to work with Africans! Some were qualified; some were not, and most of this group were not only unhappy themselves, but made life miserable for the students.[41]

Other troubling patterns also surfaced during these important foundational years. The most significant of these concerned the perspective prevalent within AIM on the role of the intellect in the Christian's life and the relationship between equality and race. We will begin by looking at the attitude towards the mind within AIM during these foundational years. Like Hudson Taylor's China Inland Mission before it, the AIM grew out of the holiness movement as propagated by

---

[39] Downing, "Our Roots", 28.
[40] Anderson, Dick. *We Felt Like Grasshoppers*, 207.
[41] Downing, "Our Roots", 43.

D.L. Moody in America and the Keswick movement in Britain.[42] This transatlantic movement held fiercely to several ideas that helped to determine the education that was to take place at RVA. First, the movement placed the salvation of the soul above all other concerns. C.T. Studd reflected this sentiment a few years later saying:

> Christ's call is… not to build and furnish comfortable chapels, churches and cathedrals at home in which to rock Christian professors to sleep by means of clever essays, stereotyped prayers and artistic musical performances, but… to capture men from the Devil's clutches.[43]

This intense concern for the soul is seen in the issues of *Hearing and Doing*, where there are more references to the spiritual state of the students than to the rest of the school's affairs combined.[44]

This single-mindedness leads directly to another concern intimately connected to the ideas expressed by Studd. The very zeal which gave AIM its evangelistic fervor often excluded other "simply good" aims. Academic pursuits were especially suspect because excellence in this realm was often linked to pride and an excessive reliance on human reason, both of which were seen as contrary to God's will for His people.[45] Therefore, because the goal of education was the conversion and sanctification of the soul, with academic excellence lying a questionable second, RVA began as a unique educational institution – one whose educational strivings were constantly kept in harness by a pervading mistrust of that very endeavor.

The second troubling attitude concerned race. The segregation found in the schools at Kijabe was not motivated by practical considerations alone. It also reflected the prevailing attitude in western culture concerning Africans, as well as the reluctant attitude of many Africans towards education. To the western mind, Africans were primitive and needed to be brought up slowly, like children. This virtually universal attitude had at least two key sources. First, in the mid 19th Century Darwin's theory of "survival of the fittest" was applied to human affairs with disastrous consequences. Social Darwinism argued that human

---

[42] Marsden, George. *Fundamentalism & American Culture*, 77-78.

[43] As quoted in Elizabeth Isichei's *A History of Christianity in Africa*, 89-90.

[44] A periodical has been published by AIM regularly from 1896 to the present. It was called "Hearing and Doing" until 1916 when its name was changed to "Inland Africa". Copies of every edition are bound in both the BGC Archives at Wheaton and AIM's archives at Pearl River.

[45] Isichei, Elizabeth. *A History of Christianity in Africa*, 89.

affairs are best left unregulated, for in a state of nature the best ideas, the brightest minds and the strongest bodies would succeed to the ultimate benefit of posterity. When applied to the practice of making colonies the end result was open and unrepentant racism. As one professor declared at the turn of the 20th Century, "The path of progress is strewn with the wreck… of inferior races… these dead people are in very truth, the stepping stones on which mankind has risen to the higher intellectual and deeper emotional life of today."[46]

The second source of this pervasive racism is exemplified by the writings of Rudyard Kipling. Kipling's perspective is especially significant because it best encapsulates the view of most missionaries during this period. Kipling was a paternalist. It was his contention that while every human being was equal, regardless of race, superior values in one society inevitably allowed that society to rise above the others. The superior society then had a moral obligation to act as teacher to its less advanced peer. While not strictly a racist, Kipling was guilty of using generalizations which, when combined and confused with Social Darwinism, led to a pervading prejudice that influenced society at every level.[47] It was a perspective that influenced the early work of AIM at every turn.

The situation was further exacerbated by the fact that even if AIM had wanted to give a comparable education to the Africans, and even if the Africans had initially pushed for the same, there were simply no opportunities in the racist European society of British East Africa for educated Africans. In short, what had already developed was a self-perpetuating web of racism that had caught AIM and was to last well into the second half of the 20th Century. In *A Short History of AIM*, published in 1903, the depictions of Africans are so horrid one wonders how the missionaries even consented to the use of the same building for both schools. It reads:

> The inhabitants of this section of Africa are of the Bantu race, and totally uncivilized, being almost entirely naked, save as their bodies are

---

[46] As quoted in McKay, Hill and Buckler. *A History of Western Civilization*, 282.

[47] It is helpful at this point to draw a distinction between the "hard racism" of Social Darwinism and the "soft/paternalistic racism" of Kipling's *The White Man's Burden*. The former believes that any inequality in the races derives from genetic inferiority, while the latter argues that any inequality derives from inferior moral/cultural values which lead to a less advanced civilization. Race is theoretically irrelevant to the "soft" racist.

covered with shells and beads or weapons of warfare… To see those naked black creatures crawling out from the low doors of their tiny huts, and note their revolting filthiness, impresses one with their moral degradation and their lost condition. Polygamy prevails… Many of the natives raise sugar cane, from which they make an intoxicating drink… Their filthiness in food matters is beyond all description, and … Their gross ignorance rather than proverbial indolence leads to frequent famines.[48]

Yet, this thread of racism which was to weave its way through RVA's history was rarely as critical in nature as the description above would have us believe, and it was always more complex. Even the harshest statements were modified by the biblical notion of equality before God and concern for the African's spiritual and physical improvement. In fact, the entire missionary enterprise had at its basis the premise that all humanity was made in the image of God. And it was this conviction, when taken to its logical conclusion, that would one day bring a demand for equality.[49]

AN ADDITIONAL ATTITUDE that can be found from the school's inception concerns the philosophy of behavior. The Holiness movement believed that beyond the initial salvation experience there was a second conversion of sorts – a process similar to what Wesley had called "sanctification". The mark of a true Christian, whether African or Anglo-American, was a life that had been externally transformed by the internal work of the Holy Spirit. The practical result of this idea was a heightened awareness of, and interest in, the external evidences of faith. This interest led to a general conception of what was the "Christian way" to behave, to dress and to live. While not directly related to RVA, the following occurrence can give the reader some idea of how this worldview translated into everyday behavioral expectations and discipline at RVA. On Sunday, May 7th 1910, Mr. Hurlburt went to Ukamba to baptize several African boys. Concerning this event, the *Hearing and Doing* of April 1910 states:

---

[48] *A Short History of AIM*, 15-19. This is available at the AIM archives, Pearl River, NY. This history was not published and the author is unknown.

[49] The truth is that while many of the early AIM missionaries come off looking quite racist when compared to the perspective of today, they were, in general much more liberal than their contemporaries.

There were two younger lads, both true, earnest, devoted Christians, as we believe from the record of their lives, Kaliuki wa Kivati and Uka wa Mukima. Each of these had for two years or more given evidence of the change of heart and life wrought by the power of God. They were asked six questions, separately, before all the people assembled.

1st. Whether they accepted and would obey all the words of God as written in His word.

2nd. If they refused to accept the affairs of the (evil) spirits.

3rd. If they refused all the evil customs of their tribe.

4th. If they refused to drink native beer and use tobacco.

5th. If they would agree not to marry more than one wife.

6th. If they would refuse to accept to accept the ithitu (native charm).

All of these were answered satisfactorily.[50]

What is evident from this passage is the realization that the founders and faculty of RVA conceived of Christianity, to a significant degree, as a list of necessary behaviors. The merits or faults of this view are not our concern – only the implications of this view upon the behavioral expectations for RVA students. Because the school had no system of disciplinary precedents and guidelines to instruct the small and irregular faculty, the implication of this view was a discipline system that had the potential to be either lovingly firm or oppressively tyrannical depending on the adult enforcing it.

The adult who was in charge of most of the discipline in the early years was, of course, Miss Hope; and while most agreed that she was strict, the majority believed her discipline was of the loving kind. Erik Barnett, who was under Miss Hope both at RVA and later at the Westervelt Home stated, "We didn't chafe at the discipline. We were there to learn as best we could. As far as I know, everyone of us had an early call to missionary service."[51] A young woman at Columbia Bible College commenting on Miss Hope's character stated, "Whatever mistakes she might (have made, the scholars) accepted that she meant it for their good."[52]

Unlike the underlying themes of AIM's single-minded evangelistic fervor and potential tendency towards legalism, the final issue was not recognizable beyond 1914. When Miss Hope first came out to British

---

[50] Banks, Howard (ed.). "A Witch Doctor Saved", *Hearing and Doing*, April 1910, p.10.

[51] As quoted in Dick Anderson, *We Felt Like Grasshoppers*, 208.

[52] Ibid.

East Africa in 1905, she came as a trained Montessori teacher. At the time many viewed the Montessori method of teaching as a cutting edge educational theory. But as we are about to see, it was also the last educational philosophy one would have expected to find at the onset of RVA's educational enterprise.

Based on her vast international experience with children, Maria Montessori believed that there were general/universal principles guiding child development.[53] The foundational Montessorrian principle was that of "self-formation". This was the idea that children have innate tendencies and interests. Because of this, the first task of the teacher was to discover each student's individual interests and then to develop a unique experientially based program for each student. With this program set in place, the student was then able to pursue their interests in *relative* freedom – that is *relative* to the highly regimented text-based education being employed in most schools at the time.[54]

With regards to the evolution of the education received at RVA throughout its history, the early use of the Montessori method of education was simultaneously peculiar and typical. It was peculiar in that the Montessori method held to a radically positive view of human nature. Because children were fundamentally both good and curious, education should be built around the nurturing of the child's natural tendencies.[55] This central Montessori philosophy was at odds with a fundamental tenet of evangelical Christian doctrine – the sinful nature of humanity. According to this doctrine, while all people are made in the image of God (and therefore capable of creativity and reason), they are, nevertheless, tainted with a natural inclination towards evil. Thus a child's tendencies should be viewed with suspicion not naïve trust.[56] When applied to education, the evangelical view of human nature assumes that children will not always want to act morally. As a result, it is unlikely that a child will eagerly seek out tedious, demanding but important work such as that of English grammar or mathematics. Simply put, in terms of educational philosophy it is difficult to conceive of two more incongruous perspectives. In that sense the existence of Montessori education during the early years at this conservative Christian institution is peculiar.

---

[53] Gupta, R.K. & A.M. Joosten (ed.). *Maria Montessori's Contribution to Educational Thought and Practice*, 44.
[54] Lillard, Paula Polk. *Montessori – Today*, 15.
[55] Ibid. 22-23.
[56] Sire, James. *Discipleship of the Mind*, 54-70.

Yet this basic contradiction between the philosophy of the mission and that of its new school is indicative of a number of themes that were to mark the next several decades of the school's history. Foremost among these themes is a lack of an educational self-consciousness. The stark contradiction between the basic religious beliefs of the mission and the educational philosophy of their school did not stand out as odd because no one thought about it. This lack of critical self-reflection naturally led to an inconsistent and incoherent educational program. The problem was only exacerbated by the fact that most of RVA's early faculty were not trained teachers and as a result usually lacked a basis for their educational practices outside of a "whatever works" pragmatism. As we will see, almost every staff member seemed to have a unique method of education, depending on his or her personal history and personality. The result was a bizarre cacophony of ideals and practices. In short, the only consistent and coherent elements in the early educational philosophy of RVA were its inconsistency and incoherence. Whatever consistency did exist most likely was the result of the unconscious philosophical presuppositions held deeply by the zealously conservative faculty.

Nevertheless, when Miss Hope returned to Kijabe at the end of 1910 the future of the school and its founding mission looked bright. With Miss Hope came updated books, chalkboards, desks, chairs and other important resources. Even more importantly though, Miss Josephine Hope became Mrs. Josephine Westervelt bringing the capable Mr. Westervelt into the school's faculty. Shortly thereafter Kiambogo was completed and student applications began to pour in from across the country.[57] An imperfect but positive foundation was in place.

IN 1905, PRIOR to the school's beginning, AIM's total missionary force sat at fifteen – most of whom were single or childless couples. In 1906, the year RVA began, AIM grew to over thirty missionaries and the next year almost doubled again to total fifty-six – including a noticeable increase in families with children.[58] Even as AIM wrestled with various internal and external challenges in the following years, never again would it shrink to its pre-RVA numbers. For the most part the mission's growth mirrored that of the school. In some instances visionary

---

[57] Anderson, Dick. *We Felt Like Grasshoppers*, 206-207.
[58] The statistics for the years prior to 1905, as well as 1906 and 1907 are taken from the chart on page 17 of Stephen Morad's unpublished Ph.D. Dissertation at the University of Edinburgh (1997).

expansion of the school allowed a potential swell in new missionaries to be realized. In other cases the expanding missionary population pushed the school to expand. But in both cases the importance of RVA to the success and growth of AIM was clearly recognizable. To the degree that AIM's work was influential in the development of the Kenya colony, the importance of this isolated and fledgling boarding school was likewise critical.

In 1911, AIM's significance in the evolution of the colony was small but growing. Approximately fifty missionaries were involved in evangelism and education around British East Africa. From those missionaries involved in education for Africans, nine schools had been started with a total enrollment of 330. By 1915 however, sixty-six missionaries were responsible for thirty-seven schools with an African student population that exceeded 2000.[59] Through evangelism and education AIM and a mushrooming number of African converts were helping to shape the colony's future.

---

[59] Ibid. Please see chart on page 301.

CHAPTER 2

WANDERING IN THE WILDERNESS: RVA FROM 1911-1933

As WE HAVE SEEN ALREADY, THE VERY EXISTENCE OF A school for missionary children had bolstered the size and status of the African Inland Mission in Kenya. In the first ten years of the school's life the African Inland Mission had grown almost six-fold, from fifteen to sixty-six missionaries.[1] Not surprisingly, as the number of AIM missionaries grew so did the mission's influence among the people groups of Kenya. Simply put, each family of children at RVA represented a missionary couple who, whether through traditional church planting, education, language translation or medicine, were helping to transform the spiritual, economic and even political culture of colonial Kenya.

Just as significant is the fact that because of the school, the children of these missionaries were now able to remain in Africa, surrounded at school and at home by the same zealous evangelical spirit that had led their parents to risk everything to come to Africa in the first place. It is not an exaggeration to say that a radical commitment to evangelical Christianity permeated the lives of virtually every adult role model the children at RVA encountered. Therefore, as they moved through their formative years most came to see the world through the lenses of a deep-seated and unadulterated evangelicalism.

---

[1] Morad, Stephen, unpublished Ph.D. dissertation, "The Founding Principles of the African Inland Mission...", University of Edinburgh (1997), p. 301.

For these children, remaining in Africa also meant being in constant contact with the people and cultures of Africa. As a result, while their parents would always feel like aliens in a foreign land, this first generation of RVA students saw Africa as their home. The indigenous languages that their parents had awkwardly translated soon poured out of their mouths as freely as English. But it was not just the grammar of a new language these children had ingested, but an entire worldview. What was beginning to take place in these RVA students was the creation of a new cultural grammar reflecting both the values of western evangelical Christianity and their African experience. Thus when this first generation of RVA students returned to Africa as missionaries themselves, as a large number would do, they signaled not only the gradual transformation of Africa but also the evolution of the goals, values and practices of the western missionary. In short, the school at Kijabe was beginning to function as a greenhouse for a new breed of missionaries whose African experience would eventually destroy old prejudices and transform the fundamentalism of their parents into a new kind of world evangelicalism.

But this did not happen overnight. The evolution towards a more global evangelicalism was anything but smooth. From 1911-1933[2] both the school and the mission struggled against a host of obstacles that would threaten not only this developing worldview, but the existence of both RVA and AIM. For the school, these hurdles included: a mission belief system suspicious of excellence in education (and indeed anything not directly related to evangelism), a plethora of uneducated educators, waves of deadly disease, cross-cultural tensions and finally a world war and global economic recession.

BEFORE EXAMINING THE role that events in Europe and America had on the life of the school, it is important to remember that if we hope to understand the development of this new breed of missionary we are best served by looking first at those forces that acted directly upon them as they were struggling to forge their identity. Because life at RVA represented the better part of the world to the first generation of missionary children, it makes sense to begin by examining the life of the school and the adults that were significant in the student's lives there.

For those growing up with high-definition television, compact disc players and the internet it may be nearly impossible to imagine the life of

---

[2] 1933 was the year when Herb Downing was brought to Kijabe specifically to develop the school into a solidly college preparatory education.

a child growing up in the 1910's and 1920's, let alone the lives of those children growing up in the isolated and raw circumstances of that generation of RVA students. By necessity, life outside of classes was made up of their natural surroundings, a romantic sense of adventure and (above all) an imagination forced to life. In truth, the sense of adventure that characterized these young students was far from imaginary. Regular events like hikes to the hidden waterfalls far into the hills above the school, or to the now famous Mau Mau caves, were genuinely dangerous. Around each bend in the trail lay the very real possibility of encounters with any number of natural predators. Even in the rowdy games of "cops and robbers" played close to the comforts of the Kiambogo building danger often came knocking. On one of many similar occasions in the late 1920's William Barnett and his sister came within feet of a leopard while playing in the thickets that skirted the campus. Luckily for them this leopard was either already satisfied or otherwise engaged because it simply stared at them for several long seconds before turning and lumbering deeper into the woods. Nevertheless, this story's happy ending could have easily had a more sobering outcome and that possibility was not lost on the students and staff of RVA.[3]

Adventure was an inescapable part of the young student's lives, but it also flowed from their lively imaginations. Without prepackaged entertainment, they were forced to create their own. Make-believe battles were often staged; some of which took on a very real tenor as boys armed with "kaffir" apple-shooting slingshots assaulted one another around the Kiambogo building. As one contemporary remembered, at times one side, lacking ammunition, would either resort to using rocks or would have to take refuge from the stinging onslaught in the catacombs under Kiambogo – often remaining there until it was time for dinner.[4]

In addition, almost as soon as Kiambogo was built, students there began the time-honored tradition of sneaking out. One night in the 1920's, Bill Barnett and some friends added to the budding tradition by going out of his second story window and sliding down the water drains.

---

[3] Interview with John "William" Barnett conducted by Robert Shuster between Mar. 29 & May 27, 1983. A recording of the interviews are available at the Billy Graham Center (BGC), Wheaton College, under CN 248.

[4] Keller, Philip. *Wonder O' the Wind*, p. 41 & an interview with Dr. Bill Barnett conducted by the author, June 30, 1998 at Pearl River, NY. Tapes will soon be available at the BGC archives. On a side note, students regularly were injured during these melees. In one case Bill Barnett opened up a large gash in the forehead of Keller as a result of a slingshot launched rock.

The purpose of their adventure says a lot about the attitudes and overall character of the students. The goal of this midnight escapade was a harmless cookout in the clearing below.[5] Whether due to the school's small size, the stringency of the rules or the moral upbringing of the students, drugs, sex and the like were almost unheard of during this period of the school's history. The vice most common among the students was violence as fights regularly broke out among the boys struggling for their place in the pecking order.[6]

The spirit of romantic adventure could even be found in the sources of food that sustained the school community. A small herd of cows that provided the milk for the community grazed on the hills surrounding the school, sometimes being menaced by irritable Cape Buffalo or the all too common leopards. Antelope from the valley were usually the meat of choice, although Cape Buffalo and even elephant were not unheard of. Because there was no refrigeration, when the station men would return from the valley with their kill, the animal was immediately divided among the station families and the school. While most of the meat was cooked and eaten within days of its arrival, some was smoked and stored for a later date.[7] Several families also raised chickens for the eggs, and occasionally the meat. Finally, the fruit and vegetables in the students' diets came from missionary gardens or local Kenyan shambas.[8] In stark contrast to life in the West, where food was quickly becoming an abstraction, this generation of missionary child grew up in an unsanitized and very real world, where sustenance came directly from labor and where life for one often meant death for another. Small as this may seem, these realities were foundational to their developing conception of life and necessarily narrowed the cultural chasm that between the missionary child and their African peer.

---

[5] Keller, Philip. *Wonder O' the Wind*, p. 41.

[6] Ibid. p.42.

[7] The school did purchase its first electric generator in 1929 which likely gave the school the ability to refrigerate its meat, allowing an increased level of security and comfort for the community.

[8] My information concerning the procurement of food through livestock, garden farming, hunting and even some gathering come from a variety of first hand accounts including: (1) an interview of John William Barnett in 1983 by Robert Schuster which can be found at Wheaton College's Billy Graham Center Archives under CN 248; (2) The Downing woman's memoir entitled, "Our Roots" also available at the BGC under the AIM collection; and (3) Githua - the Story of Dr. Ken Allen, the author of this unpublished work is unknown. The document can be found at the BGC under CN81 39-14.

Thriving in the midst of this rugged environment was a growing colony of rats. By the 1920's these rats had come to infest virtually every forgotten corner of the now ten-year-old Kiambogo building. So prevalent were these disease carrying vermin that students were paid the handsome sum of five Kenyan cents for each dead rat. Student-built traps became the trend for the young boys, while the older boys were allowed limited use of their .22 caliber rifles. John Barnett, a boarder from 1924-1931, remembered well a nightly ritual the young students experienced courtesy of these nocturnal nemeses. The ritual began when the students turned down their "hurricane lanterns" and placed them outside their doors. Next the students would stumble through the silent darkness to their corncob mattresses and cover themselves beneath the piles of thick blankets that would be their refuge from the biting chill that would nightly sweep down the hills, through the rafters and into Kiambogo,

> And then you would wait for it to start. After a while you would hear it… They would start at the end of the building and it would sound like just a rustling at first, and then it would come… like a thundering herd coming down over the ceiling, dozens of them, great big rats… some forest rats. They had gnawed holes through the ceiling and would come down the walls and next thing you know they are climbing over the top of your bed.[9]

Considering the possibility of unfriendly wildlife and the ubiquitous presence of these rats at night, it is understandable why all but the bravest avoided the precarious night journey to the infested outhouse. To accommodate the students two buckets were placed in each room. One bucket was full of fresh well water for face washing in the morning. The second empty "slosh" bucket was to be used as a receptacle for urine. On one occasion, having forgotten to replace the slosh bucket's lid, several students were awakened by the sounds of a splash and frantic scraping from inside the bucket. After quickly replacing the lid the scratching sounds died away and when the slosh bucket was emptied the next morning the students were five cents richer.[10]

IT IS IMPORTANT to remember that this adventuresome life of the students at RVA always existed within a dynamic social environment

---

[9] Interview with John William Barnett by Robert Shuster, 1983 (see note #5).
[10] Ibid.

nurtured by the mission and the school's revolving faculty. Especially during this era, when the school had yet to establish an autonomous culture, individual faculty members could have a disproportionate influence on the lives of the school's children. For better or for worse, several key individuals often determined many of the parameters within which the school was to function.

As has been the case in each era of RVA's past, this first generation of faculty were a bizarre cacophony of authoritarian, nurturing, eccentric and dynamic personalities. There were two distinct categories of faculty members during these years – those at RVA out of choice and those "serving" out of necessity. With a few exceptions, those who were coerced into teaching at RVA treated the school as a personal prison and consciously or unconsciously took out their frustration on the cause of their incarceration – the school's young pupils. By contrast, those few individuals who came to RVA out of choice were dynamic contributors to the school's evolving culture. Indeed the survival of RVA during this period of adversity can be credited to a few outstanding individuals who saw the school and its children as a sacred calling.

Like most of AIM's early missionaries, the early faculty at the school often lacked the education necessary to teach past the elementary grades, and almost always were without any formal teaching experience. As Robert Tignor has pointed out, prior to the 1930's AIM was lucky if a fifth of its missionaries had completed a four-year college degree.[11] Granted, the state of education in the United States during this period left much to be desired. Nevertheless, the marginal academic training of RVA's faculty during this era was the logical result of the anti-intellectual perspective pervasive in the fundamentalist culture from which most of AIM's missionaries came. In the Pulitzer Prize winning, *Anti-Intellectualism in American Life*, Richard Hofstadter described the reasoning that led fundamentalists to reject the life of the mind:

---

[11] Tignor, Robert, *The Colonial Transformation of Kenya*, p. 120. The lack of educated AIM's missionaries is not surprising when we remember that at this time only a tiny minority of the American population went on for post-secondary education. However, when AIM is compared to its British counterparts such as the CMS (Anglican) or CSM (Presbyterian), there is a clear distinction which can be traced directly to the more positive views of learning and reason among these two groups. Among the Church Mission Society and the Church of Scotland Mission a large percentage of the personnel were graduates of the "big four" – Oxford, Cambridge, Edinburgh or St. Andrews.

One begins with the hardly contestable proposition that religious faith is not, in the main, propagated by logic or learning. One moves on from this to the idea that it is best propagated (in the judgment of Christ and on historical evidence) by men who have been unlearned and ignorant. It seems to follow from this that the kind of wisdom and truth possessed by such men is superior to what learned and cultivated minds have. In fact, learning and cultivation appear to be handicaps in the propagation of faith. And since propagation of faith is the most important task before man, those who are as "ignorant as babes" have, in the most fundamental virtue, greater strength than men who have addicted themselves to logic and learning. Accordingly, though one shrinks from a bald statement of the conclusion, humble ignorance is far better as a human quality than a cultivated mind.[12]

Further, even when the mind was utilized, as Mark Noll points out, "the scandal of evangelical thinking... just as often resulted from a way of pursuing knowledge that (did) not accord with Christianity (such as) being blown about by every wind of apocalyptic speculation and enslaved to the cruder spirits of popular science".[13] In the case of this generation of AIM missionaries both criticisms were applicable and had an undeniable influence both on AIM's involvement in African education, and the lack of concern often given to providing a first rate education for their own children.[14] Thus, depending on the personnel "assigned" to RVA, the educational enterprise was often either not taken seriously or, if taken seriously, in a direction that was neither faithful to Biblical intent nor to the scientific method.

Having said that, one woman, Miss Muriel Perrott, stands out during this period as a voice for quality education at the school. Miss Perrott was the first teacher since Miss Hope to come to Kijabe for the specific purpose of teaching at the Academy. During her time at RVA Shakespeare and Latin were stressed within a generally humanities-based

---

[12] Hofstadter, Richard. *Anti-Intellectualism in American Life*, Vintage Press, New York: 1962, p. 48-49n.8.

[13] Noll, Mark. *The Scandal of the Evangelical Mind*, Eerdmans Pub. Co, Grand Rapids: 1994, p. 14.

[14] Examples of this anti-intellectual bent pepper the pages of Hearing and Doing, such as the dubious use of science and scriptural interpretation found in the April/May 1906 article entitled, "The Bible Hints at Scientific Facts". Evidence for the practical implications of this perspective are forth coming in the look at AIM's African schools and the course of education pursued at RVA.

British curriculum.[15] Tiny and slightly hunchbacked, Miss Perrott was not an imposing figure, yet her love for the students and teaching made a powerful impression on those who attended the school at this time. Philip Keller acknowledged his debt to her stating, "amid this struggle there was one person who by her quiet strong love saved me from utter ruin... She gently came alongside to let me get a glimpse of Christ in her life... And at the same time she encouraged in me a great love of fine literature, good books and great authors."[16] Another contemporary concurred, "She knew education and she knew kids... she made school work enjoyable, she made it live."[17] Even after she left AIM and the school, Miss Perrott displayed a deep commitment to her students writing many of them consistently until her death some forty years later.[18]

The legacy of Miss Perrott certainly lived in her students, many of whom went on to careers of considerable stature.[19] In four critical years Miss Perrott established a standard of excellence that slowly began to permeate the school's value system. As a result, in spite of fundamentalism's anti-intellectualism, RVA began to turn out students who not only held to the evangelical values of their parents, but also had the academic tools to move beyond the efforts of their zealous parents.

Yet the legacy of this small and unheralded British schoolteacher did not end with academics. Indeed, up until the late 1970's it was impossible to attend RVA without being directly touched by Miss Perrott's efforts. Convinced that the British system represented the very best in education, Miss Perrott saw to it that its tried and true traditions were implemented at RVA. As head teacher from 1924 until 1927, Miss Perrott instituted the two-house system. The two houses, named Stanley and Livingstone respectively after the noted explorers, had a variety of functions. First and foremost they acted as teams which competed with each other in intra-school athletic competition. The value of team sports

---

[15] Interview with Dr. Bill Barnett (see previous notes).

[16] Keller, Philip. *Wonder O' the Wind*, p. 40.

[17] Interview with Dr. Bill Barnett by the author at Pearl River, NY on June 30, 1998.

[18] Both Keller and Bill Barnett commented that they and others received letters right up to Muriel Parrot's death.

[19] Among the less than thirty students at RVA at this time, several went on to become doctors, at least two were noted authors and several more made a name for themselves as successful farmers and military men (one of the Allen children, Johnny, became a hero as a fighter pilot with the RAF during WWII). This is in addition to the high percentage who returned to Africa as missionaries.

in character building led Miss Perrott to introduce to the school rounders, cricket and several other British sporting activities.[20] While both uniforms and the two house system were discontinued in the late 1970's and early 1980's, the significant British influence upon the school lives on in the sports of field hockey and rugby, the prefect system and countless other traditions. Indeed, just beneath the surface of virtually every aspect of the community's culture lays some relic of Old Britannia. Miss Perrott left RVA for a personal furlough in 1931 and never returned. Despite the brevity of her term at the school, her role in the development of its unique culture cannot be overestimated. Had she returned to RVA it is likely the school's British flavor would have been even more pronounced.

Academically, the school's early faculty were a mixed bag. The same can be said of the first faculty in terms of personal character and psychological stability. Like most of the early faculty, Mr. North and his wife felt called to Africa to preach the gospel, but found themselves forced into a teaching role for which they were neither academically nor psychologically prepared. These deficiencies did not have to mean failure at RVA. However, Mr. North's personality, combined with an unwillingness or inability to relate to the students, led directly to a failure to gain the student's respect assuring catastrophe as an educator. In just one instance North was sliding down the Kiambogo banister (hardly the action of a typical administrator) when a student, "Doc" Propst, hit him in the seat of the pants with a slingshot-propelled marble. Because of North's universal unpopularity no student ever gave information as to the perpetrator of the crime and "Doc" Propst lived to play another day. While the "Doc" Propst incident does not necessarily imply a lack of respect among the students, a second example illustrates the degree to which North's leadership had brought the school dangerously close to anarchy. In one instance North tried to use his position of authority to retain the warthog tusk of student Earl Andersen. When the students rallied against North's authority he fell back on the only thing left – physical force. In a bizarre event that Darwin would have been proud of, North invited some of the older boys down to a clearing beneath the Kiambogo building and challenged them to a fight for authority.[21] The

---

[20] Information on the beginning to the two house system can be found in Entwistle, p. 14; the Dr. Bill Barnett interview; A speech by Shelley Arenson at RVA during the 1996-96 school year, among others.

[21] Interview with "Doc" Propst conducted by Rich Dilworth, Aug. 9, 1997. The tape is in possession of the author and will shortly be available at the BGC archives. Up until the late 1970's the field beneath Kiambogo was referred to as

tenure of the North family at RVA might be the most glaring example of the consequences of allowing inept and unwilling faculty run the school, but it is not the only one.

Much like the Norths, the Andersons came to the school as a pair of latter-day-Jonahs. Being forced to work in a capacity for which they were ill prepared served to exaggerate the emotional instability and tyrannical tendencies lying dormant in the couple. To begin with, contemporaries had real questions about Mrs. Anderson's psychological stability. One student from the time politely concluded that, "Mrs. Anderson did not appear completely normal".[22] Mr. Anderson compensated for any appearance of vulnerability with an authoritarianism straight out of a Dickens' novel. Corporal punishment, already used at RVA, became all too common for any number of major or minor infractions. It was concerning the Anderson period that student Philip Keller compared his life as an RVA student to an imprisoned Masai whose unnatural and brutal confinement had "shattered" his inner spirit.[23]

The Anderson's social problems spilled over into their relationships with their fellow staff members. The school board minutes of September 24, 1928 reveal a fierce and often petty struggle for control of the school between the Andersons and the outstanding British teacher Miss Perrott. It is evident from the minutes that Mr. Anderson had been treating the school as his own private kingdom with its limited resources such as the school's newspaper being retained by Anderson for his personal use. Duties that he saw as an inconvenience, such as teaching first aid classes or planning the school's recreational time, he outright refused to do. Finally, Anderson tried to give his wife positions which had already been offered by the mission to others. In one such case, he inexplicably removed Miss Perrott from her Sunday School duties and replaced her with his wife.

When confronted by the board concerning negligence towards his responsibilities at the school, Anderson claimed his personal need to study Swahili needed to take precedence. In addition he argued that his duty to attend to his wife's "condition" did not allow him to carry out his menial tasks at RVA – although these things did not infringe upon his ability to administer the school. In a judgment that reflects both the

---

"Bully Battlefield", but few if any knew the origin of the title. See taped interview of Joyce Baker, May 1999 by the author – available at the Billy Graham Center, Wheaton College, under the Papers and Materials of Phil Dow.
[22] Interview with Dr. Bill Barnett by the author, June 30, 1998 (See note #3).
[23] Keller, Philip. *Wonder O' the Wind*, p. 39.

wisdom of the school board and its confidence in Miss Perrott, the board used Mr. Anderson's words to take away from him control over the school's workings. Using language dripping with irony, the board insisted that due to his wife's condition, Mr. Anderson should not do anything beyond the very tasks he had previously deemed beneath him. As if to pour salt into the wound, Anderson was asked to conclude the meeting by leading the prayer.[24] Three months later the Andersons were "relieved" of all their duties at the school.[25]

During the Anderson's rough run at RVA several people stood out as nurturing adults and fine educators. As we have seen, one of these was Muriel Perrott, but she was not alone. Miss Slater, the housemother from 1927-1930, was another such person. According to the students, the tiny Miss Slater fit her role perfectly. Her obvious compassion for these children who were separated from their parents resonated with the boarders at RVA. Cookies and games on Saturday night and other budding traditions gave the building once described as, "a gaunt, gloomy edifice…"[26] a sense of warmth and security. Despite being the lone adult in charge of up to 30 students (many taller and stronger than she) Miss Slater was able to keep "perfect order". As one person remembered, "she trusted you and believed in you. This brought out the best in a person".[27]

Finally, Mr. Gabbott stands out as another one of the adults at RVA that gained the affection and admiration of the young students during these years. It is thus a bitter irony that a fatal flaw in Gabbott's character led to perhaps the greatest tragedy of the young school's history. It was evening and Gabbott's young children were noisily careening around the family's quarters. At the end of a tiring day Gabbott was unusually irritable and yelled at his children to quiet down. They obeyed for a time, but soon playfulness had again won the day and their father's words were forgotten. As the noise reached a climax Gabbott allowed his anger and irritation to get the better of him and

---

[24] RVA School Board Minutes of Sept. 24, 1928, available at the school, Kijabe, Kenya.

[25] RVA School Board Minutes – Dec., 1928, available at the school, Kijabe, Kenya.

[26] Keller, Philip. *Wonder O' the Wind*, p. 38.

[27] *Githua*, The unknown author was certainly a child of Dr. Ken Allen and a student at RVA during the 1920's. Information on Ms. Slater is principally on page 28. The document is available at the BGC archives under CN81 39-14. After leaving RVA, Ms. Slater for many years ran AIM's Mayfield guesthouse in Nairobi.

before anyone knew what happened Gabbott had slapped his young son hard enough to knock him off balance and into a basin of scalding hot water being prepared for bathing later in the evening. Despite Gabbott's quick rescue, the burns to his child were deep and covered virtually every inch of his small body. Within a few days, Gabbott's son was dead leaving the family and the school community profoundly shaken.[28]

Individual personalities such as Muriel Perrott, Miss Slater, Charles Hurlburt and Mr. Gabbott made an indelible impression on this generation of students at RVA. Along side the children's parents, these faculty members helped nurture in many of this generation a vibrant evangelical faith. They also played a critical role in filling the student's African childhoods with pleasant memories, something that should not be overlooked. Combined with the adventure inherent in Africa, these elements in the missionary children's lives led many to return to Africa as missionaries themselves. Thus, in large part due to the existence of the Rift Valley Academy, a critical and often overlooked pattern was beginning – the phenomenon of the second generation missionary.

WHILE THE FORCES of ardent faith and individual personality were changing the lives of the school's students, larger forces were shaping the context within which the school and the school's faculty functioned. In many ways 1914 exemplified some of the powerful outside forces that were at play in the daily life of the school. To begin with, the less than robust health of Mrs. Westervelt took a significant turn for the worse late in the year. Doctors in Kenya believed she had a heart condition intimately connected to the high elevation of Kijabe. At least one doctor was convinced that Mrs. Westervelt had no more than two years to live and recommended an immediate return to the United States. When the Westervelts reluctantly left Kijabe[29] the impact on the

---

[28] Interviews with Dr. Bill Barnett and "Doc" Propst both include this story. See earlier notes for more information on these interviews. The devastated family left RVA soon after the incident. Rumors that Gabbott experienced some sort of a temporary breakdown cannot be substantiated, but sometime after the tragedy the school board asked the Gabbotts to return to RVA. Their return appears to have brought a deep sense of healing to both the family and the school community.

[29] After leaving RVA and returning to America the Westervelts lived in both Siloam Springs, AR and at Columbia Bible College, SC. During much of this time they ran a home for RVA students who had come to America to finish their last years of high school before beginning college. The story of the Westervelt House is a book on its own.

stability and quality of education at RVA was palpable.[30] The departure of one of the school's founders and first teacher coincided with the outbreak of WWI. Despite Kijabe's relative isolation, the war had an impact on the school in multiple ways. On the most practical of levels the war exacerbated the ongoing problem of staffing the school. Several new missionaries who might have unwillingly replaced the Westervelts at RVA were forced to delay their trip due to the precarious nature of wartime sea travel.[31]

The emotional and psychological upheaval caused by the departure of the Westervelts and the unsettling news of a growing world war had at least one unexpected consequence. Late in 1914 a religious revival of sorts swept through the school during which all but three of the students either converted or made recommitments to Christianity.[32] The war era also saw a wave of epidemics hit the school. At least three times between mid 1915 and late 1916 the school was forced to close because of various "contagious diseases"[33] many of which were genuinely life threatening due to the primitive nature of tropical medicine at the time.[34]

Despite the boiling of patriotic zeal and some limited fighting on the border with German East Africa (Tanzania), prior to 1917 British East Africa had managed to remain relatively untouched by the tragedy that had engulfed most of Europe. Because missionaries and colonists from these antagonistic countries remained thousands of physical miles from the trenches and mustard gas-soaked reality of WWI, most remained colleagues in cultivating the physical and spiritual potential they envisioned in East Africa. However, by May of 1917 this began to change and Britain announced the drafting of all British and Canadian men living in Kenya. This included Kijabe AIM missionaries Dr. Kenneth Allen, Rev. McKentrick[35], Aleck Alexander and Gordon Stephenson. The primary task of the missionaries was to assist in

---

[30] Anderson, Dick. *We Felt Like Grasshoppers*, 207 & Downing Memoir, p. 30.* (See note #24 in chapter 1).

[31] "The Rift Valley Academy", *Inland Africa*. July-Dec. 1916, p.7.

[32] Banks, Howard (ed.), "The White School", *Hearing and Doing*. April-June 1914. Also see Entwistle, p. 12.

[33] Although the implication is that there were several diseases/viruses that impacted the school community typhoid is the only one mentioned by name in either of the sources cited in note #10.

[34] See note #6.

[35] Rev. McKentrick did not actually serve with the British forces due to the serious illness of his wife at Kijabe.

leading the native "Carrying Corps" that had been founded by Dr. Arthur of the Scottish Mission.[36]

"Carrying Corps", staffing problems and religious revivals aside, the AIM community remained focused on the primary task of spreading the Gospel. In that sense World War I did not significantly change things. The one major exception to this rule occurred thousands of miles from the quiet isolation of the Rift Valley Academy. In August of 1917, off the coast of South Africa, the British ship *City of Athens* was hit by a mine and sunk. Among the passengers were nineteen AIM missionaries. Raymond Davis, one of the survivors, wrote home to his parents saying, "We were hit (at) 3:30 P.M., and the last we saw of the ship, she was… propeller high in the air, and bow under the water. It went out of sight at 4:40 P.M. just about sunset, with the sky all aflame with gorgeous colors… leaving a few frail lifeboats on the open sea, about 25 miles from land."[37] The frail lifeboats struggled to stay afloat into the darkness as the frigid Antarctic waters seeped through the vessels' cracks. Late in the night a rescue ship miraculously came upon the scattered castaways, but not before one lifeboat had sunk claiming at least ten missionaries, including six missionary children likely set to begin studies at RVA later that year.[38]

Outside of the tragic sinking of the *City of Athens* the War did not directly claim the lives of any associated with AIM and the Rift Valley Academy. Nevertheless the impact of the war on the school was profound, even if not always obvious. Within ten years of the war's conclusion the Kenyan Colony, AIM and RVA had all seen substantial changes that were a direct result of the conflict.

Among the most obvious changes in Kenya was a dramatic increase in the number of European settlers. Prior to the war, colonists in Kenya were few but could boast some of the most aristocratically pure blood in Europe.[39] As a result there was a clear distinction between the pious and poor missionaries and the oft-titled and opulent settlers. The relative

---

[36] Editor Unknown, "White & Native A.I.M. Workers Drafted to Fight Germans", *Inland Africa*. July 1917, p. 1

[37] This letter from Raymond Davis to his parents was reprinted in the Nov. 1917 issue of *Inland Africa* under the title of, "Missionaries Write of Ocean Disaster", p. 8-9.

[38] Ibid. p. 9.

[39] Edgerton, Robert. *Mau Mau: An African Crucible*. P.11. Edgerton argues that the British settlers to Kenya were the wealthiest ever to leave England's shores. So many aristocrats came to Kenya that the Norfolk Hotel was referred to as, "the House of Lords".

numerical strength of the missionary element was erased in 1919 when the British government launched the Soldier Settler plan. Retiring officers were entered into a lottery which might mean a portion of free underdeveloped bush land in the Kenyan highlands.[40] If, as some have argued, it was the railroad that had originally opened Kenya up to settlement, it was the lottery that made extensive settlement a certainty. With the Soldier Settlement plan, British East Africa was on its way from a remote missionary outpost to an enticing new white frontier.

A small number of these former British soldiers also came out to Kenya as missionaries. Indeed, several retired servicemen brought their perspective to RVA in the 1920's as teachers or administrators. The nature of their influence is not surprising. Militaristic discipline, already a tendency within the school, became the norm peaking with Mr. Anderson's placement as principal in 1927. In these days, "everything was military. Before each meal the students would stand stiffly in a line, from tallest to shortest, for inspection."[41] Appearance and hygiene of each student were thoroughly appraised before all could file into Kiambogo for the meal. Acclaimed author and conservationist Philip Keller concurred stating that during his first years at RVA, "a veritable catalogue of rules, regulations and endless restrictions imprisoned me as surely as any victim behind bars."[42] Enforcement of this "veritable catalogue" was carried out with varying degrees of corporal punishment. Yet this strict discipline was only half of the picture, as the women of the community such as Muriel Perrott and Miss Slater balanced out the militarism by showering gentle comfort onto the vulnerable missionary children.

STANDING IN STARK contrast to the Victorian sensibilities of the missionaries was the lifestyle of the earliest European settlers to Kenya. The moral climate of the colonial culture greeting the new wave of settler

---

[40] Huxley, Elspeth. *Nine Faces of Kenya*, p. 95.

[41] Interview with Dr. Bill Barnett at Pearl River, NY on June 30, 1998. The interview was conducted by the author. Tapes of the interview hopefully will be available at the Billy Graham Center shortly.

[42] Keller, Philip. *Wonder O' the Wind*, p 38. Philip Keller has now passed away but was the author of multiple books including *A Shepherd Looks at Psalm 23* and *Wonder O' the Wind*. The latter is an autobiographical account of his childhood in Africa. As will be pointed out later, as Keller grew older, his experience at RVA improved considerably - especially when contrasted with his final years of secondary school spent at an unnamed British school in Kenya - an experience he described as "a living Hell". *Wonder O' the Wind*, p 56.

soldiers was less than modest. Whether its cause was wealth, excessive leisure or a spirit of adventure run amuck, the growing community of settlers in Kenya had earned a reputation for rampant hedonism. In "Happy Valley" heavy drinking and drugs (especially cocaine and morphine) were prevalent; and sexual hijinks were "so common that it seemed everyone slept with everyone else; then, after a period of repose, did so again."[43] In at least one home, weekend guests were required to switch partners at least once during the weekend.[44]

Instead of raising the moral ethos of Happy Valley, the lifestyle of the military newcomers to Kenya comfortably adapted to the culture already in place.[45] This is not to say all white settlers in the Kenya Colony were entirely hedonistic, for some settlers stood out as examples of moral rectitude and self-discipline. Indeed, even the most morally degenerate settler was at least viewed as a hard worker. Nevertheless, those settlers who rejected a morally licentious lifestyle were the exception to the rule.

This celebrated immorality had a role in bringing out and accentuating the isolationist tendency already within AIM. While close to the railroad for the purpose of efficacy in evangelism, RVA was noticeably isolated from the hubs of European settlement. This chosen isolation from the sinful world grew in step with the increasingly numerous and degenerate settler community. To those living at Kijabe, interaction with the world was limited to African evangelism and the acceptance of some settler children to the Academy (a decreasing reality as settler schools began to develop around the Colony). In a very real sense, life at RVA had taken on the feel of a monastery. And for better or worse that "other worldly" perspective became ingrained in the young students.

WELL BENEATH THE surface of things, WWI acted as a crucible in yet another way. The war radically altered Western Civilization's view of the world and the people who made it up. Apparently isolated or not, those at Kijabe were to be influenced more by this intellectual battle than by any struggle fought with guns and bombs. Prior to WWI Western Civilization was brimming with idealism, optimism and self-assurance. Because of this, virtually every example of Western Culture was given blanket approval, especially those involved in the

---

[43] Edgerton. P. 17.
[44] Ibid.
[45] Ibid.

humanitarian quest of civilizing the backward peoples of the world.[46] Much of this was destroyed along with most of Western Europe in the Great War. Having witnessed, or taken part in such apparently purposeless killing and massive destruction, Christendom was forced to reconsider its claim to moral superiority. Unfairly or not, traditional Christianity was saddled with much of the responsibility for this fallout.

At the same time Science, long the rising darling of the western world, finally laid sole claim to the mantel of humanity's hope. If God could not save us, perhaps we could save ourselves. Reason, science's highest value, pushed faith from a position of respect to that of a quaint pastime and finally to outright silliness. Biblical scholarship was the most clear-cut example of this attack on traditional supernatural Christianity. Using the tools of science, Higher Criticism brought into question some of the most sacred beliefs of Christianity.

The impact of this revolution in western values on AIM and RVA was not immediate, but it was substantial. First, the idea of missions itself came under fire. For a variety of reasons non-Christians and liberal Christians found missionaries either arrogant, ignorant or a combination of both. Three reactions to this attack on Christian missions stand out. First, many westerners increasingly questioned the truth claims of Christianity and thus its valid authority in culture. Not surprisingly, this response necessarily led to a decreased enthusiasm for the missionary enterprise, for once the power, goodness or truth of an idea was questioned, the thought of exporting it became nonsensical. The best example of this is the Princeton missions conference. By 1928 the number of college student volunteers for missions had dropped from 2,700 in 1920 to 252.[47]

A second reaction to the pervasive assault on orthodox Christianity was found in the liberal and culturally flexible Christianity that was coming to dominate most American denominations. This liberal response proceeded from an overarching faith in the progress of Western Civilization. Religion was not an end in itself, but a tool used to serve

---

[46] Hudson, Winthrop S. *Religion in America.* p. 297. Even as late as 1918 President Wilson felt free to give a resounding nod to the missionary effort. In the August, 1918 edition of *Inland Africa* there appeared an open letter from Wilson stating among other things, "I think it would be a real misfortune, a misfortune of lasting consequence, if the missionary programme of the world should be interrupted...I hope you will feel at liberty to use this expression of opinion in any way that you think best. Cordially and sincerely, yours, Woodrow Wilson".

[47] Hudson, p. 344.

the end of human progress. The Layman Inquiry represents a practical application of this perspective. Financed by Rockefeller Jr., it sought a cross-cultural dialogue in which each religion was equally valid and seen as a valued part of an eventually unified world faith. The Inquiry concluded, "(Christians) must be willing to give largely without any preaching, to cooperate wholeheartedly with non-Christian agencies for social improvement."[48] This Social Gospel promoted the ethics of Jesus without regard for the outdated and slightly embarrassing notions of miracles, Christ's divinity or any other exclusive truth claims of Christianity.

If the liberal response to the challenge of changing contemporary culture could be described as an uncritical embracing of that culture, the third response, the birth of fundamentalism, was a total and rigid rejection of it.[49] As it happens, AIM is perhaps the best example within the missionary movement of this response to the challenges of modernity. With good reason AIM viewed many of the currents within Post-WWI mainline Christianity with extreme skepticism. In a religious climate characterized by an almost trendy, intellectual hubris, AIM clung fiercely to a simple faith in an unchanging God as found in the Bible.[50] Compounding this response was the strong tradition within AIM of Premillennial Dispensationalism with its propensity of interpreting most wars and natural disasters as evidences of the end of the world.[51] Thus the cultural crisis in America had the effect of accentuating and radicalizing strong inclinations already apparent in AIM.

THE AMERICAN CULTURAL crisis had an impact on life at RVA in at least two important ways. First, for the African Inland Mission all activities that were not obviously evangelistic in focus came under intensified suspicion. The children at RVA had a first hand chance to view this sentiment in action. Some liberal advocates of the Social Gospel had made their way out to Africa with other mission groups during this period. Because humanitarian activity was seen by this group as an end in itself, this work had an intensity of focus that resulted in a dramatic increase in the quality of African education, agricultural

---

[48] Ibid. p. 345.

[49] Marsden, George. *Fundamentalism and American Culture*, p.85.

[50] Oliver, Roland. *The Missionary Factor in East Africa*, pgs. 227-28. Oliver shows here how far AIM was moving when it had difficulty working with other Protestant missions due to its equating anything "High Church" with modernism and thus an attack on true Christianity.

[51] Tignor, Robert. *The Colonial Transformation of Kenya*, p. 120.

programs and the like.[52] Many at Kijabe (including the school's faculty) acknowledged this success but asked, "What good is it for a man to gain the whole world, yet forfeit his soul?"[53] One AIM missionary in a letter written during this period said as much, "I cannot believe that God brought us out here to educate these people in worldly wisdom so that they can get big salaries as clerks, etc. God called us to give them the Gospel and there our duty begins and ends."[54] As a result, even AIM's extensive involvement in African education was increasingly disparaged in favor of church planting and other clearly spiritual endeavors. To the growing minority of educated Africans this shift was easily interpreted as complicity with the settler community's desire to keep the African majority subservient to the European minority.[55]

This development did not come without significant internal struggle. Charles Hurlburt, AIM's field director from 1901 to 1925[56], and the founder of RVA, was gravely concerned about any movement away from African education. To Hurlburt, African education was not only a tremendous gift to the people AIM sought to serve, but more importantly the most effective tool for evangelism. Writing in *Inland Africa* in 1924, Hurlburt pleaded, "The cry of the people is for the mission to give them schools. No other equal opportunity to give the Gospel to the people is offered in Africa. From these schools nearly all of our converts have come. Shall the AIM enter this door?"[57]

Soon after this report was published the Home Director and several other influential members of the Home Council were asked to resign. These resignations were preceded by the resignation of then RVA principal William Blaikie and followed by Hurlburt himself in 1925.[58] It

---

[52] Morton, Andrew. *Moi: The Making of an African Statesmen*, pgs. 53-54.

[53] *The Holy Bible* (NIV) Mark 8:36.

[54] A letter written by Rose Horton of the AIM to H.D. Campbell March 23, 1931. Quoted in Tignor, p. 277.

[55] Harry Thuku's speeches and writings during this period are especially critical of missionaries and, what he saw as, their complicity in the colonial subordination of the African. Standing against Thuku and some of the young educated revolutionaries were a growing number of Christian converts who saw the missionaries as having brought some sort of spiritual and intellectual emancipation.

[56] Some sources put Hurlburt's resignation in 1924, but the precise date is not critical to the point here, which is the appearance of a "forced" resignation due to Hurlburt's moderate view on the role of "social" service in Christian missions.

[57] Hurlburt, Charles, *Inland Africa*, July 1924, pgs. 1-3.

[58] Tignor, Robert. *The Colonial Transformation of Kenya*, p. 123-124.

is not clear if all of these resignations were related, but what is clear is the massive impact these departures had on AIM and RVA. Because of the strength of evangelical fervor among AIM's fundamentalist constituency, and the resulting need for an educational institution for the missionary's children, it is probably an exaggeration to say that AIM and RVA would not have come into being without Hurlburt, but such a claim certainly has some credence. It was Hurlburt who brought AIM from a floundering and anemic vision to arguably the largest missionary organization in British East Africa. Further, the very idea of a school for missionary children was Hurlburt's, based on the needs of his own children. It was his vision that convinced Miss Hope to devote all her missionary career to the creation of such a school.[59] This same visionary was behind the plans for Kiambogo, the selection of staff members to teaching positions, and virtually every other important decision concerning the direction of the school during its first twenty years. This is not to say that the faculty and students did not significantly shape RVA's culture and traditions, but they did so within a general framework established and sustained by Hurlburt. RVA survived and even grew slightly in spite of considerable odds and much of the credit for this is due to Hurlburt's strong presence and vision. When he left AIM in 1925 RVA temporarily floundered in a leadership vacuum.[60]

If Hurlburt had meant so much to the mission and the school, and if his resignation brought with it a period of precarious instability, an explanation of Hurlburt's departure may provide some clues as to why RVA developed as it did over the next decade. Why did the de facto founder of AIM and RVA leave his life's sacred calling – a calling he had risked all for? To this day considerable controversy surrounds Hurlburt's acrimonious resignation from AIM. Along with the controversy have come a variety of theories to explain his decision – all of which have some foundation in the historical record. The most substantial and persistent causes center around Hurlburt's health and the controversies within the mission over: (a) the use of education in evangelism, and (b) what was meant by AIM's self-characterization as a "faith mission". Each of these issues undoubtedly pushed Hurlburt towards his decision, but none of these alone seems to have had the power to cause such a dramatic move. Indeed, it gradually becomes

---

[59] Anderson, Dick. *We Felt Like Grasshoppers*, p. 205.
[60] Entwistle, Roy. (Unpublished Masters Thesis – Seattle Pacific College, 1968) *The Rift Valley Academy, Kijabe, Kenya, From 1946-1966: Problems and Progress*, p. 15. However, Entwistle simply acknowledges a significant deterioration at the school, but does not attribute it to Hurlburt's resignation.

evident that even these causes combined were not necessarily sufficient to bring about his eventual resignation. There had to be something more. To get to the bottom of the controversy it is necessary to first briefly explore the three most compelling causes suggested thus far.

The cause most often put forward in official AIM literature, as well as those closest to Hurlburt, is that of failing health.[61] Indeed, if you travel down the chain of communication far enough it is possible to find stories of brain damage and even mental illness, both of which seem to have no evidential basis. Yet as with most fanciful stories, there is an element of truth in these tales. Illness certainly was one factor in Hurlburt's resignation. Starting in 1917 and then again in 1919 and 1920 he had lengthy and serious bouts with various tropical diseases.[62] After leaving Kijabe in 1925 Hurlburt spent six months in England recovering from yet another serious illness.[63] Clearly his health was a significant concern. However, Hurlburt's health had been inconsistent for his entire career and never before had illness been enough to deter this visionary pioneer. Indeed, within a year and a half of his resignation Hurlburt had founded a new mission to Africa and accepted a post at the Bible Institute of Los Angeles that he held until near his death in 1936.[64] It is conceivable that health concerns did force Hurlburt to leave Africa, but it does not adequately explain his resignation from AIM.

As we have already seen, Hurlburt had become convinced in the 1920's that African education was not only valuable in itself, but represented the most effective means of evangelism – AIM's driving purpose. His willingness to embrace these apparently humanistic means brought Hurlburt into conflict with an Home Council in more intimate contact with the American Modernist controversy – the cultural battle that had polarized the American church into its fundamentalist (conservative) and Social Gospel (liberal) camps. There is no question

---

[61] Multiple sources make this claim including most AIM literature on the resignation and Hurlburt's own family. (Telephone interview with Win Hurlburt, May, 10, 1999 by the author). Win is the grandson of Charles Hurlburt, and himself a lifetime missionary to Africa and something of a legend in his own right.

[62] Morad, Stephen. (Unpublished Ph.D. Dissertation, University of Edinburgh, 1997) *The Founding Principles of the AIM and their Interaction with the African Context in Kenya From 1895 to1939: the Study of a Faith Mission*, p. 162 footnote.

[63] Telephone interview with Win Hurlburt, May, 10, 1999 conducted by the author.

[64] Ibid. & Tignor, Robert. *The Colonial Transformation of Kenya*, p. 122.

that the increasingly reactionary Home Council feared the same slide into, what they felt was, empty humanitarianism on the mission field that they had seen take place at home.[65] This point was made abundantly clear in the two years surrounding Hurlburt's resignation. In 1924 Hurlburt left no doubt that he believed AIM's future must be tied to African education, devoting almost his entire *Inland Africa* "Annual Report" to this issue. The direction AIM did take immediately after Hurlburt's departure shows just how large the gulf was between Hurlburt and the Home Council on this issue.[66] Almost immediately after taking over as the new Home Director of AIM, H.D. Campbell wrote emphatically that, "Undue stress (was) being laid on education."[67] Even when the efficacy of continuing some service projects could not be ignored, they were seen as a necessary evil. In a letter to C.F. Johnston on May 14, 1928 Campbell grudgingly conceded that, "Incidentally some service, so called social, will result, but it will not be the main part of our program."[68]

It is not surprising that relative to other mission and government schools, AIM's African schools remained substandard - a fact not lost on many African students who began seeking out other schools whenever possible. AIM's refusal to accept government funds (another policy Hurlburt came to oppose) also had a role in the eroding quality of AIM schools.[69] But the question remains – was the clash over education as a means of evangelism enough to push Hurlburt out of the mission? Just as in the case of his health, Hurlburt had experienced similar struggles within the mission over specific policies and evangelistic means; and while the education issue was quite possibly one of the largest of these internal battles it alone did not appear to have the strength to topple his leadership.

---

[65] This is the argument put forward most forcefully in Robert Tignor's *The Colonial Transformation of Kenya*.

[66] Morad, dissertation, p. 305.

[67] Campbell, H.D. July 1925 edition of *Inland Africa*.

[68] As quoted in Tignor, p. 278.

[69] Tignor, Robert. *The Colonial Transformation of Kenya*, p. 122. Tignor is convinced that Hurlburt had come to the conclusion that the future of missions was in education and hoped to bring AIM fully into the educational fray. Morad also cites a telling letter by AIM missionary George Rhoad which states, "all over the field murmurings are heard that indicate we have not only lost the confidence of the government, but of large sections of the native people also." (Morad, p. 308 notes).

In his well-documented doctoral dissertation Stephen Morad puts forth an additional compelling cause for Hurlburt's resignation – the controversy over the meaning and implementation of the mission's "faith basis". Like the China Inland Mission, the Christian Missionary Alliance and several other Keswick influenced movements, AIM was founded on the belief that if men and women were "called of God" and doing his will, that same God would provide for their physical needs. Under Hurlburt, AIM took this idea to its logical extreme stating that because God knew the mission's needs, to ask sympathetic would-be-donors for financial support displayed a lack of faith.[70] In other words, much of the mission's sense of divine sanction came from what it saw as a total reliance on supernatural intervention on their behalf. When supporting funds were flowing in, the "faith basis" could act as a tremendous source of encouragement for the missionaries. But when funds slowed to a trickle, as often did happen in the early days, calls for moderation were quick to follow. Dissenters from Hurlburt's position argued, did not God use people to further His purposes? If not, why were they in Africa at all? Those who questioned Hurlburt's radical "faith basis" argued that acknowledging the needs of the mission publicly did not remove it from reliance on God's provision.[71]

Constantly present beneath the surface, in 1925 the "faith basis" issue exploded into an all too public argument between Hurlburt and the new AHC (American Home Council) leader H.D. Campbell. It was Hurlburt who first accused the AHC of compromising the faith basis by publishing the mission's needs in their paper *Inland Africa*. He argued that, "the most artful solicitation is a strong and pathetic statement of need without direct appeal. It may gain money but it leaves out God, and whatever comes is a direct result not of God's divine action but of man's ingenuity."[72] The AHC ardently denied having left the faith basis and Campbell shot back implying that Hurlburt's attack was "unchristian" and something more like a "fetish" than a substantial claim.[73] Despite meetings between the AHC and Hurlburt in 1926[74] the perceived rift between the two was too great and the separation became permanent.

---

[70] Morad, Stephen, p. 92.

[71] Ibid., p. 99.

[72] Letter to the Committee of Direction, Oct. 8, 1925, as quoted in Morad, p. 115.

[73] As quoted in Morad, p. 117.

[74] Although Hurlburt had officially resigned in 1925 there were hopes on both sides that there could be reconciliation and thus meetings were held, but to no avail.

But was the debate over the faith basis the critical cause behind Hurlburt's departure? One way to answer this question is to ask how real this controversy was. To an outsider the debate must have appeared ridiculous – two groups fighting over ever so slight differences, while agreeing on the essence. But to Hurlburt any slight deviation from a fundamental founding principle represented a compromise – and in the Christian life there could be no compromise. Thus the real question is, did the AHC's position represent a deviation from the mission's principle? The answer, while not without nuance, is no. Campbell, perhaps shaken by a policy that even had the appearance of evil reemphasized the "faith basis". And until Campbell stepped down as AHC director over a decade later no change had been made to the "faith basis" in the AIM constitution. In other words, while full of theological fervor, the controversy was a red herring – a guise under which a plethora of building tensions based on new issues and changing circumstances could be dealt with. The struggle over the faith basis was real, but its essence was an all too worldly power struggle between a younger generation and an aging patriarch slowly losing absolute control over the mission he had done so much to build.

The continuing revolution in transportation and communication technology had brought the mission's constituency and home councils closer to the once distant fields. In addition to faster, more reliable sea travel and trans-ocean communication cables, the automobile had begun to speed up and shrink the world. Even Kenya was impacted. The first car had arrived in Kenya in 1914 and by 1928 Nairobi was a motorized town.[75] With these and other technological developments came an increased demand for accountability and thus a shift in the power structure from the "on the spot" director Hurlburt, to the American home councils.[76] In addition, the tiny mission Hurlburt had done so much to develop had now expanded beyond the ability of one geographically isolated leader to successfully direct. From a lone missionary in 1900 to well over fifty in 1925, AIM was no longer a tiny focused enterprise and

---

[75] Aseka, E.M. "Urbanization" found in William R.Ochieng's *Themes in Kenyan History*. Heinemann, Kenya Ltd. 1990, p. 57. The first car owned by an AIM missionary was a Ford driven by the Roe's in Machakos. Based on a telephone interview with Hurlburt's grandson and long-time missionary to Africa on May 10, 1999 by the author.

[76] It is interesting to note that a similar change in the pattern of the power structure was found at this time in the English Colonial Office. For more on this see Gunn and Duignan's *African Proconsuls*.

new methods of administration were needed.[77]   In the end, Hurlburt's controversial resignation was an ironic indication of his success.   The mission had grown beyond him.

The immediate impact on the school of Hurlburt's resignation and the American cultural crisis is telling.   From a peak of nearly fifty students in the early 1920's, enrollment by 1928 had fallen to eighteen.[78] Further, without Hurlburt's relatively pro-education stance the school was left in the hands of a mission whose general attitude towards quality "worldly" education was one of suspicion if not outright hostility.   This attitude is not surprising considering the education level of early AIM missionaries.   In the early 1920's of the 48 missionaries known, only five had four-year college degrees and of those it is likely that only one was ever a teacher at RVA.[79]

As we have seen, despite the fact that the educational enterprise was increasingly viewed as a necessary evil, the academic program at RVA was not entirely neglected.   By 1928 the mission recognized that some permanent leadership was required to keep the school from collapse.   As a result they established a school board – thus partially filling the leadership vacuum created by Hurlburt's resignation.   Yet, much of the credit for the school's perseverance during this period must be given to AIM's British missionaries who were not as influenced by the American cultural crisis.   In fact, without the outstanding efforts of the academically minded British missionary, Muriel Perrott, it is difficult to imagine what the school would have evolved or devolved into.

THE AMERICAN CULTURAL crisis also had an impact on the way AIM missionaries interacted with the culture they had come to serve and live in.   This development was also watched closely, if not consciously, by the students at RVA.   As discussed previously, most of the first generation of AIM missionaries looked at Kenyan traditional culture through the lenses of soft racism.   Without excusing this perspective, it is important to note that the missionaries lived in an era dominated by racism and generally were less prejudiced than their settler peers.   There were at least two reasons for this.   First, the underlying egalitarianism of Christianity meant that ultimately God loved the Kenyan peoples as much as he loved the missionaries.[80]   Second, the

---

[77] Morad, Stephen, pgs. 17&301 (diagrams).

[78] Entwistle, Roy, pgs. 14&15.

[79] Tignor, Robert, p. 120.

[80] While Christians have regularly been blinded by the cultures they are a part of, to argue that Christianity is inherently racist is to ignore the entire New

nature of their interaction was that of a paternalistic teacher-pupil relationship, as opposed to the exploitive master-servant relationship employed by many settlers.

Having said this, early AIM missionaries came to Africa with the assumption that African traditional culture was inferior at best and often explicitly evil. As early as 1914 AIM joined other missions in speaking out against female circumcision - something they viewed as a heinous example of a depraved culture. WWI exaggerated this impulse. While some missions began shying away from a canonization of western culture, AIM (for a time) became even more aggressive on cultural issues. As they grew more outspoken the African churches were forced to choose between western cultural Christianity and traditional African cultural beliefs and practices.[81]

At the same time that AIM was hardening its position on cultural practices, currents within the African communities were moving in the opposite direction. WWI had allowed thousands of African soldiers a view into the realities of western civilization. What they saw destroyed the facades of white superiority that many of them had previously accepted. In many cases, the Africans who fought in WWI were given tasks demanding similar ability and responsibility to that of the "superior" white soldiers. In addition, the African soldiers had seen scared white men die in the same way that black men did. Some African soldiers had even slept with white prostitutes, something unthinkable in Africa.[82] In short, the war had begun to destroy the myth of African inferiority that the white community had worked so hard to establish.

Perhaps most significantly, missionary schools were providing education to an increasing number of bright young African students who, when educated, began to question any claims of inherent inferiority the colonial culture had tried to instill. Even in the midst of the Hurlburt controversy, AIM's presence (albeit half-hearted) in the African educational enterprise was numerically significant. The shock of the war

---

Testament and do a serious injustice to the writings of Paul, "There is neither Jew nor Greek, slave nor free, male nor female, for you are all one in Christ Jesus" – Galatians 3:28, *Holy Bible*, (NIV).

[81] Andrew Morton in, *Moi: The Making of an African Statesmen*, (p. 56) described the internal struggle the young Moi (himself a convert to Christianity through AIM missionaries) experienced as he faced the time of his age group's circumcision day. Moi solved the dilemma by having the simple operation performed in a western style hospital and forgoing the traditional rituals associated with the practice.

[82] Edgerton, Robert. *Mau Mau: An African Crucible*, p. 15.

and education on the African perspective was heightened by the increasingly repressive measures being instituted by the colonial government in the attempt to make Kenya attractive to European settlement. A new system of taxation acted as indirect coercion of Africans into lives of forced labor. Further, an identification card called, "Kipande" quickly became a symbol to the increasingly politically conscious African community of their servile status.[83] Nevertheless, the culture of white superiority continued to grow in arrogance. Stories of white cruelty were commonplace and usually not investigated or prosecuted. The students at RVA were well aware of the culture growing up around them. One student at the time witnessed a local white farmer – a Major Smith – kill one of his workers with a rungu[84] for laziness and then comment that, "He was just an African".[85] Instances like this, when put alongside the Biblical mandate of equality before God and loving thy neighbor, produced acute cognitive dissonance in many of the young missionary students. In time this dissonance forced into being a new conception of race and culture in these children.

The combination of these factors made an uprising of some form likely if not inevitable. In 1921 a young missionary-educated Kenyan named Harry Thuku began speaking out against the white colonial government and against the missionary complicity in the oppression of the Kikuyu. Thuku was most adamant in protesting the "hut and poll" taxes that had forced some Kenyans into servitude; and the land policies of the government that he declared boldly were theft – plain and simple.[86]

Thuku's open accusations stirred a quietly boiling pot of discontent and provoked a government response. Thuku was promptly arrested and detained without trial. The colonial government's actions triggered the first political protest of its kind in Kenya. Confusion surrounds the initial moments of the events. Anywhere from several hundred to several thousand angry protesters had made their way to the Nairobi cell where Thuku was being held. As the crowd grew more belligerent the 150 African policemen standing guard outside the cell understandably became agitated. Like the American Boston Massacre it is uncertain

---

[83] Berman, Bruce & John Lonsdale, *Unhappy Valley*, pgs. 111 &113.

[84] A Rungu is a traditional weapon (usually associated with the Masai). It is a thin baton with a heavy knob at the top. A blow to the head with a rungu can be fatal.

[85] Interview with John Barnett (see previous notes).

[86] McKentrick, Fred, "The Thuku Movement in East Africa", *Inland Africa*, June 1927, pgs. 1&2.

who fired the first shot or why. Regardless, the shot was fired and both the crowd and the police panicked. The East African Standard reported twenty-five dead when the chaos had subsided, but some African eyewitnesses claimed the death toll was well over one hundred. Standing in the crowd was another missionary educated Kikuyu named Johnstone Kamau – later known as Jomo Kenyatta – the first president of the Republic of Kenya.[87]

While many missionaries were sympathetic to the African concerns, the anger and the violence elicited a variety of divergent responses. AIM's response to the Thuku movement is telling and does much to explain later tensions between the mission and the Kenyan community around it. In their publication *Inland Africa* of June 1927, Rev. McKentrick described Thuku as a "bitter... self-willed and rebellious lad" who had been dismissed from the church.[88] While acknowledging the very real evils taking place in Kenya, AIM (true to its belief that political leaders are to be honored) chose to side with the established white government. This willing submission to the "authorities established by God",[89] which continues to be deeply ingrained in AIM's belief system, was not viewed as neutral by many of the Kenyans with whom they worked. To them AIM's "apolitical" position was blatant acquiescence to evil. This apolitical stance, when coupled with AIM's increasing assault on female circumcision and other traditional cultural practices produced a growing gulf between the mission and its Christian converts.

The schism reached its worst point in 1929. During this year the cultural crisis within Kenya prompted nearly ninety percent of AIM's converts to leave mission churches and begin churches of their own[90]. The crisis also seems to have been behind the gruesome murder of AIM missionary Hulda Stumpf in her Kijabe home. A part-time staff member at RVA, Stumpf's primary work was with African women. AIM's uncompromising position on female circumcision had made her

---

[87] MacPhee, Marshall, *Kenya*, p. 71 and Robert Edgerton, *Mau Mau*, p. 42. Edgerton, as always cites those sources which will allow the greatest dramatic effect in the retelling. Nevertheless, the basic facts are agreed on by both authors (and a plethora of additional accounts).

[88] McKentrick, Fred, "The Thuku Movement in East Africa", *Inland Africa*, June 1927, pgs. 1&2.

[89] Romans 13:1, *The Holy Bible* (NIV).

[90] Harlow, Vincent, E.M. Chilver and Alison Smith, *The History of East Africa*, p. 364.

infamous among some Kikuyu who resented the rejection of their traditional practices.[91]

While graphic details of the murder were not spelled out in official AIM literature, a variety of tales continue to this day. Many who were students at RVA during this period claim the murder was of a sexual nature, perhaps including Ms. Stumpf's circumcision.[92] Indeed, *Inland Africa's* veiled account of the murder hints at the aggregiousness of the incident, "Alone in her little house at night she had been brutally, inhumanly murdered." It goes on to say, "With our knowledge of Africa we would say that this was the work only of some degenerate man."[93] Yet the doctor first to examine the corpse claimed that no circumcision had been performed, nor was there evidence of sexual assault or mutilation of any kind.[94] Whether it was of a sexual nature or not, what is clear is the link both the Kenyan and missionary communities drew between the murder and the circumcision controversy – every account that survives ascribes the motive to the controversy. This fact makes an already tragic event bitterly ironic, for it was Hulda Stumpf who more than a year before the murder had begun to publicly question AIM's rigid perspective on African cultural practices that were not explicitly unbiblical – specifically female circumcision.[95]

The murder shook the communities and produced two contradictory outcomes. Positively it forced AIM to take a long look at its perspective on traditional African culture and ultimately adopt a less condemning position on some practices – an attitude that was to be most apparent among those second generation missionaries who had experienced the controversy as children. In addition, the murder caused a backlash within the African community that brought reconciliation between AIM and some of its converts. Less positively, the murder was the first significant block in a wall of fear that threatened to separate the

---

[91] "Editorials" *Inland Africa*, Feb. 1930, p. 8. It should be added that not every AIM missionary towed the party line with regards to female circumcision. The Stauffachers working in Masailand believed that cultural practices that did not directly conflict with the Christian message should not become distractions from that message. They echoed the Apostle Paul that "in Christ there is neither circumcision nor uncircumcision". This is found in Robert Tignor's *Colonial Transformation of Kenya*, p. 253.

[92] Interviews with Dr. Bill Barnett, "Doc" Propst and others all concur in this view.

[93] "Editorials" *Inland Africa*, Feb. 1930, p. 8.

[94] Morad, Stephen, p. 24.

[95] Ibid.

missionary and African communities. In addition to psychological barriers, metal bars were installed on missionary compound windows and makeshift alarm systems were put in place.[96] This fear of physical violence was then added to the complex collage of variables at work at RVA during this period including: the adventuresome life enjoyed by the young students, the school's frontier-like circumstances, the eclectic personalities and behavior of the faculty, and a whole host of cultural, political, intellectual and theological currents which penetrated the community's relative isolation. But in the end, what are we to make of the Rift Valley Academy during the years from 1911 to 1933?

BECAUSE PART OF RVA's significance lay in its role in attracting and retaining missionary couples with children, any test of the school during this era necessitates a look at the relative importance of the AIM in the evolution of the Kenyan cultural and political context. Unlike the first ten years of the school's existence, during the 1920's and early 1930's AIM did not experience dramatic growth. That is not to say it had ceased to expand, for it had grown steadily but slowly to a size of approximately one hundred missionaries in 1933. It is to say, however, that the explosion of the missionary population generally anticipated in the 1910's did not materialize. There are several reasons for this. First, the missionary impulse, so strong prior to WWI had been dealt a powerful blow in the late teens and twenties by WWI and the disillusionment that was to follow. The result was that not only were fewer people considering missions, but less money was being sent to support those already in the field. Second, as we have seen, despite the efforts of a few outstanding individuals, RVA had yet to coalesce into a first rate school to which missionary parents could comfortably send their children. The anti-intellectual and "other worldly" biases of the fundamentalist culture had much to do with this. That same fundamentalist culture also led to the internal divisions within the mission concerning African education that, in turn, limited AIM's involvement in the larger African educational enterprise. Yet, these things said, it is important to remember that even while battling these internal demons, AIM still rivaled the largest Protestant missions in Kenya, and the existence of RVA was largely responsible for that resilient strength.

The Modernist controversy in America also created in AIM a shell-shocked defensive mentality that often translated into isolationist

---

[96] Interview with Dr. Bill Barnett (see previous notes).

behavior. AIM's involvement in the Protestant Missionary Alliance diminished during this era; and as a result, the effectiveness of the overall Protestant missionary enterprise was hampered. Like the proverbial ostrich with its head buried in the sand, AIM sought to go about its business with little regard for the evolving cultural and political context they were a part of. This isolationism was characteristic of not only fundamentalists during this period, but the American zeitgeist as a whole; and can be seen perfectly in the self chosen, "island unto itself" existence of the Rift Valley Academy during this era. The murder of Hulda Stumpf and the increasing antagonism being directed at AIM from its own converts did, however, begin to shake the mission from its self-induced slumber. By 1933 both the school and the mission were willing to move in a new direction – a new direction that was fueled in large part by the return of many of the first generation of RVA students.

In any era one test of a school is the students it produces. Of course, such a test is somewhat flawed as it downplays the massive impact familial, cultural and individual circumstances play in the path the school's students later choose. Nevertheless all schools do have an influence – and certainly few schools can claim as profound an influence as this isolated western boarding school in the heart of Africa. If you can tell a tree by the fruit it produces, what were the fruits of the school's efforts? What lives did the school help produce?

Even a cursory study of the students coming out of RVA during this period reveals several conclusions. First, in interviews, letters and the limited published accounts concerning these students, there is virtually no mention of the girls who took their education at RVA. There is nothing mysterious about this omission. Consistent with the prevalent concept of the traditional Christian family, many RVA women went on to Bible schools and married, becoming wives and mothers.

Not surprisingly there is far more information available about the boys of this era, and what this information reveals is rather impressive. Granted, not all of the school's students went on to live admirable and noteworthy lives. At least one alumnus became an officer of the infamous Kenyan penal system and battled alcoholism his entire life before dying an embittered and lonely man in Tanzania.[97] Yet, thanks to the British influence, most RVA men overcame the anti-education bias prevalent in fundamentalist missionary circles and went on to higher education of some kind, many to attain advanced degrees. From this group came a high percentage of doctors, most of who returned to Africa

---

[97] Ibid. (Dr. Barnett was speaking of the elder Allen boy in this story).

as missionaries. Among these were the legendary names of Dr. Philip Morris (an outstanding eye surgeon in Kenya); Dr. Bill Barnett (a longtime AIM doctor in Africa); and "Doc" Propst.[98] The school also turned out a disproportionately large number of renowned authors including: Charles Ludwig (*He Freed Britain's Slaves*) and Phillip Keller (*A Shepard Considers the 23rd Psalm*, among others).[99] Reflecting the extent to which the beauty of the African habitat had shaped his values, Keller also was widely heralded as a world leader in the conservationist movement. The school even produced one of the RAF's heroes during the Battle of Britain – Johnny Allen.[100] Finally, whether as doctors, teachers or traditional church planting missionaries, an overwhelming number returned overseas to work in developing countries. And this has been perhaps the most remarkable trait of the school's graduates. From this time forward generation after generation of RVA alumni returned to Africa as missionaries, many of whom were to make a remarkable contribution to the Kenyan church and culture.

Much of the credit for the extraordinary lives of these RVA students certainly must go to the parents, their faith, and the Kenyan culture these children grew up in. Yet, if Rogers and Hammerstein are right and, "nothing comes from nothing" somewhere in the disjointed, makeshift and (at the time) often second-rate RVA education "there must have been something good".[101]

---

[98] Ibid.
[99] Devitt, Edith. *On the Edge of the Rift*, p. 82.
[100] Interview with Dr. Bill Barnett (see previous notes).
[101] Rogers & Hammerstein, *The Sound of Music*, 1965 (Movie Version).

CHAPTER 3

THE FIRST WAVE OF RETURNING RVA ALUMNI: RVA FROM 1933-1945

By 1933 RVA HAD BEEN IN EXISTENCE FOR OVER A quarter of a century, but as an institution it was just beginning to mature. Of course, this does not imply the school's earlier history was insignificant. Nothing could be further from the truth. Before the arrival of Hurlburt's small party in 1901 the African Inland Mission was comprised of a dejected bachelor. By 1933, thanks to Hurlburt's leadership and the presence of the fledgling Rift Valley Academy, AIM had grown to be the largest American mission in Kenya with a contingent of at least 50 missionaries at any given time.[1] Only the British societies, whose children could be trained at the few colonial schools, were larger. Between the Protestant and Catholic missions, Kenya had gone from having a miniscule Christian population in 1900 (0.2%) to a significant minority by 1933[2]. And converts were not the only examples of Christianity's mushrooming influence in the colony. Even with the obstacles presented by waning missionary zeal in the west

---

[1] Morad, Stephen. "The Founding Principles of the African Inland Mission and Their Interaction with the African Context in Kenya From 1895-1939: the Study of a Faith Mission". Unpublished Ph.D. dissertation, University of Edinburgh, 1997. Charts of pages 17&301.

[2] Barret, David (ed.) *The Encyclopedia of World Christianity*, "Kenya", Oxford Univ. Press, 1982. No data is available for this era, but most estimate that somewhere between 15-20% of the African population would have considered themselves Christian in 1933.

after WWI and the faltering global economy during the early 1930's, mission schools and medical centers continued to proliferate across the colony, transforming the cultural landscape. As early as 1921 AIM was responsible for 122 African schools, with over 2,700 students, staffed by either Euro-American missionaries or the over 200 Kenyan teachers that had been trained by these missionaries.[3]

The cultural transformation brought by Christian missionaries was extremely complex in nature, always being shaped by both the indigenous cultures that were accepting it and the British colonial system within which it took place. Increasingly missionaries were at odds with the settler community and the colonial government who openly questioned the "prudence" of educating and Christianizing the "natives", something that most now acknowledged would undercut the settler's dominant economic and political position. The one thing that all "Europeans" could agree upon was that the work of the missionaries was profoundly reshaping African culture in Kenya. To the extent that this change was the result of the African Inland Mission work (and significant influence cannot be denied) the Rift Valley Academy played a central role. Yet, despite its absolutely essential support role for the American missionary project, the school's development had not been closely attended to.

It was almost in spite of itself that the Rift Valley Academy survived its first generation of existence. In retrospect it is clear that many of the school's difficulties were a direct result of the fundamentalist worldview that lay at the core of the community. This worldview that seeped through virtually every pore of the community produced a school with a generally reluctant faculty, meager resources and few aspirations for its future. Yet, that same fundamentalist culture also produced a positively dynamic brand of Christianity, profoundly committed to living a life worthy of Christ's calling. Some of these individuals were extraordinarily gifted and used these gifts to meet the emotional and educational needs of the slowly growing band of missionary children. Without this small group of dedicated educators, it is difficult to imagine the school's survival to this point.

Yet, ultimately RVA survived for one reason – it was needed. Even those who were most adamantly against using missionaries to teach white children had to concede that the entire American and Independent[4]

---

[3] Morad, Stephen. "The Founding Principles of the AIM", p. 301.

[4] The term "Independent" includes all missionary groups not associated with the Catholic, Anglican or Mainline Protestant churches. They were usually of

missionary enterprise would have been significantly weakened without such a school. Therefore, although Herb Downing's "call" in 1933 to lead the school might have been privately denigrated, no one put up a fight. It needed to be done.

LIKE NO ONE before him, Herb Downing was tailor made for the role of RVA's principal. Downing's life up to 1933 had prepared him for the task in at least two ways. Most importantly he was among the first of the school's former students to return as a missionary himself. As a native of Kijabe he understood the dynamics of the quirky school community and the African culture surrounding it. In 1905 he had been one of the first Americans born in East Africa. Due to his father's role as field director with AIM, Downing's childhood and primary education were all at RVA. In fact, he was not away from Kijabe for any extended period of time until he left as a teenager to complete his high school and college education in America.

As a child growing up at Kijabe, Downing had spent considerable time with the children of the African Christian leaders his father worked with. As a result of these relationships he picked up the Kikuyu language almost as early as he did English. Downing's command of the language and culture of the Kikuyu spoke eloquently of his respect for the equal humanity of the Kenyan people that his Christian faith espoused. But more than that, Downing's mastery of Kikuyu and Swahili connected him intimately to the culture and people of the area – opening doors and facilitating goodwill in ways unimaginable to those outside the circle of trust created by the bond of language. Like some of the other RVA students who returned to Africa after college, genuine interpersonal experience with Africans, when combined with the egalitarian Christian ideals of his parents, had overcome the racism that many of the earliest missionaries had come to Africa with. Downing's ability to see past skin color and the myriad cultural obstacles that stood between the European and the African was not lost on the Kenyan community surrounding RVA. This attitude of mutual respect provided opportunities for AIM and RVA that might have otherwise been impenetrable. Simply put, Africa was his home.[5] But his Kijabe

---

Fundamentalist or Evangelical stock and by this point comprised a substantial and growing minority (40%) of the total missionary population.

[5] Information on Downing's childhood at Kijabe can be found in a variety of places. I have relied primarily on interviews with Downing and his son Glen. Both interviews are on tape at the Billy Graham Center Archives. The Herb Downing interview was conducted in 1983 and is found under CN 251. The

education was not the only thing that made him well suited for his coming role at RVA.

As a college student Herb had decided upon the field of education, hoping some day to return to teach in one of AIM's African schools. For Downing, this meant first getting some experience in America. From 1928-1933 Herb taught in the Pennsylvania public schools. Because of his unique perspective and natural leadership ability he was quickly put on track to become an administrator. By the time he decided to return to Kenya in 1933, the twenty-eight year old Downing had already served as a Vice-Principal of a public junior high school in Western Pennsylvania.[6] Thus his insight into the mission community, the Kikuyu culture and the larger multiracial Kenyan culture combined with his experience as an educator to make him an ideal choice to be RVA's principal.

DESPITE THE FAMILIAR geography and some recognizable faces, the Kenya that Downing and his young family returned to was not the one he had left. In truth he was never entirely separated from the evolution of Kenyan society for he certainly must have read AIM's *Inland Africa*. However, these accounts were written primarily to describe the progress of evangelism, and thus rarely betrayed the depth of the political, social and economic turmoil in which that evangelistic work functioned. Therefore, while he had heard of the Thuku movement (1922) and Hulda Stumpf's murder (1930), Downing had missed the dynamic and substantive change the colony had experienced in his absence. Thus, for this Rip VanWinkle the real education was about to begin.

Surrounding the isolated glimpses Downing must have read in *Inland Africa* was an increasingly complex society experiencing profound change. At the center of this change was the larger Protestant missionary community. While AIM had determined to let nothing distract it from the work of evangelism, other Protestant groups had begun to get involved in the internal politics of the colony. The Church of Scotland under the leadership of Dr. Arthur is perhaps the best example of the broad perspective employed by several of the other Protestant missions. While not disregarding evangelism, the Scottish mission had at its core the belief that loving your neighbor had practical and physical

---

author conducted the Glen Downing interview on May 29, 1999 at Buck Creek Camp, WA. It can be found in the Papers and Materials of Phil Dow at the BGC Archives.
[6] Ibid.

consequences. This fundamental belief led directly to their extensive educational program and the conviction that the economic and political good of the African majority should be a primary concern. Therefore when in the early 1920's the administration of Governor Northey sided with Lord Delamere's vision of a white man's Kenya, the missionaries voiced their concern to the colonial office in England. A bitter dispute between the British Protestant missions and the settler community ensued culminating in a decision by the colonial office at Whitehall which came to be known as the "white paper".[7]

Issued in July of 1923, the white paper sided with the missionaries stating in one decisive sentence that the concerns of the African community in Kenya "must be paramount".[8] It was a dramatic triumph for the Protestant missions and the African community for whom they spoke. The white paper had the effect of devastating the fragile relationship between the settler and missionary communities. To be sure, on an individual basis friendships remained, but the bridge between the two communities had been destroyed and would not be mended. Kenya pioneer John Boyes summed up settler sentiment stating, "The primary mistake, from which all of the trouble springs, and to which all missionaries seem to be officially compelled to subscribe, is that the African Negro is, or can be made by education, the moral and intellectual equal of the white man."[9] The settler community saw clearly the implications of the missionary project and it stood in direct conflict with their own. Shortly thereafter the Church of Scotland confirmed their desire to encourage self-determination by promoting the emergence of indigenous church leadership – something AIM had also been slowly moving towards. In place of external authority the Church of Scotland Mission (CSM) set up a church officiating body called the Kirk Sessions which gave defacto control of church affairs in Kenya to the Kenyan church.[10] The implication was obvious and had direct political ramifications. Africans could and should begin to assume the leadership over their own destiny.

---

[7] Murray-Brown, Jeremy. *Kenyatta* (2nd Ed.), George Allen & Unwin, London: 1979, p. 88.

[8] Ibid, p. 89.

[9] Kennedy, Dane. *Islands of White: Settler Society and Culture in Kenya & South Rhodesia*, Duke Univ. Press, Durham: 1987, p. 162.

[10] Murray-Brown, p. 90 & B.E. Kipkorir, *Imperialism and Collaboration in Colonial Kenya*. Kenya Literature Bureau, Nairobi: 1980, under Anne King's, "J.W. Arthur and African Interests".

The growing independence and confidence of the African population, resulting in part from the Protestant missions in Kenya, was exemplified by the development of a dynamic syncretism that combined Protestant theology and symbolism with the African community's customs and political circumstances. Nowhere was this more evident than in the symbolism surrounding Harry Thuku – the exiled leader of the 1922 uprising. In the teahouse banter of Nairobi and in African church sermons Thuku began to be seen, in quite literal terms, as the African Moses – God's deliverer who would come back to liberate the captive tribes of Kenya.[11] So deeply had Christian ideals and symbols begun to influence Kenyan culture that even the more militant Kikuyu organization, the Kikuyu Central Association (KCA), choose as their theme, "Pray and Work".[12]

Downing had also been absent during the last tumultuous years of Charles Hulburt's tenure as AIM's leader. Prior to Hurlburt's resignation his growing commitment to African education had led to a cooperative effort on the part of the protestant missions to begin a first rate university preparatory high school for the best African students.[13] While AIM's involvement in the school after Hurlburt's departure was nominal at best, in March of 1926 the Alliance High School quietly opened its doors. Its apparently timid beginning, however, should not mask the significance of this one school in the development of the colony's future. For the first time missionaries were explicitly educating Africans for positions of leadership in society – in a society that did not yet exist. The sober minded settlers resented the vision of the protestant missionaries and for good reason. By 1947 the Alliance High School had an academic record that equaled or outshone the best of the British schools and when the first cabinet ministers of the newly independent Republic of Kenya sat down in 1963 a full three-quarters of them were alumni of this single institution.[14]

---

[11] *Kenyatta*, p. 99.

[12] Ibid, p. 104.

[13] Oliver, Roland. *The Missionary Factor in East Africa*, Longmans, NY: 1952, p. 227-228. The proposal for the school surfaced in 1915 and was accepted in 1918 by the four largest protestant missions: the Church of England (CMS); the Church of Scotland (CSM); the United Methodists; and AIM. AIM even under Hurlburt was the most reluctant of the missions due to its fear of modernity and liberal theology. It was, nevertheless, behind the plan.

[14] Kipkorir, B.E., "Carey Francis at Alliance High School, Kikuyu 1940-1962", p. 113.

Throughout history and across cultures, whenever a significant new set of ideas is introduced into a culture, the status quo is upset. When this happens there must be uncertainty as individuals struggle through the changing reality for a new identity. By introducing the beliefs and values of Christianity and western education, the missionary movement had profoundly shaken the status quo of traditional Kenyan culture. Christianity and western education would have caused a cultural crisis together, but a third element proved to be the wild card – for it virtually guaranteed the crisis would include violence (something the other two did not in any sense encourage). The change of the economic system from one based on subsistence farming and pastoralism to one of industrial agriculture and cash cropping displaced many Kenyans. Taxes enforced by the Northey administration also pushed thousands of other Kenyans out of the countryside and into the market economy and the growing towns.[15] From all over Kenya individuals from virtually every tribe began to make their way into Nairobi – either out of economic necessity or because of the lure of the new life it promised. These Kenyans were individuals between worlds. They had been cut off from the values of the past without fully adopting those offered by the Christian missionaries or the often-extravagant settlers. Congregating in dirty teahouses in the African sections of Nairobi these displaced discontents began to develop into a new brand of African which Downing could have only partially anticipated – the missionary educated, cosmopolitan and discontented young generations of which Harry Thuku and Jomo Kenyatta were prototypical.[16]

The tension that now permeated Kenyan politics looked like it would dissipate when the settler friendly administration of Northey came to a close in the mid 1920's. Yet when Sir Edward Grigg replaced Northey in 1925 life for the African community went from bad to worse. Under this disciple of Smuts and Rhodes the goals of the white paper were consciously ignored in favor of settler concerns.[17] As a result, anger quietly boiled among the young and destabilized African community, increasing in step with the growing arrogance of the settler community.

Added to the tense atmosphere among the cultural groupings in Kenya were the challenges facing the missionary community. The American stockmarket crash of 1929, and the domino catastrophes in

---

[15] Edgerton, Robert. *Mau Mau: An African Crucible*, pgs. 14-16; *Kenyatta*, p. 87-88 & especially Bruce Berman and John Lonsdale, *Unhappy Valley*, James Currey Ltd. London: 1992, pgs. 114-115.

[16] *Kenyatta*, p. 83.

[17] Ibid, p 104.

Britain and elsewhere, had plunged the western world into economic and political turbulence. As a "faith mission" – AIM was particularly vulnerable to the rising and falling fortunes of the Anglo-American economy.[18] As the depression spread and deepened, the dedication of those financially supporting the missionaries was sorely tested. Ultimately, as Roy Entwistle pointed out in his 1968 M.Ed. thesis, many of those supporting the missionary movement decided that under the circumstances their first loyalty must be to their families and communities at home. As a result, AIM funding dropped to a point where some missionaries were forced to become entirely self-sustaining – growing their own vegetables, hunting their own meat and so on. For RVA this meant two things. First, many missionary families already in Kenya could not pay their school fees. And second, numbers of would-be-missionaries hoping to begin work in Kenya simply could not raise the funds necessary to come out to Africa. These two realities combined, leaving the community impoverished and the school's size small.[19] Herb Downing inherited a barely breathing school, supported by a small and faltering mission community, itself surrounded by a dramatically altered and increasingly tense colonial context.

HERB DOWNING AND his wife Mildred arrived in 1933 just in time for the new school term. Despite the fact that much in Kenya had changed since he left, Kijabe remained isolated and apparently untouched. To the casual observer, life at RVA continued much as it had when he was a student. Positively, despite the depression, the school's student body had stabilized at around thirty students. Less positively, the school's faculty problems had continued and in 1933 the thirty-four students enrolled had no teacher.[20] Therefore, Downing's first duty as school principal was to teach alongside his wife until other staff could be found to allow him more time to devote to the school's development.

Another significant similarity between the school that Downing had known and the one he now returned to was the age of the students. No

---

[18] As a reminder, a "faith mission" is one, usually rooted in the Holiness movement, that believes that God will provide for every need that is within His will. Therefore to publish needs or wants in order to solicit financial support is to take away reliance on God as well as evidence of supernatural intervention – if indeed the necessary funds come in without publicizing the need.

[19] Groves, C.P. *The Planting of Christianity in Africa*, Volume 3, Lutterworth Press, London: 1958, p. 138. Also see Entwistle's M.Ed. Thesis "The Rift Valley Academy...", p. 17.

[20] See Herb Downing interview available at the BGC Archives under CN 251.

students were admitted before the age of seven and almost no students remained at the school past the age of fifteen. These ages are significant for several reasons. First, many of the students boarding at RVA were very young. Psychologists have confirmed what common sense told the early missionaries in Kenya, that long periods of separation from loved ones could be tremendously trying on children of any age - and certainly the younger the age the greater the potential emotional trauma.[21] Indeed it was to significantly lessen this period of separation that the school had been established in the first place. Nevertheless, the accounts of heavyhearted parents saying goodbye to weeping children that are prevalent in missionary memoirs from this time reveal the pain of parents and children as they learned to live with separation from loved ones.[22]

Those in charge of RVA were only too aware of the pain of the missionary families and for the most part made a concerted effort to minimize the loneliness the children experienced. For starters, RVA chose a full year school schedule which allowed families a month of vacation together after each three-month school term. In addition, in spite of the militaristic ethos of the school, dorm life and school activities were consciously guided by an attempt to provide students with an extended family. Finally, while boarding was easier for some than it was for others, everyone realized that the alternatives were either the family's return to America or the return of the children to America or Britain – alone. This could mean not months but years of separation from family. Therefore to most, all things considered, RVA was the preferable option.[23] The long-term impact of the separation on the young boarders varied depending on the circumstances and idiosyncrasies of individual families. To try and make any definitive statement on the health or harm

---

[21] Some relatively recent studies on the effects of separation upon the missionary child at boarding schools are: Wickstrom, D.L. "Self-esteem and dependence in early, late and non-boarding children" (1978) and David Schipper, "Self concept differences between early, late and non-boarding children" – unpublished dissertation, Rosemead Graduate School of Psychology (1977). Both are found in Edward Danielson, *Missionary Kid – MK*, William Carey Library: 1984. Other similar studies confirming these results are found in Kelly O'Donnell and Michele Lewis O'Donnell (eds.) *Helping Missionaries Grow: Readings in Mental Health and Missions*. William Carey Library: 1988.

[22] One of many such examples is found in "Githua" the unpublished story of the Allen family in Kenya. It can be found at the BGC Archives under CN 81; 39-14. The lifelong struggles of son Bill Allen with homesickness and loneliness are tied directly to the trauma of boarding at RVA at such an early age.

[23] Just one of the many places this argument is made is in Edith Devitt's book, *On the Edge of the Rift*, University Printers, Langley, BC. Pgs. 80-86.

of boarding for this era of student would be to move onto highly speculative territory. However, if we judge the long-term impact of the experience by looking at the lives of these students (such as we did earlier) it appears that few were irreparably damaged. The number of students from this era who returned to Africa as missionaries and sent their own children to RVA is a testament to the generally healthy experience they had. For whatever reason the positives of the RVA experience seemed to overcome the pain of homesickness many of them experienced.[24]

Nevertheless, the tender age at which RVA's first students began boarding is an important reminder of the painful separation students and parents experienced in the school's early years – a pain that lies at the heart of the missionary experience, then and now. Yet, it is also a reminder of the important role the school played in limiting the even greater separation the families would have been forced to confront had the school not existed. This potential separation would have forced the missionaries to choose between two equally sacred callings – that of parents and that of missionaries. It was a dilemma that could have dramatically curtailed the number of Christians willing to enter the mission field. As Herbert Downing acknowledged in 1946, "the existence of school facilities on the field for children of missionaries has been instrumental in producing valuable missionary personnel".[25] In the mind of Downing and a growing number of others the role of missionary education for the success of the entire missionary enterprise was, "vital".[26]

The age of fifteen is also significant for similar reasons. As the equivalent of an old-time, one-room schoolhouse, RVA in the 1930's often lacked both the books and the qualified faculty necessary to prepare its students for entrance into post-secondary education.[27] It was assumed by most that at fourteen or fifteen the students would leave

---

[24] See the concluding pages of chapter two and the conclusion of this chapter for considerable evidence of healthy and fruitful lives RVA students went on to live.

[25] Downing, Herbert C. "The Education of Missionaries' Children", *Inland Africa*, Jan/Feb. 1946, pgs. 7-8.

[26] Ibid.

[27] In his interview H. Downing recalls using the same science text for three years in a row – a physiology text of all things, which he says he virtually memorized. Similar stories are found in *Devitt's On the Edge of the Rift* and the "Doc" Propst interview (Also available at the BGC Archives under the Papers and Materials of Phil Dow) among other places.

RVA for either a British boarding school (an option most did not consider as they hoped to prepare for American universities) or school in America. For those students returning to America this would mean living with relatives, in Christian boarding schools or at the Westervelt House. Such a separation was traumatic by itself, but this transition was not just an extended separation from their family. It was a separation from the entire world of their childhood. Thus, when the young students returned to America or England they returned to a world they did not understand and one that could not even begin to understand them.

The same phenomena remains today, but it can hardly be equated with the cross-cultural trauma experienced by pre-WWII RVA students.[28] Even with improving communication and transportation technology, Kenya in 1933 remained in relative isolation. No planes daily shuttled Americans and Britons into and out of Kenya. No telephone lines connected Nairobi to London or Los Angeles, let alone Kijabe. This isolation from the "home" cultures produced two apparently contradictory realities. First, the pieces of European or American culture that did slowly seep into the white society of Kenya were often colored and synergized by the entirely exotic culture already in place. In one of the more extravagant examples of this cultural synergy, one Lady Feilding asked her husband to build their home in the Kenyan highlands based on the mythical treehouse in her favorite British fairy tale Peter Pan. The result was a bizarre and sprawling piece of Anglo-architecture, plucked awkwardly in the Kenyan wilderness, today known as the world-famous Treetops Hotel.[29]

Second, Kenya's isolation sometimes led some Europeans to such an extreme attempt to retain their western cultures that elements in British or American Kenya were often more British than Britain or more American than America. Whether it was the staging of the annual horse races at the Ngong track outside of Nairobi, strict golf course etiquette and attire at the Limuru Club or the ceremonies surrounding the

---

[28] An increasing number of studies have been done in recent decades concerning the psychological health of missionary children. Those studies have strongly supported the conclusion that the early missionary community came to intuitively – if the child was to make the readjustment into their "home" culture it was important that the child have a strong familiarity with that culture prior to re-entry. Thus the third culture created at RVA might act as a bridge between cultures, thereby giving students a greater opportunity for a successful life in America.

[29] Amin, Mohamed, Duncan Willets and Brian Tetley. *Journey Through Kenya*, p. 121.

traditional "fox" hunts, British colonists fervently kept alive traditions of Old Britannia that were, at the same time, losing ground in the New Britain. Simply put, the British or American culture that existed in Kenya was often decades behind its long-since-evolved parent culture. Either way the culture the missionary children grew up with in Kenya was almost entirely unintelligible to their peers in America or Britain; and the same could be said in reverse.

If the age of seven represents the separation experienced by the boarders at RVA, and if fifteen represents the lonely return by most to now alien cultures, the picture of life for this era's missionary child is rather bleak. Yet to leave it there is to miss the critical piece of the puzzle – namely the experience of the students at RVA between the years of seven and fifteen. The frustration of students common to schools everywhere and some painful realities specific to boarding aside, most of the letters and memoirs that remain reveal a generally content student body at RVA. In the words of one of RVA's early students, hers was, "an exceptionally happy and privileged one".[30]

PRIOR TO DOWNING'S arrival the experience of the students was often similarly positive, but in many cases it was positive in spite of a school culture that seemed bent against such a pleasant outcome. As we have seen, the school's lack of structure and vision had led to an inconsistent experience, one largely dependent on the peculiarities of the adults that fate had often forced on the school. Downing hoped to change this. He understood that for most missionary and potential missionary families, a run-down and haphazard boarding school held little more attraction than no school at all. Simply put, the better the school, the more freedom Christian families would have to consider a role for themselves in missionary work. By setting in place traditions that could sink beneath the changing cosmetic façade of the school and into its soul, Downing aimed to create a lasting and positive culture – one that could thrive regardless of who sat in the principal's office or assigned the classroom work. Although Downing was American, his childhood in the colony meant that his worldview was an international blend of British, Kenyan and American perspectives. Not surprisingly, the school structure and traditions he sought to put in place at RVA reflected this unusual cultural heritage.

---

[30] The daughter of Lee Downing wrote these words in an unpublished account of the Downing family at Kijabe entitled, "Our Roots", p. 1. This can be found at the BGC Archives, Wheaton IL.

As has been noted, the curriculum of the school to this point was not strictly British or American, but had been determined by the availability of textbooks and faculty. Quite often British faculty had taught from American textbooks or vice versa. As a temporary fix, this fluctuating arrangement had been tolerated, but as other European schools began to crop up around the colony with government support and a consistent curriculum, the inadequacies of such an approach became apparent. American textbooks or teachers often failed to adequately prepare students for the Cambridge Exams that determined a child's ability to continue to top secondary schools and universities in the British system. Because RVA had wanted to be affordable for the children of missionaries they had, from the beginning, charged settler children double the fees for AIM children. As the mission gave little money to the school, RVA had become reliant for its survival on the extra income generated by the tuition of settler students – all of whom needed to take the Cambridge exams. In addition, the high percentage of British AIM missionaries were growing less satisfied with the mixed curriculum which they perceived to be hurting their children's future educational prospects.

So dissatisfied were the British AIM missionaries that by 1937 plans were in place for a separate school run by the British Home Council for British missionary children.[31] Because the settler children would likely leave RVA for its British equivalent, taking with them funds essential to the maintenance of RVA, the proposed school was a very real threat to the future existence of RVA. In a letter to RVA parents on April 15, 1937, Downing acknowledged as much expressing grave concerns over the imminence of, "the British Home Council's (school)... in competition with RVA". The danger to RVA was palpable as Downing continued, "our buildings and equipment are getting further and further behind the standard set by other European schools in Kenya". There needed to be significant changes soon or RVA would cease to exist, leaving the growing number of American children without a school, thereby threatening the ever-expanding American missionary influence in Kenya. In a move that displayed Downing's openness to the British system and the danger to RVA he concluded with "a proposal to combine the two projects ... and missions."[32] A questionnaire was sent out to

---

[31] RVA School Board Minutes, dated 3/26/37. The same ideas are found in Downings letter to RVA parents, dated April 15, 1937. Both documents are found in the RVA archives, Kijabe.

[32] This letter of April 15, 1937, again, is available at RVA in the school's archives.

parents asking if they would prefer an entirely British curriculum taught by British teachers or if a more intentionally British, but still mixed, curriculum would suffice. From all indications, Downing was ready to dramatically rearrange the school in order to keep an AIM school – regardless of the cultural emphasis - as an option for missionary children. Fatefully, the results of the survey revealed a missionary population willing to accept a modified mixed curriculum, so long as the goal of the school was preparation for the British Cambridge Examinations.[33]

The British influence on RVA at this time was also clearly seen in the sporting activities initiated under Miss Perrott. Upon Downing's encouragement Dr. Davis built a tennis court and gave lessons to the students. The British sports of field hockey, cricket and rounders were also stressed. Because equipment was scarce, some enterprising students created their own sticks and bats out of local trees. The small numbers of students meant that almost everyone was needed in order to play a decent cricket or hockey match. But, of course, this full participation is exactly what Herb sought.[34]

In addition to an emphasis on sports, Downing sought to instill a sense of discipline, tradition and school pride through the introduction of school uniforms. The boy's uniforms were the traditional British khaki while the girls wore gray jumpers, white blouses and red bows.[35] The decision to use uniforms was hardly novel in Kenya. The British schools that had begun to pop up around the Kenya colony in the thirties all instituted uniforms in keeping with the values of tradition, discipline and comradery the English system was built around.[36] Thus the colonial context naturally led RVA to a similar policy. Yet the choice of uniforms also is indicative of the direction the school was to take in the next few decades – a direction seen in at least one other system Downing instituted in the 1930's.

Downing held to the conviction that if a person did a bad thing, it was all right (even good) to feel bad for doing it. What has been vilified as "guilt", Downing believed was evidence of a healthy conscience –

---

[33] RVA School Board Minutes, dated 4/27/37. Available from the RVA archives.

[34] Entwistle, Roy. Unpublished M.Ed. Thesis at Seattle Pacific College (1968) entitled, "The Rift Valley Academy...", p. 18.

[35] Ibid. p. 19.

[36] The most important white school in Nairobi at this time was the newly opened Prince of Wales School (1931). The availability of a British curriculum, in addition to RVA's inconsistent ability to take in more students led to an absence of non-missionary students from the time of Hurlburt's resignation up till 1940.

assuming that that guilt led the person to accept the forgiveness Jesus offered, and thus to the restored wholeness that God wanted for everyone. Most attempts to shift blame away from the individual would have struck Downing as blatantly dishonest and ultimately tragic. In the conservative protestant worldview, attempts to ignore or excuse individual sin, and thus guilt, allowed people to sever their conscience. This not only left the individual ultimately empty and unsatisfied but also kept them separated from God, all the while putting a candy coating on actions that hurt others. Downing's was an entirely self-consistent belief system that allowed people to honestly face moral failure because repentance brought with it healing. Yet, to the person who did not believe in a forgiving God the consequences of such a system appeared cruel.

Under Downing, a system of rewards and punishments was instituted based on this worldview. It was a program he also hoped would bring consistency and fairness to discipline at RVA. In this system students would receive "black marks" for breaking a rule. The greater the infraction the more black marks were given. If a student reached a certain number of black marks, they received some form of corporal punishment. On the bright side, at the end of the school term the number of black marks were added up and those students who had received less than the preset limit were given a party. The party, called the Rendezvous or "Mutton-Guz", originally included a lamb roast and games and was eagerly anticipated by the students – that is those who had behaved themselves. The mischievous or malicious could only sit in their rooms waiting for the next term and the hope of taking part in the next term's party. Said one student; "Finding out someone was going to be excluded from the Rendezvous was like learning they had been convicted of some great crime" – which was exactly Downing's intention.[37]

Choosing a discipline system that included corporal punishment, "black marks" and other apparently harsh measures was conservative even in the 1930's, yet it was not out of step with the main stream of western educational practice. The Progressive school of education initiated by Kilpatrick at Columbia had yet to have any substantial influence on the average America school. It was not until late in the

---

[37] A Letter from Lois (Danielson) Carlson, a student at RVA during the Lehrer era (1936-1955), to the author written in 1997. The letter is in the possession of the author but will eventually become part of the Phil Dow collection at the Billy Graham Center Archives at Wheaton College, Wheaton, IL.

1940's that the feel-good, self esteem-driven, Progressivism gained dominance in America.[38] Characteristically, Kijabe was isolated from the latest educational trends and Progressivism did not disturb RVA's educational culture until the late 1960's. But more will be said on that at the appropriate time.

Within two years of Downing's arrival the school had begun to develop a new sense of itself and even a quiet pride in its existence as a community. A forty-eight foot cedar flagpole was cut as a symbol of the school's growing pride.[39] Yet, if the new seeds Downing had planted were to take root there needed to be some semblance of consistency and quality in the faculty, and over this area Downing had no control. Because of RVA's inferior position in the AIM hierarchy, Downing had almost no say in who was sent to teach at the school. He could neither recruit nor refuse teachers. He could only wait, hope and then do the best with what he was given.[40] Happily, Providence once again smiled on the school when the Lehrers came to RVA.

"MA" AND "PA" Lehrer arrived as dorm parents at Kijabe in 1936 and stayed, almost uninterrupted, until 1955.[41] Unable to have children of their own, the Lehrers were a couple looking for children to raise, and at RVA they found children who desired parental nurturing as much as they wanted to give it. No parents are perfect and certainly the Lehrers misstepped from time to time. Nevertheless this stern but warmhearted couple filled a significant void in the lives of the school's students.

Pa Lehrer was a strong and physically fit man whose enjoyment of the outdoors was only equaled by a curious intellectual bent. The well-read Lehrer displayed a mind that, for the AIM missionaries of the day, was unusually independent and free ranging.[42] Lehrer's strong mind and body combined with a genuine affection for the children to produce a

---

[38] Hirsch, E.D. *The Schools We Need: Why We Don't Have Them*, Doubleday, NY: 1996. P. 50-52.

[39] Entwistle, p. 18.

[40] Interview with Glen Downing conducted by the author at Buck Creek Camp, WA on May 29, 1999. Available at the BGC Archives under the Papers and Materials of Phil Dow.

[41] Entwistle, p. 80. The Lehrers took their only leave from RVA during a furlough to America from 1950-52.

[42] Interview with Charles Skoda by the author at Buck Creek Camp, WA May 29, 1999. Charles was a boarder at RVA, living with the Lehrers for eleven years. Charles remembered clearly that Carl Jung, of all people was a favorite of Lehrers.

father figure almost universally admired. As one student remembered, "He had an uncanny ability to command respect and obedience without saying a word".[43] During the regular Saturday and Sunday afternoon hikes on which Pa Lehrer took his charges, he "walked with great dignity and a steady pace with… kids of all shapes and sizes strung out behind him".[44] The hikes provide us with a wonderful insight into Pa Lehrer and the culture that he helped create at RVA.

The routinely rigorous hikes were not simply to allow energetic and rambunctious students some positive release. Significantly, they were an education in their own right. Thanks to the spontaneous tutorials that poured out of Pa Lehrer, the young scholars gained a deep appreciation of the trees, birds, grasses and animals of the Kenyan highlands. It is no wonder that so many of this era's students became active conservationists.[45] Yet for all the learning that happened these hikes were never forced educational experiences. More often than not playful "caffy-apple" fights would break out among the students under Lehrer's smiling, watchful eyes. The children needed to be able to be children and Lehrer understood this, yet they all knew to keep their adventures within certain bounds. Whether out of either fear or respect, few trespassed these apparently well-understood limits.[46]

The same mixture of fun and instruction seemed present in even the most routine of daily events – the community meals in Kiambogo. At meals, manners and etiquette were taught and modeled by the Lehrers even while certain childish freedoms were amusingly tolerated. Each meal would begin with the students standing at attention behind their assigned chairs.[47] Pa Lehrer, dressed as always for the evening meal in a dark dinner jacket and a bow tie, would say the blessing and the feast of food and conversation would begin.[48] Proper table etiquette was strictly

---

[43] Letter from Lois (Danielson) Carlson to the author in 1997. Lois boarded at RVA under the Lehrers for six years. The letter is in the possession of the author but will be found at the BGC Archives in the Papers and Materials of Phil Dow.

[44] Ibid.

[45] Letter from Ruben Schwieger to the author on June 14, 1997. Ruben was a boarder at RVA for 10 years and lived under the Lehrers for seven of those years. The high percentage of "naturalists" / "conservationists" was noted by Charles Skoda in the Buck Creek Camp interview cited above.

[46] Letter from Lois Carlson to the author in 1997. Letter in possession of the author.

[47] Letter from Ruben Schwieger to the author on June 14,1997 as cited above.

[48] Letter for Josephine Downing to the author in 1997. This letter will also shortly become part of the Papers and Materials of Phil Dow at the BGC

enforced, but inevitably bartering among the students or stories of the day's activities would drive the volume of conversation above the appropriate level. When this happened Pa Lehrer, "with his characteristic aplomb... would rise from his chair, tap a bell on the table in front of him, and say, 'Alright, let's get it out of your system' and lead the students in 'Three Cheers'."[49] It was a wonderful game for the students who were trying to make each "hurrah" louder than the one before it. Once this was over there would be a period of silence for ten minutes that was strictly enforced – no talking whatsoever. For the students, being disciplined had never been so much fun.

"Ma" Lehrer was neither intellectually nor physically vibrant. Her chronically swollen ankles labored under a "full figure" and kept her from the vigorous hikes her husband led. Yet, her physical impediments did not keep her from her many duties around campus – to the consternation of those less virtuous students. Among her duties were the monitoring of study halls, rest hours and the planning of Saturday evening games. Whether because of her police role or her emotional unpredictability, Ma Lehrer did not enjoy the degree of veneration her husband did.[50] The picture painted of her by the students of the period is one of an ever-vigilant spy, always on the prowl for the more mischievously inclined. One student wrote years later that during the rest hours, "Ma Lehrer seemed to be able to hear us misbehaving" despite the several stone walls separating them.[51] Another student recalled, "always being in trouble because of my restlessness (during study hall)".[52] Nevertheless, the students knew she meant well and that "covered over a multitude of sins".[53]

Archives. Josephine was a student at RVA for approximately eight years from 1936-44.

[49] Letter from Lois Carlson to the author in 1997. See previous citations. The Lehrers allowed students to trade food items between themselves. This barter economy could evidently become amazingly complex, sometimes including meal arrangements weeks ahead or alternative unspecified favors.

[50] This general sentiment was given by Skoda, Baker, Carlson, Honer and others. Nevertheless each of them clearly appreciated the role Ma Lehrer ultimately played in their lives.

[51] Letter from Ruben Schwieger to the author on June 14, 1997. See previous notes.

[52] Letter from Lois Carlson to the author in 1997. See previous notes.

[53] Paraphrased from the *Holy Bible (NIV)*, 1Peter 4:8. Sometimes a botched task done with all the earnestness that love can produce means more than a perfect product. This sentiment seems to ring true with regards to the affection Ma Lehrer received in spite of her personality and, at times, actions.

Ma Lehrer's role as chief of police was balanced by that of games mistress. Games night fell on Saturday night and was the highlight of the week for many of the students. Some of the games like the economically named, "The Prince of Paris Has Lost His Hat and Doesn't Know Where To Find It" were relatively tame. Others however were wildly entertaining. Red Hot Poker was one of the later. Usually a large bucket was placed in the center of the main lounge from which all the furniture had been cleared away. The students would then form a circle, linking hands and wrists, and the melee would begin. The goal was simple – knock over the bucket in the center using the body of some unfortunate peer. Insult was then added to injury as the battered victim was eliminated from the game. The circle would begin again slowly, but soon bodies would be flailing recklessly around the room with remarkable speed. This continued until only two people remained – the one with the best mix of dexterity, flexibility and strength usually prevailing. Strangely, in this context of raucous revelry Ma Lehrer thrived. Said one student, "I think she had as much fun as we did".[54]

From all accounts the Lehrers were marvelous house-parents, but with at least thirty children there was unavoidably an institutional quality to their nurturing and this was not always pleasant. The harsh realities of institutionalism were most evident in discipline. One outcome of the traditionalist protestant philosophy of discipline was a limited form of corporal punishment. This had long been a part of the workings of RVA but during this era it gained an unnecessarily ugly public aspect that for moments turned the school into something resembling a medieval public execution. For serious offenses or an accumulation of "black marks" the students were "beaten on the buttocks on Saturday evenings in front of the whole school".[55] Mirella Ricciardi (Rocco) in the book *African Saga* wrote, "It was a terrifying experience… with tears in my eyes, I watched Dorion (her older brother) being caned".[56] Settler child Frank Sutton recalled, "you used to get thrashed every time you got ten (black marks) in front of the whole school which, I thought, was an incredibly nasty thing to do… but there we are, that is how it was."[57] That is, indeed,

---

[54] The quote and the entire paragraph above it come from the Carlson letter cited above.

[55] Ricciardi, Mirella, *African Saga*. William Collins Sons & Co., London: 1982, p. 91.

[56] Ibid.

[57] Frank Sutton kindly answered my questions onto tape from his home in Nairobi, Kenya. This tape is a part of the Papers and Materials of Phil Dow at the BGC Archives, Wheaton, IL.

how it was. Yet this apparently Dickensonian cruelty must be put alongside the sense of concern and fairness that even those being disciplined attributed to the Lehrers. Sutton himself remembered the Lehrers as "wonderful people".[58] Ruben Schwieger perhaps summed up best the prevailing student sentiment writing, "we truly loved them for we knew they loved us".[59]

The consistency and quality the Lehrers brought to RVA became even more critical to the school's success when Herb Downing and his family returned to America in 1938 for what was supposed to be a one-year furlough. When World War II broke out in 1939 the danger of ocean travel trapped the Downings. They would not return until January of 1947.[60] During this nine year period, as a series of staff came and went, only the Lehrers remained to sustain the momentum of the still small school.

LIKE THE FIRST World War, WWII fundamentally reshaped the world and altered the lives of everyone living in it. Kenya was certainly no exception. Each segment of the population was profoundly affected by the war, but that affect differed significantly based on the unique concerns and circumstances of the particular group.

The initial reaction of the African Kenyans to the latest European war says much about the political and cultural climate of that community. Among the most educated and politicized, WWII revealed an important division of feeling. In the simplest terms, some supported Britain and some supported the anti-Britain - Germany.[61] For the majority of Africans who supported Britain in World War I the horrific murder of Hulda Stumpf and the events of the late 1920's had represented an ironic turning point in their perspective. Many displayed a deep-seated sense of sadness over the bitter antagonism that surrounded these events and sought reconciliation with the Christian missions from which they had become estranged. Often this reconciliation also

---

[58] Ibid.

[59] Letter from Ruben Schwieger to the author on June 14, 1997. See previous notes.

[60] The Entwistle Thesis, p. 80 and the Herb and Glen Downing interviews all agree on the dates and circumstances surrounding the Downings absence from RVA.

[61] This historical reality is brought to life in the Kenyan novelist Ngugi's story of the development of African nationalism and identity, *Weep Not, Child*. On page six, one character exclaims, "ah! Hitler that brave man, whom all the British feared…".

included a renewed loyalty to the nations that the mission groups loosely represented.[62]

Harry Thuku is perhaps the most conspicuous example of this reconciliatory response. Even before the more radical KCA openly applauded Hitler and the Fascist alliance, Thuku had broken away to form the moderately pro-British Kikuyu Provincial Association (KPA) in the hopes of pursuing ultimate self-rule through cooperation instead of revolution. This was a curious response considering the nine years of forced exile and detainment (without trial) that Thuku endured under British rule. Yet, it was a fairly consistent one by those who had been converted to Christianity or had been educated in mission schools. Significantly, those Africans representing this reconciliatory perspective joined up in numbers to fight for Britain.[63]

Others, namely the KCA minority, were vocal in their anti-British sympathies. Like the Italian and German expatriates in Kenya their biases cost them their freedom. The leadership of the KCA was all interned at the beginning of the war. Only Kenyatta, who was studying in England, and had married a Briton, remained free.[64]

Between forty and one hundred thousand black Kenyans were a part of Britain's war effort. Their loyalty to the mission's home countries was one reason for this, but a variety of promises by the British also convinced those whose ears still echoed with stories of WWI's misery that this time things would be different.[65] In some ways things were different. For one, WWII marked the first time Kenyan troops had fought for Britain outside of the colonies. Brigades of Kenyan King's Rifles fought in Ethiopia, Madagascar and even as far away as Burma. Kenyan troops were most conspicuous in the Ethiopian and Somali campaigns where they made what one military historian called, "the longest and swiftest advance in military history".[66] The considerable success the soldiers experienced added confidence and a more cosmopolitan perspective to the already ripening will for self-determination that the Christian missions had been so instrumental in

---

[62] C.P. Groves, p. 215. Evidence of this reconciliation is also found in the AIM account of Hulda Stumpf's funeral where, "man letters… from the natives were read (expressing their gratitude to Miss Stumpf)". *Inland Africa*, May 1930 written by Leroy Farnsworth.

[63] MacPhee, Marshall C. *Kenya*, Praeger Pub. NY: 1968, p. 93 & Edgerton, p. 45.

[64] Murray-Brown, *Kenyatta*, p. 210.

[65] MacPhee, p. 93.

[66] Moyse-Barlett, Lt.-Col., *The King's Rifles*, p.521 as quoted in MacPhee, p. 93.

bolstering. The soldiers' loyalty and success also reinforced the fragile fraternal bond growing between the colonial government and the African community. As a gesture of good faith, the detained KCA leaders were released in 1943; and in 1944 an African was given a seat on the colonial legislative council for the first time.[67]

The first Kenyan on the legislative council, Eliud Mathu, was aligned to Thuku's moderate KPA (now known as the KAU). Like so many of Kenya's future leadership, Mathu had taken his secondary education at the missionary-run Alliance High School and went on to university at Oxford.[68] He represented what many Christian Kenyans hoped would be the future – an articulate moderately pro-western African, rooted in Christian teaching and firmly committed to the improvement of his community's well being. When Sir Mitchell arrived as the new colonial governor in 1944 that bright future looked close to becoming a reality. Mitchell had just finished overseeing the implementation of a new multi-racial system of government in Java and had made statements asserting his intention to seek a similar course in Kenya.[69] But all was not roses under the quiet that had settled over the colony during the war. Even as most were busy about the business of life in the now maturing British colony, extreme elements within both the African and settler communities continued to ferment. It is to the settler community we will now briefly turn.

For the settler community, WWII was a period of unprecedented prosperity. There were at least three reasons for this economic boom. First, between the first and second world wars an infrastructure had been put in place by the colonial government that was both efficient and expansive. Virtually every fertile region of Kenya had ready access to a reasonably reliable railway system and roads were increasingly common. This infrastructure gave cash crop farmers the opportunity to look for markets outside of East Africa. Second, experimental farming had by this time firmly identified coffee, tea, sisal and other staple crops as ideally suited to the Kenyan climate. Therefore the once hit or miss farming prospect in Kenya turned into a consistently profitable enterprise, that is, if there was a demand for those crops.[70]

The necessary demand came somewhat unexpectedly shortly after the war began when the once all-powerful British navy was soundly

---

[67] MacPhee, p. 96 & Murray-Brown, p. 218.

[68] Ibid, p. 96.

[69] Ibid. p. 97.

[70] Murray-Brown, *Kenyatta*, pgs. 225-226

beaten in the Pacific and Atlantic. The demise of British naval power effectively ended the Empire because it severed the lines of trade between Britain and many of its remaining colonies. Therefore, previously peripheral colonies like Kenya were suddenly turned to as an indispensable producer of food and supplies for British troops in their regions. This was particularly true for Kenya as an invasion of Italian held territory in Somalia and Ethiopia looked inevitable.[71]

Another unavoidable result of Britain's supply crisis was the industrialization of the Kenya Colony. The significance of this development cannot be overstated. Prior to 1939 the role of the colonies in the imperial system had been as suppliers of raw materials. Although it was never highly profitable in practice, in theory this relationship was meant to give Britain's industries cheap materials, keeping it near the top of the world's industrialized nations. As a result, all prior attempts by the colonies to develop anything beyond absolutely essential industries had been rejected. Suddenly, Britain needed the colonies to industrialize and to Britain's pleasure they responded with surprising speed. In the end, Britain owed part of its survival during the war to colonial industry, but colonial industry also cost Britain its empire. Through even limited industrialization the colonies achieved a level of self-sufficiency that would allow them to break free of England. The question now was who would run the colonies in the post-colonial era. The stage was set for a struggle between the settler community and the largely missionary educated Kenyan elite.[72]

Economically WWII was a bonanza for the settler community. Because of Kenya's relatively advanced infrastructure and central location, it was also utilized as a training base for troops that would be taking part in the African campaigns. Finally, and for many of the same reasons, Kenya was chosen as an ideal location for the African campaign's POW camps. This sudden influx of soldiers and POWs combined with Britain's unexpected supply crisis to create a demand for the settler's products that exceeded their wildest expectations. Within five years the colony's domestic exports nearly doubled.[73]

The period of WWII was also one of unprecedented hysteria within the European community in the colony. With the exception of a few bombs proported to have been dropped by lost Italian pilots along

---

[71] Ibid.
[72] Ogonda, R.T. "Industrialization" in William Ochieng's *Themes in Kenyan History*, pgs. 73-77.
[73] Murray-Brown, *Kenyatta*, pgs. 225-226.

Kenya's coast, no fighting actually took place in Kenya.[74] Nevertheless, fears of fascist infiltration ran rampant for a time during which radical Kenyans, like the KCA, and settlers of German and Italian extraction, were detained without trial and at times exiled until the war's conclusion. This was often done merely on suspicion of disloyalty. The hysteria was not always without cause, but its effect on the settler community was disturbing as friend imprisoned friend and children were forcibly separated from parents.[75]

In one instance, Italian Mario Ricciardi was arrested by his friend and neighbor and separated from his wife and children for the entire war. In addition, Dorion, his eldest child, was removed from the British Kenton College the same night and all property that was in his name was confiscated. Within days this wealthy and well-liked settler family was broken up, financially weakened and socially isolated. This story was repeated regularly throughout the colony as the hysteria rose to a crescendo.[76]

The war's frenzy affected the school community at RVA, often in humorous ways. Despite the near impossibility of an Italian raid on this strategically irrelevant American outpost, a bomb shelter was built near the middle of campus to protect the community from the imminent Italian attack.[77] In addition, amongst other "necessary precautions" windows were taped to keep light from escaping the buildings at night and alerting enemy aircraft.[78]

Despite the irrational fears that gripped the community from time to time, the overall response of the school to the wartime circumstances was admirable. While boarding schools in Nairobi closed in the face of rumors of an Axis attack, RVA stoically went about its business – and this despite the fact that Herb Downing and other key faculty were trapped in North America and Europe and funds for running the school had dwindled to nothing. More remarkable still, RVA stood up against colonial and settler pressure and accepted dozens of non-missionary children who had been shunned by the British schools for political reasons. During the war almost two thirds of the school's thirty-plus students were from non-missionary homes – many of whom were from

---

[74] Shel Arensen's Address to the Rift Valley Academy student body in 1997.

[75] Ricciardi, Mirella, *African Saga*, p. 76.

[76] Ibid. Pgs. 76-78.

[77] *Kiambogo* (the annual yearbook of RVA), 1956, "History"

[78] Interview with Charles Skoda by the author on May 29, 1999. The tape of the interview is now at the BGC Archives under "Papers and Materials of Phil Dow".

nations with ties to the Axis powers.[79]   Because the school was so desperate for staff to meet this need, AIM reversed another longstanding policy and allowed several of non-missionary women to live at the school with their children in order to assist in the teaching.[80] Ironically, these women, whose husbands were often abroad fighting for the British, taught the children of their enemies. As a result, one would expect heightened tensions between many staff and students related to nationalistic fervor. But from all indications the tenor of life at RVA more closely resembled that of an apolitical family - the unprecedented diversity notwithstanding.

If RVA acted as a leper colony of sorts for the rejected and discarded among the settler community, it also actively reached out to the British soldiers and settlers on the community's periphery. Soldiers were regular guests of the Devitts and other Kijabe missionaries. The Devitts, in turn, were the guests of the army, preaching in their chapel services on Sundays.[81]   For AIM missionaries the war, with all its misery, nevertheless gave them an opportunity to show Christian charity. Even more important, they believed it brought people face to face with inherently spiritual questions and therefore created hearts and minds unusually receptive to their message. It is not surprising that *Inland Africa* is littered with stories of settler children and soldiers converting to Christianity at RVA during the war.[82]

In addition, for the older students and their parents the war raised to the forefront the question of how to best complete their secondary education. An ocean liner to America or Britain was simply not an option. One such ship carrying AIM missionaries to Africa had been sunk early on in the war and several AIM men were imprisoned in German POW camps as a result.[83]   Yet, the school was in no better position to provide the final years of education than it had been in 1938. Nevertheless, unusual circumstances generated unusual measures and several students chose to take the Cambridge Examinations in Nairobi in lieu of pursuing an American high school diploma. Ken Downing and his wife tutored these few students and the results were respectable as the

[79] *Inland Africa*, Sept./Oct. 1941 "From the Regions Beyond".

[80] Entwistle, Roy M.Ed. Thesis, p. 19 & Skoda interview.

[81] *Inland Africa*, Sept./Oct. 1943, "William L. Lester".

[82] *Inland Africa*, Jan./Feb. 1945, "Ivy and Kenneth Downing"; *Inland Africa* Jan./Feb. 1942 "Letters from the Prison Camp" & *Inland Africa* Sept./Oct. 1941, "From the Regions Beyond".

[83] *Inland Africa*, Jan./Feb. 1942, "Letters from the Prison Camp".

students made honors in several subjects.[84] Thus while they could not be considered RVA's first graduates, these few students made it clear that completing high school in Kenya was both preferable to returning to North America and feasible for future RVA students. These realizations, therefore, helped lay the groundwork for Herb Downing's educational vision upon his return in 1947.

IN A SMALL, even ambiguous way, the school also made a statement against the colonial/settler status quo in the area of racial justice during WWII. In 1945 the school discovered that one of its newer settler students, David Dibbens, was of mixed race.[85] In the segregated, hierarchical culture of colonial Kenya the question of racial purity was seen as essential to the continued psychological dominance of the tiny white minority. A person of mixed blood was therefore rightly seen as a threat to the system. As a result, David was viewed as a social outcast by both the European and African communities, and unequivocally denied access to European schools.

When RVA and the larger colonial community discovered David's racial heritage the school was forced to make a choice. The pressure from the European community to remove David from the school was intense. Allowing David to stay would have subtly, but unmistakably undermined the racial status quo and further antagonized the large settler community already convinced that the education and Protestant egalitarianism of the missionaries was "ruining the natives". Still, in the end, in a sheepishly worded statement, the board decided to allow David to remain at RVA – for the time being.[86]

It would be a mistake to infer from this example that RVA or AIM were awakening to their responsibility as Christians to actively promote social justice – for, to the school's shame, had David's racial background been known earlier all indications were that he would have been kindly refused admission. However, when the issue came looking for them, RVA did respond positively and in a modest way helped to undermine the strict racial hierarchy upon which the colonial Kenyan culture was built.

The Dibbens case is significant for it reminds us that the question of race was at the very center of the missionary enterprise in the colonial

---

[84] Letter from Josephine Downing to the author in 1997 – the three female students who took the Cambridge Exam were Jean Nixon, Lucile Anderson and Josephine Downing.
[85] RVA School Board Minutes, dated 12/12/45. Available at RVA.
[86] RVA School Board Minutes, dated 1/8/46.

African context. There was perhaps no issue that was more complex, and there was certainly no issue that was of greater significance to missions in Kenya, than that of race. It goes without saying that a missionary's view of race was fundamental to everything they did on the field. If a missionary saw the African as merely quaint or inherently simple-minded both the means and ends of their missionary efforts would necessarily look different from the missionary who came to Kenya in humility believing they were no better or worse than the African brothers and sisters they had come to serve – being loved and created "of one blood" by the same God. As we have already seen in the case of Herb Downing and his peers, RVA was quickly developing into a greenhouse of future generations of missionaries. The Dibbens case thus becomes even more critical to our story as it forces us to ask what view of race was being nurtured in the minds of those children who would do much to shape the future course of the developing church in Africa.

When considering the existence of racism at RVA it is important to remember that RVA, despite its best efforts, did not exist in a vacuum. As part of a colonial context, RVA existed within a colonial worldview that was not just racist, but reliant on an assumed racial hierarchy. So ingrained were racial assumptions that even the educated and relatively enlightened Elspeth Huxley wrote matter-of-factly that, "(African brains) have a shorter growing period (and possess) less cunningly arranged cells than the brains of the Europeans (which explains the) fundamental disparity between the capabilities of his (the African's) brain and ours". Significantly, it was this worldview that acted as a filter through which Europeans (many missionaries included) interpreted their personal experiences. Finally, the reality at this time was that Africa, technologically speaking, was light-years behind the Euro-American world. The inescapable fact was that as members of a preliterate society, the Africans in Kenya lacked many of those skills and values that the west had set up as the standards for what was good. The result was that without any other source for truth outside of experience and reason a racial hierarchy not only appeared to be possible but was eminently reasonable. It is not surprising then, that Europeans coming to Africa expecting to see ignorant and dark savages saw just, and only, that. With their racist worldview thus being apparently confirmed by personal experience there began a demoralizing and self-fulfilling prophecy. Africans were not fit for positions that required intelligence or responsibility and so were not trained for such. Having not been trained for such positions, Africans were not fit for them and so the self-perpetuating system developed. Once initiated the system became assumed. African inferiority was just a fact of nature.

Battling with experience and reason as powerful sources of truth in the missionary epistemology was the concept of revelation in the form of the Bible. And while experience and reason certainly influenced the way the missionaries interpreted the Bible concerning the question of race, the basic underlying biblical assumption of equality allowed some missionaries to take a leap of faith – to think and act outside of the assumed racial paradigm. By being actively involved in African education around Kenya and by accepting David Dibbens to RVA, AIM was signaling that it was at least partially out of step with the colonial racial worldview. Every bit as significant was the example of equality set by some members of the faculty – not least of which was the principal Herb Downing.

However, that said, the message being sent to the students at RVA concerning race was far from consistent and quite often in line with the colonial worldview. In fact, the pattern of African socio-economic subservience that could be found throughout Kenya was mirrored in the daily life of the school where the only Africans the students came into regular contact with were those who did their laundry, cooked their meals and washed their dirty dishes. Whatever might be preached in chapel, the school's labor system consciously or subconsciously confirmed to its band of aspiring missionaries the natural inferiority of Africans. And when inferiority is assumed contempt is never far off.

The confusing blend of contradicting messages unintentionally sent by the school resulted in an equally bewildering pattern of behavior by its students. Student volunteer evangelism teams were at times made up of the very children who consistently derided the "stupid wogs" that they lived among. Yet, every student who showed contempt for the Africans around them did so while simultaneously watching the lives of those few faculty members whose faith in action was translated into a genuinely egalitarian life and perspective. These students also wrestled with the question of race while regularly hearing a biblical message of equality that pricked and prodded their still sensitive consciences. Not surprisingly, the confusing clash of perspectives and experiences resulted in an acute and disturbing cognitive dissonance. Many decades after the fact, Stan Barnett remembered with shame how, with machetes in hand, several of his RVA classmates made bone-chilling sport of chasing frightened Kikuyu women in the forests above the school. Only one of his peers refused to take part in the twisted game. That student was David Dibbens.[87]

IN SUM, BETWEEN 1933 and 1945 RVA began to move away from being a haphazard and ill-equipped school towards being a first rate institution – one that would be a comfort to missionary families deeply devoted to their children's growth and happiness. Although various external obstacles limited the school's growth during these years, a steady American and independent missionary presence thrived in Kenya that helped to produce a growing Christian influence in the evolving Kenyan culture. By 1948 over 30% of the African population were self-designated Christians and even greater numbers were being influenced directly or indirectly through the missionary schools.[88] That influence, with its inherent belief in the brotherhood of humanity and commitment to education, also acted to destabilize the political and cultural colonial system. In short, this still small school was playing a surprisingly significant role in the now dramatically unfolding story of modern Kenya.

---

[87] Personal interview with Stan Barnett at Buck Creek Camp, WA, May 29, 1999.
[88] Barret, David (ed.), *The Encyclopedia of World Christianity*, "Kenya". Oxford University Press, Nairobi: 1982.

CHAPTER 4

PAX AMERICANA, MAU MAU AND KENYAN INDEPENDENCE: RVA FROM 1946-1963

PROFOUND CHANGES CONFRONTED ALMOST EVERY person living in the post-war world. Modern technology and the expanding presence of capitalism meant that even minor events in one country could have international ramifications. Like no other time in history, the post-war era demanded a global perspective.[1] For Kenya, and everyone living in it, a new paradigm was required. The possibility of developing in quiet isolation apart from the expanding world system was gone forever.

On a grand, geopolitical scale, the once glorious empire of Great Britain, weakened significantly even before the war, was now little more than a shell of its former self. With reluctance, the United States filled the vacuum created by Britain's decline. In the words of one historian, "By the end of WWII the United States had emerged as the most formidable military and economic power in the history of the world".[2]

---

[1] For the purpose of this chapter, the term "post-war" will refer to the years between the end of WWII and Kenyan Independence – 1946-1963.

[2] Pierard, Richard V., "Pax Americana and the Evangelical Missionary Advance" in Joel Carpenter and Wilbert Shenk (eds.) *Earthen Vessels*, Eerdmans, Grand Rapids: 1990, p. 155. This statement can, of course, be debated on multiple grounds; but taken in absolute terms, it is difficult of contend otherwise.

After one hundred and fifty years of virtually unbroken and chosen isolationism, America was now pushed into the world spotlight. As one government official solemnly remarked, the United States could, "never again be an island to itself".[3] For even the most peripheral of the world's regions, this usually meant some form of American cultural and political influence. Therefore to fully appreciate the change in Kenya during this period it is important to understand the changing American culture that was beginning to influence Kenya and the rest of the world.

Strangely, the American public warmed quite quickly to their new prominence in world affairs. This sudden willingness by Americans to reject isolationism was the result of two related developments. First, Americans had seen WWII as a triumph of freedom and democracy over the evils of fascism. Unlike its morally questionable antecedent, the Second World War was seen by many as a clear battle between good and evil, right and wrong. In saving the free world, Americans acknowledged that the United States had necessarily assumed a role of moral leadership that was global in scope. Thus, much in the same way that Britain had believed in its civilizing mission at the turn of the century, the Americans now picked up the torch of civilization with their uniquely American missionary zeal.[4]

It is significant that despite having unprecedented power after WWII America did not set up colonies to enforce its vision of a better world – their values would not permit such a blatantly undemocratic system.[5] As John Gaddis has convincingly argued, American interventionism in world affairs from WWII to the 1960's was simply a natural outcome of its national core values of democracy and self-determination. Even the potentially coercive American commitment to "open market capitalism" did not immediately overwhelm these inherently anti-imperialistic values. In short, because of their unavoidable centrality to world affairs, in 1946 Americans began to turn their eyes outward as they had never done before, yet they did so without imperial ambitions.[6]

The rise of the Soviet Union as a threat and foil to American core values was a second reason Americans were suddenly interested in international affairs. If America was now forced to carry the torch of

---

[3] Secretary of War Stimson as quoted in James T. Patterson's *Grand Expectations*, Oxford University Press, NY: 1996, p. 82.

[4] Patterson's *Grand Expectations*, chapters 4&5.

[5] Granted, between the years of 1895 and 1908, the US did experience a bout of imperialism of the old fashioned kind, but just as quickly it recoiled from that and receded back into its traditional isolationism.

[6] Gaddis, John, *We Now Know*, Oxford University Press, NY:1997, pgs. 6&7.

freedom, the greatest threat to the freedoms of democracy and self-determination was Communism. Therefore, quite reasonably, the stronger the enemy appeared, the greater the concern Americans had for world affairs. The hysteria surrounding Senator McCarthy and the Communist threat in the 1950's is only the most glaring example of the passions the Soviet threat posed in the hearts and minds of average Americans.[7]

COMMUNIST RUSSIA ALSO acted as a foil to the deep-seated American Christian tradition. The rise of "atheist" Communism thus helped fuel a wave of spiritual revivalism that had begun to sweep over Christian America after the war. The increased spiritual fervor in America caught many by surprise because it appeared to come out of nowhere. The liberal social gospel of the mainline Protestant denominations that had defeated the Fundamentalist elements during the 1920's and 1930's seemed firmly established as the dominant American religious tradition. Yet, the religious establishment had little to do with the waves of revival that reshaped American culture after WWII.[8]

Beaten and left for dead, the fundamentalists had retreated to the American periphery. The battle with liberal Protestantism in the 1920's had shown them to be intellectually naïve, which resulted in widespread ridicule and ostracism by the opinion makers of elite culture. Thus in the minds of many Americans, intelligent people could not be Fundamentalists. Nevertheless, the simple truths of orthodox Christianity still rang true for millions of Fundamentalists; and for a generation these forgotten and discounted believers quietly entrenched themselves along the fringes of American culture.

During this time many Fundamentalists simply held on more tightly to their beliefs, choosing to ignore the culture that had rejected them. Others, however, began to develop an increasingly cogent and intellectually impressive apologetic. Referring to themselves now as "evangelicals", this zealous group of articulate orthodox Protestants began resurfacing in the early 1940's. The National Association of Evangelicals (1942) and Youth for Christ (1943) were just two of the national organizations that announced the tremendous grassroots strength of the "new evangelicalism".[9]

---

[7] This point is made in different ways, and to different ends, in Patterson's *Grand Expectations* and Gaddis' *We Now Know*.

[8] Carpenter, Joel, "Propogating the Faith Once Delivered" in *Earthen Vessels*, pgs. 92-132.

[9] Pierard, Richard V., "Pax Americana…" in *Earthen Vessels*, pgs. 160&170.

The rise of Evangelicalism was closely linked to the increasing importance placed on the family unit in the post war period. As Winthrop Hudson writes, " seldom had the joys of home and family been more cherished and celebrated".[10] When combined with the rise of "atheist" Communism and this profound nostalgia for the family, evangelical Protestantism caught a wave of religious revivalism that revolutionized the American cultural landscape. Hollywood reflected the spirit of the times by producing Christian-themed blockbusters such as Quo Vadis (1951), The Robe (1953) and Ben Hur (1959). In 1954 Eisenhower signed legislation that added the words, "One nation under God" to the Pledge of Allegiance. And finally a year later, Congress attached the phrase "In God We Trust" to American currency.[11]

But evangelicalism was not simply the latest installment of American civil religion. Most evangelicals, while regularly mixing patriotism with religious fervor, nevertheless remained profoundly "other worldly". No one better exemplifies this reality than Billy Graham. Unquestionably the symbol of American evangelicalism, Billy Graham's simple message was the forgiveness of individual sin, by God, through the death and resurrection of Jesus, for all who believe. Further, the Evangelical message was inherently universal in scope and thus was easily wedded, not only to America's increased extroversion, but also to the age-old Christian missionary enterprise.

In short, America's new dominant role in world affairs forced the nation to break from its isolationist tradition. This new impulse was exacerbated by the simultaneous rise of the Communist threat to America's core values. Both of these geopolitical realities, in turn, helped fuel a grassroots protestant revivalism, already underway, that both revolutionized the American cultural landscape and invigorated the missionary spirit. The result was a dramatic surge in the number of American Protestants considering the "call" of foreign missions. And, by 1946 those answering this call were overwhelmingly the conservative "other worldly" minded evangelicals.

The numbers illustrate the increasing missionary zeal of American Protestants in quite dramatic terms. In 1911 Americans made up less than a third of the missionaries worldwide with a total of 7,239 out of 21,307. Forty-five years later, in 1956, the American missionary presence had exploded in both real and relative terms. The numbers of

---

[10] Hudson, Winthrop, *Religion in America* (4th Ed.), Macmillan, NY: 1987, p. 352.

[11] Patterson, *Grand Expectations*, p. 329.

American missionaries had risen over 300 percent from 7,239 to 23,058; and the relative percentage of American missionaries to the overall missionary population had also increased from twenty-five percent in 1911 to sixty-six percent in 1956.[12] Perhaps nowhere was the increased American missionary involvement felt more fully than in Kenya.

There are several reasons for Kenya's appeal to this new wave of American missionaries. For one, the colony's infrastructure had grown up considerably during the war, making access to the remote unreached peoples much easier. Further, the strong missionary presence already in Kenya also meant that continental, and even global, headquarters for mission groups were often placed in Nairobi making Kenya a hub of missionary activity. And finally, Kenya was home to the school most capable of providing the evangelical spiritual nurturing and American academic training demanded by this new generation of intensely family-oriented American evangelical missionaries.[13] That school was, of course, the Rift Valley Academy. Yet, at the end of the war RVA had neither the faculty, the physical structures, nor the necessary curriculum to accommodate the potential tidal wave of missionary families to Kenya.

As IF ON cue, Herbert Downing returned to the Rift Valley Academy in 1947 fresh from the increasingly evangelical American context. Trapped in America by the war from 1939 to 1947, Downing had experienced first hand the mounting missionary spirit of American Protestantism. Already acutely aware of the importance of RVA to the success of the missionary enterprise before his sojourn in America, Downing had also witnessed the growing devotion to "the family" in conservative protestant circles during the closing years of WWII. Therefore, convinced that the Rift Valley Academy's role in the missionary movement would dramatically increase in the coming years, Downing developed a vision for the school's future he hoped would allow the American missionary potential to flower into a reality.

The clearest expression of Downing's vision for a post-war RVA came in an article written by him in 1946 for *Inland Africa*. The article, entitled appropriately enough, "Education of Missionaries' Children"

---

[12] All the above statistics are taken from the chart in Pierard's "Pax Americana" in *Earthen Vessels*, p. 158.

[13] The ambiguity in curriculum that had defined the school as "Anglo-American" prior to WWII was removed in favor of an entirely American curriculum due to the rise in the American missionary impulse after the war's conclusion.

was the first time in fifty years of AIM literature that the importance of "MK" (Missionary Kid) education had been explicitly highlighted. To be sure, short mention of the school could be found from time to time buried in the back pages of mission newsletters, but usually only in connection to the conversion of students, religious revivals or the outbreak of one disease or another. Of course, the missionaries themselves were well aware of the school's ups and downs, but because RVA was not considered directly part of the mission's uncompromising evangelical purpose it did not usually merit mention. In fact, because the school took mission resources and personnel that might have gone towards evangelism, it was almost an embarrassment to many in AIM – a family secret better left in the closet.

Therefore Downing's high profile article serves as evidence of a genuine shift in the way this stoic "faith mission" looked at their own work and the importance of caring for the needs of their children. Downing began the article with the obvious but significant statement that, "the question of education for the children of missionary parents is as old as the first missionary family".[14] The article concluded with perhaps the most telling shift in thinking – a blatant plea for qualified teachers to teach at RVA. In Downing's words, "They (the missionary children) need the best trained, most consecrated Christian teachers that can be had".[15] More remarkable still was the request for the funds necessary to improve the school's facilities. Again Downing wrote, "They deserve the best of equipment for their training that money can buy".[16]

Yet, amidst this considerable shift in perspective, it is important to point out that the education of missionary children was still not seen as something necessarily worthy of attention for its own sake. Downing was clear that attention to MK education was valuable for two reasons. First, RVA allowed missionaries with children to remain on the field; and second, RVA could act as a training ground for the next generation of missionaries. Towards this end Downing remarked, "When the time comes for their (the RVA students') return to the mission field, the knowledge of native customs and language which they acquired in their childhood is an invaluable asset to them as missionaries and to the

---

[14] Downing, Herbert, "Education of Missionaries' Children" in *Inland Africa*, Jan/Feb of 1946, p. 7.

[15] Ibid. p. 8.

[16] Ibid.

mission as an organization. Some are returning even now to the mission field".[17]

Downing's suggestion that RVA might act as a greenhouse for the next generation of AIM missionaries warrants consideration. Already within AIM, family dynasties had begun to appear which seemed to give credence to Downing's contention. His own family was a case in point. Downing and his brother Ken had both grown up in Kenya and attended RVA; and both had returned with AIM to Kenya as missionaries and had sent their own children to RVA. During the forties and fifties RVA was also home to the third generation of the Barnett, Andersen and Propst/Stauffacher families – among others.[18] This pattern of RVA-educated American missionary children returning to East Africa as missionaries stands out as unique among the missions in British East Africa. Of course, other mission groups did experience the return of a smaller percentage of their children to East Africa, but rarely as missionaries. The famous Leakey family of Kenya is an extraordinary example of this fragile trend among the other early mission groups in the colony. Most, if not all, of the children and grandchildren of the pioneer Anglican missionary Rev. Leakey returned to Kenya after their university education in England to permanent residence (and ultimately citizenship) in Kenya. Their contributions to the fields of anthropology and paleontology are world renowned; and their involvement in Kenyan politics continues to be substantial.[19] Yet, where the children of AIM missionaries returned to Kenya as missionaries, the children of the other missionaries (if they returned at all) usually came back in a non-religious capacity.

This striking pattern of missionary dynasties in AIM is undoubtedly the result of several concurrent causes. However, most of the causes for the return of missionary children to Kenya (such as the desire to return to the land of their youth) are to be found in other mission groups as well. There is, however, one variable that separates AIM from its peer organizations. Of all the mission groups working in Kenya only AIM had created a school for their own children, rooted in their peculiar Protestant Holiness worldview, and run by their own missionaries. In short, based on AIM's track record and its contrast with other mission groups, Downing's contention that RVA acted as a greenhouse for future missionaries seems undeniable.

---

[17] Ibid., p7.

[18] AIM personnel records kept at the Mission's headquarters in Pearl River, NY.

[19] See the autobiography of Richard Leakey, *Only One Life*.

THE EXISTENCE OF RVA led to a pattern of missionary dynasties within AIM and the American missions. These dynasties gave AIM's work in Kenya a continuity that no other mission group could match. This continuity, in turn, provided AIM with the colony-wide recognition, acceptance and influence that only familiarity and longevity could bring. As we have already seen, by WWII AIM's constant presence had begun to influence Kenyan culture through the mission's increasing number of converts and flourishing African schools.[20]   Yet the numbers alone cannot adequately portray the extensive influence RVA and AIM had already had, and were going to have in the years following WWII. Indeed, every statistic represents the story of an individual life – one that was changed by contact with AIM.   While not representative of every trend found in AIM converts, the story of Kapkorios Toroitich arap Moi is particularly noteworthy as an example of the mission's powerful and enduring influence in Kenya.

In 1907 an Australian bachelor named Albert Barnett, believing God had called him as a missionary to Africa, boarded a New York-based steamship headed for Kenya. When the vessel stopped in Genoa, Italy a young Swedish woman (also going to Kenya as a missionary with AIM) boarded the boat. It was love at first sight and, after getting married, the young missionary couple began to raise a family while they worked among the Tugen clan near Lake Baringo in the western part of Kenya.[21] Because of hostile opposition from colonial officials, the Barnett family relocated from Kapbarnet to a former Maasai region called Eldama Ravine.[22] As their children grew up the question of education naturally surfaced and the logical solution was the new AIM school at Kijabe. The existence of RVA allowed the Barnetts to continue their work among the Tugen without hampering their children's futures.

The opportunity to stay in Kenya also had implications on the children's evolving worldview. Through their lives both at home among the Tugen and at RVA, the Barnett children developed an affection for the Kenyan people and their boarding school; but above all, they developed the intense devotion to the evangelistic Christianity that

---

[20] For statistics please refer to the conclusion of the previous chapter entitled, "Quietly Stirring the Pot".

[21] Interview with Dr. Bill Barnett at the home of Dr. Ted Barnett in Pearl River, NY on June 30, 1998.

[22] Morton, Andrew, *Moi*, Michael O'Mara Books Ltd., London: 1998, p. 48. It is important to note that the name "Kapbarnet" means, "place of Barnett" in honor of the family.

seemed to spring naturally from the lives of their parents and the soul of the mission. The school thus had a dual purpose. One purpose was to allow missionaries with children to remain in Africa working with the Kenyan people; and the second was to help develop a new generation of missionaries to one day continue the work of their parents. With the Barnetts, and a large number of AIM missionary families, both purposes were served. Albert and his wife Elma set up a mission station at Eldama Ravine, building there a strong foundation for future work among the Tugen in the region; and each of their four children returned as AIM missionaries, two of whom (Paul and Erik) were to continue to work among the Tugen at Eldama Ravine.[23]

Like many of the AIM missionaries with children at RVA, the Barnetts were helping to shape the nation's future. In 1934 a ten-year-old Tugen boy came to the Barnett's mission station from a village in the region with a desire to be educated. Like a growing number of African children of this era, when Kapkorios Toroitich arap Moi entered into the AIM mission school community the course of his life was dramatically altered. The school ethos was consistent with the stark discipline characteristic of the mission that ran it. The day began at 6:00 a.m. with prayers followed by a rigorous detail of the chores necessary to sustain the community. These included working the vegetable gardens and hauling gallons of water up from the river almost a mile from the mission station. These tasks consumed the morning and it was not until the afternoon that Moi and his co-ed peers sat down with Elma Barnett to learn their letters. Outside of games in the late afternoon, the remainder of the day was no less rigorous.[24] Simply put, life at AIM's mission school was neither frivolous nor leisurely, but that did not keep more students like Moi from arriving regularly in the hopes of receiving an education at the mission school.[25]

Contrary to some strains of historiographical folklore, AIM never forced the Tugen (or any other people group) into their schools or churches; such a position would have been in contradiction to almost every tenet and tendency of the highly individualistic protestant faith missions. Instead what stands out is the remarkable lengths to which many students went in order to gain an education in the mission's schools. Moi's own sister, Rebecca, was among a generation of students who literally ran away from their village in the hope of a better life at the

---

[23] AIM personnel records available at AIM headquarters in Pearl River, NY.

[24] Morton, Andrew, *Moi*, pgs. 48-49.

[25] Ibid. pgs. 49-50.

mission. With Moi's help Rebecca stole away from her village, walking for hours through the dead of night to the mission station and a new life. Recalled Rebecca, "My generation was now at school and I would have been left out if I hadn't gone…It (AIM's mission station) was an exciting place to go, a place to be educated, explore Christianity and achieve our goals in life."[26]

Like others of his generation, for the young Moi Christianity became more than just a means to an education. In 1936 he was baptized by another AIM missionary, Rev. Dalziel, and took the Christian name, Daniel.[27] As a bright and hardworking Christian student, Daniel arap Moi continued to distinguish himself. The AIM missionaries encouraged Moi's burgeoning leadership by making Moi the teacher for the younger students' regular Bible studies. Finally, urged on by the Barnetts, Moi and his friend Gideon Tarus passed their exams and went on to the nearby government school at Kapsabet. Yet AIM's influence on the young Moi did not end there. Most school breaks found Moi in the home of either the Barnetts or the Bometts.[28] In seeking out these Christian families, Moi gave evidence of a continuing desire to develop his leadership abilities. By this time Albert and Elma's RVA-educated children were returning to Kenya as missionaries themselves. Their two eldest sons, Paul and Erik, were to build on the strong relationship the Barnett family had with Moi and his generation of Tugen Christians. As Moi rose through the ranks of schoolboys, becoming the government school's captain in 1942, the two generations of Barnetts continued to act as spiritual counselors and confidants.[29]

Upon completion of his training at the government school Moi turned down an offer to attend the Alliance School and chose instead to become one of Kenya's first African teachers.[30] Thus RVA-educated Paul and Erik saw to fulfillment the first fruit of their parent's labor – the rise of the educated African teacher/leader. It was this generation of missionary-educated African leaders that would soon usher in a new era in the colony's history.

The role of Paul and Erik Barnett in the lives of Moi and his generation was no less significant than that of their parents. Yet instead

---

[26] Ibid. p. 49.

[27] Ibid. p. 52.

[28] The Bometts were the leading African Christian family in the region, having also been converted and discipled by AIM missionaries (with children at RVA).

[29] Ibid. pgs. 55-58.

[30] Alliance High School was the elite African school in the colony run by the alliance of protestant missions of which AIM was a founding member.

of serving in the role of teachers and authority figures, this new generation of AIM missionaries (having grown up as peers with their African counterparts) acted more as spiritual counselors to the growing network of indigenous Christians. This relationship can be seen in each of the major rites of passage Moi went through as a young man. Erik officiated at Moi's wedding to Helena Bomett in 1950 and Paul christened the couple's first two children.[31] Moi's rise to the role of teacher in an African-run-school is symbolic of the dramatic changes that had already come to Kenya through RVA and AIM. But the influence of this AIM-educated African Christian leader was just beginning. Thirty years later the fourth generation of Barnetts (then students at RVA) witnessed Moi take the oath of office to become Kenya's second president. It is hard to imagine this lasting and fruitful bond between the Barnett family and Moi without the years of consistent contact and mentorship provided by the several generations of Barnett missionaries to Kenya. And it is equally hard to imagine this type of consistency, or any of the missionary dynasties that AIM produced, without the existence of RVA. Finally, it is important to remember that while the story of Daniel arap Moi is among the most dramatic and controversial examples of RVA and AIM's influence on Kenyan history, variants of this tale were being repeated in thousands of individual Kenyan lives around the colony.[32] By the early 1950's an entire generation of young Christian teachers, clergy and political figures were making their way into positions of influence in the rapidly changing colony.

BECAUSE IT CAN also give us insight into life at RVA during this period, it is worth examining the type of education that Moi and his African peers received at the AIM schools. First, influenced deeply by the Keswick/Holiness movement, AIM missionaries believed that the mark of a true Christian was a life which had been externally transformed by the inward work of the Holy Spirit. In practical terms

---

[31] Ibid. p. 67.

[32] Moi stands out as a controversial example of AIM's influence in that depending on who you are taking to Moi is either a misunderstood saint, a good but simple victim of evil manipulators or a master politician – meaning a person willing to say and do whatever it takes to remain in power. History will need time to sort out this complex man, but based on his peaceful handing off of power to the opposition party in the historic elections of 2002 one must conclude that he is, at worst, something of a mix between the above three options.

this idea led to an emphasis on external evidences of faith.[33] True to AIM's holiness theology, a strict morality pervaded the African school communities. In many cases boys and girls were kept totally separate with the hopes of ensuring sexual purity among the students. Rigid guidelines were to be followed when male and female students "courted" including constant missionary chaperoning and parental approval.[34]

The separation of male and female students had another purpose as well. Consistent with both African culture and the traditional American model of a Christian family, the boys and girls were given separate chores during the morning hours that were in keeping with the proper gender roles the missionaries expected the students to fulfill as adults. Still, it is important to remember that this apparently restrictive gender based system was nevertheless a radical departure from the male-dominated Tugen culture. While the chores for girls did differ some from those of the boys, the fact is that girls were being educated in the same classrooms and with the same curriculum. Under the cultural circumstances, a more radical statement of equality was difficult to imagine.

The enforced separation of the sexes in AIM's African schools was mirrored at RVA during this period as well.[35] In fact well into the 1950's the rules governing interaction of the sexes at RVA were positively draconian. A line, quite literally, divided the school into two, with boys on one side and girls on the other. Even brothers and sisters were allowed together only on rare occasions such as when sharing letters from their parents. As one of the third generation of Barnetts at RVA remembered, "a lot of us grew up with a sort of guilt complex about girls (because of the rigid rules concerning the sexes)."[36] The distinct gender roles apparent at the African schools were even more obvious at RVA where the girls were given almost no freedom to roam the wilderness surrounding the school and were actively encouraged to pursue feminine

---

[33] Marsden, George. *Fundamentalism and American Culture*, Oxford University Press, NY: 1980, p. 77-78.

[34] Morton, Andrew, *Moi*, p. 54.

[35] This became even more noticeable after WWII as RVA made a concerted effort of develop a high school. As the school began to grow substantially in numbers, and in the average age of its students, new policies were needed to confront the specifically adolescent issues the school board was now beginning to confront.

[36] Interview with Dr. Stan Barnett by the author at Buck Creek Camp, WA on May 28, 1999. The interview is on tape at the Billy Graham Center Archives, Wheaton College, IL under "the Papers and Materials of Phil Dow".

hobbies such as sewing. This is in contrast to the rough athletics and hunting excursions planned for the boys. Joyce Baker remembered that, "the boys could roam freely, catch a ride into Nairobi (and the like), while the girls couldn't do anything alone."[37] The clear distinction AIM drew between the sexes was generally consistent with the traditional African culture the school was surrounded by and directly in line with the brand of Protestantism dominating the American cultural landscape directly after WWII.

Another similarity between the AIM education Moi and his peers received and that being provided at RVA was the anti-intellectualism we have already found in RVA's history. American pragmatists to the core, AIM had never viewed education as an end in itself. Confirming this perspective, one of Moi's schoolmates, Gedion Tarus recalled that, "the (AIM) missionaries were not interested in academic achievement but to change the individual who would go back and convert others".[38] Therefore when compared to the caliber of schools run by the Anglican missions, the AIM institutions often appeared second-rate. Nevertheless, the education AIM provided was often still an important stepping stone for many young Kenyans who, Tarus continued, "saw the mission as a kind of rebirth".[39] Daniel arap Moi, who went on to become one of the first African school principals and later the second president of Kenya was not the only notable graduate of AIM's African schools. In fact, what stands out amidst the generally substandard reputation of the AIM schools is the number of leaders that came out of the system.

As we have seen in Downing's 1946 article, this "souls first" approach to education also remained predominant at RVA during the post-war period; and strangely the same unexpected achievement is evident in the RVA graduates. The percentage of doctors and academics that RVA produced in this era is astonishing in light of the anti-intellectual bent of the school. Among the many outstanding graduates of this era were David Johnson (Ph.D. in Anthropology – University of Chicago); John Skoda (Ph.D. in Engineering – University of California at Berkley); and Gerald May, longtime president of the University of New Mexico.[40] Such a distinguished record makes sense only when we

---

[37] Interview with Joyce Baker by the author at the Buck Creek Camp, WA on May 28, 1999. Also available at the BGC Archives.

[38] As quoted in Morton's *Moi* on pgs. 53-54.

[39] Ibid.

[40] Interview with Charles "Skipp" Skoda by the author at Buck Creek Camp, WA on May 28, 1999. The interview is available on tape at the BGC Archives under "the Papers and Materials of Phil Dow".

consider the intense Christian commitment that characterized many of the school's post-war graduates. The success they experienced, ironically, must be traced to the same brand of evangelical Christianity that discouraged intellectual endeavor. In short, their drive to serve God to the best of their ability led them to pursue for Christian purposes what other schools pursued for individual glorification. Established with specifically Christian service in mind, the spirit of the school motto, "Omnes Christo" (All for Christ), was applied liberally and unleashed a hardworking, talented and uniquely equipped group of young men and women onto the world – many of whom were to live lives of excellence and substance.

An additional observation concerning Moi's education under the Barnetts (and the African education received under AIM generally) is particularly significant because it cuts to the heart of the African Christian's response to the cultural crisis of Mau Mau, now just around the historical bend. While ignorance and sensationalism had characterized AIM's earliest responses to traditional African culture, the murder of Hulda Stumpf in 1930 awakened the mission to the growing calls by its own missionaries to adopt a more conciliatory attitude towards African culture.[41] By the time Moi and his peers reached the age of circumcision, with its culturally profound ceremonies, AIM's attitude had softened some. Nevertheless, many conservative African Christians and missionaries continued to believe that undergoing the traditional ceremonial rites was tantamount to apostasy. In contrast, non-Christian Africans, with ever-increasing fervency, declared that to refuse circumcision was to reject one's identity as an African.

Like many of the young AIM educated Kenyans, Moi was pulled in both directions at once. His response represents the compromises sought by most of the AIM converts. By choosing to undergo the circumcision procedure, but in a western style hospital and free of the traditional rites associated with the ceremony, Moi walked a moderate middle road that was nonetheless fully in line with his Christian faith.[42] This decision signaled the desire most of AIM's African converts had to hold to their African identity, but only to the degree that that identity was consistent with their faith. Such a decision did not sit well with many of Moi's Kikuyu, Meru and Embu peers – especially those who had not received

---

[41] As noted previously the Stauffachers were especially vocal about the need to respect African traditions that were not directly in conflict with the Bible; and Hulda Stumpf herself had made a public statement to the same effect less than a year before her murder.

[42] Morton, Andrew, *Moi*, pgs. 56-57.

an education and were increasingly frustrated by the changes taking place around them. Yet for the African Christian, the internal tension between their Christian faith, the traditions of African culture and the realities of modern politics, was only to increase as independence neared. Indeed, this tension was later to be displayed most dramatically when Moi, as Kenya's second president, struggled to reconcile his faith with the pressures and demands of realpolitik.

Thus when Herb Downing returned to Kenya in 1947 a fierce battle for the colony's soul was well underway. Understanding the importance of the missionary community in that struggle, and RVA's importance to that community's consistency and effectiveness, Downing set about the task of turning RVA into a first rate institution with a visionary fervor unprecedented in the school's history.

DOWNING BELIEVED THAT if the missionary effort was to see a full flowering, RVA must be able to provide education up through the 12th grade that was of the finest caliber possible.[43] It is here that we get our first clues as to the mysterious academic success of the students coming out of AIM's "anti-intellectual" schools. Downing was passionate that RVA develop into a superior school, but not because there was anything inherently good about excellence in education, but instead because the better the education the school provided, the greater the influence RVA students might have as Christian witnesses to the next generation of Africans. It was a subtle but significant change in perspective from AIM's earliest missionaries and reflected the considerable influence the "new evangelicalism" in America had had on the young principal. Whereas education was viewed with suspicion by many of AIM's fundamentalist pioneers, it was now seen as a neutral means to a positive end.[44] To the degree that RVA students latched on to this higher spiritual goal of education, they embodied a zeal for learning that surpassed that of students from schools that viewed education as an end in itself.

With this "new evangelical" vision of education as his inspiration, Downing began to will his dream into reality. Like Hurlburt and Hope

---

[43] Interviews with Herb Downing (by Robert Schuster in 1983 and available at the Billy Graham Center, Wheaton, IL under "AIM") and Glen Downing by the author, available at the BGC Archives under "the Papers and Materials of Phil Dow".

[44] The sentiment is seen in Downing's *Inland Africa* article, "Education of Missionaries' Children", Jan./Feb. 1946, p. 7. Also see Elizabeth Isichei's *A History of Christianity in Africa*, p. 89.

almost fifty years before him, Downing believed that expanded facilities were essential to the school's growth and success. With this in mind a building program began "in faith" that the necessary funds would materialize. Over the next decade a series of new buildings sprouted up around the campus including: the laundry facility (1950); the first section of "Titchie Swot" (the Elementary School); the Stevenson dormitory for grade school girls (1956); the Principal's residence; the first wing of the Westervelt dormitory for high school boys; and the Jubilee Hall (1955). In addition to these "permanent" buildings, several "semi-permanent" structures were erected to house the British and Kenyan troops during the Mau Mau crisis in 1952 and 1955 that were later converted into the school store and the science room.[45]

Downing's building program did not progress without complications. A lack of funds kept one faculty residence without a roof for two years.[46] More significantly, the school was closed for an entire term in 1951 to make major renovations on the aging Kiambogo building, including the replacement of a dilapidated and genuinely hazardous roof.[47] The most significant setbacks to the school's expanding facilities were the result of fires – one to the newly built Stevenson dorm in 1958 and one to Downing's own home, then named Suswa.[48] The Stevenson dorm fire is noteworthy because it illustrates, in a darkly humorous way, the potential for spiritual legalism that has been one of the enduring failings of the school.

The fire's origin remains something of a mystery, but when several students did notice it, the flames were still small enough that it might be put out. In a panic, the girls called the home of a station family where a large number of the missionaries were meeting. The mother answered the telephone and, hearing the voice of a student emphatically stated, "We are in a prayer meeting and should not be interrupted!" and promptly hung up. The now hysterical girls nonetheless obeyed the

---

[45] Many of these buildings have been replaced. The Westervelt dorm was expanded and then replaced by the current science building. What was called "Kedong" (Titichie Swot) was expanded considerably. And the once mundane but inoffensive Jubilee Hall was replaced by the ominous looking Centenniel Hall in the mid 1990's. See *Inland Africa*, Sept./Oct. 1950, "The Training of Missionary Children – Part I", p. 2&3; *Kiambogo* (the RVA yearbook) – 1958 "Campus", pgs. 10-11; and Entwistle Thesis, p. 24.

[46] *Inland Africa*, Sept./Oct. 1950, pgs. 4-5.

[47] Downing, Herb and the RVA school board, "Letter to Parents No. 3" dated, Feb. 23, 1951. Available at RVA.

[48] Entwistle, p. 36.

missionary lady and, as the righteous group continued to pray for the school, watched as the dorm burnt to the ground.[49]

The considerable building program launched by Downing in the post war years revealed an important component of his overarching vision for the school's educational program. Betraying the strong British flavor of his own RVA education, Downing was convinced that competition was a good and necessary part of a first rate school. As post-war student John Morris remembered, "Everything was competitive".[50] Downing believed competition pushed students beyond what they thought they could achieve and developed the qualities of teamwork, perseverance and communication in the competitors. Team sports were ideally suited to achieving these character goals, and thus, a sloping hill near the middle of the school's campus was turned into the flat clearing that became the school's principal sports field. Beginning in 1956 and using only a small bladed tractor, students and faculty carved out a large field overlooking the Kedong Valley.[51] The entire project was not fully completed until 1964.[52] Nevertheless, between 1957 and 1963 the partially completed field provided ample room for the House Competitions that gained considerable importance during the post war era.

The Livingstone and Stanley House athletic competitions had been around since Muriel Perrott's sojourn at RVA in the mid 1920's, but during the post-war years (1946-1963) the House Games eclipsed every other extracurricular activity at RVA. The Houses chose mascots, created cheers; and developed a corporate culture that helped shape the students in each house.[53] Nights before major competitions were filled with all the excitement of Christmas Eve, as colonies of butterflies invaded the stomachs of the eager young students. In one episode when a vigilant house parent happened upon a group of Stanleys, indulging in one of their customary pre-event feasts of sodas, sweetened condensed milk and bread, the students were soundly berated. The house parent, taking the House Games every bit as seriously as the students, scolded

---

[49] Taken from Shel Arensen's speech to the faculty and students of RVA upon commencement of the Stanley and Livingstone House Games during the 1996-1997 school year. A tape of this speech is available at the BGC Archives, Wheaton, IL under "The Papers and Materials of Phil Dow".

[50] An interview with John Morris by the author at the Buck Creek Camp, WA on May, 29, 1999. The tape of the interview is in the possession of the author.

[51] *Kiambogo* 1956-57, "Events", p. 39.

[52] Roy Entwistle's letter to the author, dated Sept. 15, 1997. The letter remains in the possession of the author.

[53] *Kiambogo* 1956-57, "Stanley House" & "Livingstone House", pgs. 10&11.

their captain for "leading these young boys astray with surfeiting the night before the big day of important games".[54] Nevertheless, from all accounts it appears the students managed to overcome their "surfeiting" and the occasionally grave faculty member to enjoy themselves thoroughly.

Prior to the 1960's the school was not large enough to supply high school sports teams, and therefore athletic competition at RVA continued to be dominated by the House system. By 1960 however, the school had grown enough to allow for limited inter-school competition. Due to its American flavor and the small number of players needed, basketball seemed the logical choice for RVA's first interscholastic team. There was, however, one problem with the choice. No other schools in the British colony played basketball. In the end, RVA was eventually able to find competition against men's teams from the American Consulate in Nairobi and the British troops remaining in Kenya from the Mau Mau emergency, but a lesson was learned.[55] The choice of basketball also shows the degree to which the community had become an island unto itself, aware of only those external forces that directly affected its existence. That is not to say the students and faculty at RVA were oblivious to the changes taking place in Kenya – for as we are soon to see, the Mau Mau emergency was partially a result of their presence in Kenya and directly affected life at the school from 1951-1954. It is only to say that the American missionaries and the students at RVA tended to isolate themselves from the rest of the expatriate community, relating primarily to the African community and amongst themselves.

Like all good generalizations, there were plenty of exceptions to this isolationist tendency, most of which were born out of practical necessities. RVA's experience of fielding a basketball team awakened them to the necessity of developing British team sports. By 1963 RVA was able to field a rugby team under the coaching of South African, Dave Reynolds. It was through this quintessentially British team sport that a new tradition of interaction between the American RVA and the European and African schools was begun.[56]

The first game was played on the field of the Kijabe Primary School against St. Mary's School from Nairobi. Future principal, Roy Entwistle, remembered the, "gray wet day well. Virtually every RVA student and

---

[54] Art Davis' letter to the author, dated June 6, 1997. The letter remains in the possession of the author.
[55] *Kiambogo* 1959-60, "Sports – Basketball", p. 45.
[56] *Kiambogo* 1962-63, "Rugby", p. 57 and Entwistle letter of Sept. 15, 1997 to the author.

all staff members turned out to see 'our boys' battle St. Mary's to a 24-13 win".[57] Even though St. Mary's was fielding its second team, the feat was remarkable considering that RVA had a total of 45 high school boys to chose from against St. Mary's hundreds. Entwistle continued,

> I (was) standing in front of two priests from Saints and (heard) them say, 'These American boys are going to do well in this game once they learn it.'... We went on to post a 7-1 season and the next year... we began playing the first teams. (There was a) tremendous school spirit that was evident... From the start (Dave Reynolds) drove the concept of pride into the boys and they seemed to play above their heads in almost every game.[58]

In time rugby would become synonymous with RVA in the minds of the Kenyan schools. Enthusiasm for rugby also provided evidence of the diversity of cultures that were at work in the evolving "third culture" at RVA.

FROM ITS VERY beginning the school community at RVA was a blend of different, and at times conflicting, cultural impulses. As the American presence grew in the 1950's, the pendulum of cultural influence began to swing strongly in that direction. Several new practices that were initiated during the post-war period serve to highlight this point. Mainstay American school traditions such as a school yearbook (1957), a student council (1958), a school song, and the evangelical equivalent of a prom (the Junior-Senior Banquet – 1956) were all introduced during this era.[59] Yet, other cultural influences continued to help shape the school culture as well. Although in a muted form, the British influence that had been dominant in the earliest years of the school, continued to be important. The prefect system that had been informally used since 1953 was solidified in 1958 with the formal election of head prefects and written guidelines outlining the system's purpose and day to day functioning.[60] School uniforms adopted in

---

[57] Entwistle letter to the author, dated Sept. 15, 1997. The letter is in the possession of the author.

[58] Ibid.

[59] See the respective *Kiambogo* editions, available at the Rift Valley Academy.

[60] *Kiambogo* 1957-58, p. 39 and *The RVA Student Handbook* (1958), p. 9.

imitation of the colony's British schools continued to be used and added to (school blazers were introduced in 1965).[61]

Finally, the setting and culture of hinterland Africa also added to the unique world that was post-war RVA. The spectacular panorama afforded by the Great Rift Valley and abundant wildlife continued to be central to the RVA experience. A feeling of exotic adventure still pervaded the place. Leopards and buffalo continued to roam the rustic campus and the game that thrived in the valley below remained the school's primary source of meat. In short, the effect of the African setting on the distinct culture at RVA remained significant.

Yet the African culture itself can hardly be discounted. This culture could be found anywhere from informal games such as "Musa", which were based on the Kenyan experience, to the cafeteria's recipe book which included African staples such as ugali and irio. More significantly, the slang that was used during this period (and has continued to evolve to the present) was perhaps the most poignant example of the varied and authentic African experiences many of the students brought from their upcountry homes to the school community. Phrases and words from Swahili, Kikuyu, Luo and any number of indigenous African languages, combined with British idioms and American English to create a pigeon English unique to RVA and symbolic of the distinct third culture that, by the post-war years, had developed a life and worldview of its own.[62]

WHILE THE LARGER American, British and African cultures were profoundly significant in their influence, it was the revitalized subculture of evangelical Christianity that wielded the greatest influence on the culture developing at RVA in the post-war years. Before investigating the influence of this subculture it is first necessary to define it. As historian Mark Noll has observed, evangelicalism has never been static, "always being made up of shifting movements, temporary alliances and the lengthened shadows of individuals".[63] Still British historian David Bebbington has isolated four ingredients consistently

---

[61] Entwistle, Roy. M.Ed. Thesis at Seattle Pacific College. The blazers were restricted to the high school boys, reflecting a British "pecking order" mentality that was also strong evidence of English cultural influence.

[62] The slang that began to play such a role in the school's unique vocabulary continues to grow and evolve to the present and will be discussed at more length in a later chapter.

[63] Noll, Mark. *The Scandal of the Evangelical Mind*, Eerdmans, Grand Rapid: 1994, p. 8.

central to evangelicalism: crucicentrism (a focus on Christ's redeeming work on the cross), biblicism (a reliance on the Bible as ultimate religious authority), conversionism (an emphasis on the 'new birth' as a life changing religious experience); and activism (a concern for sharing the faith).[64] Each of these characteristics was, from the school's inception, so ingrained in the culture that they hardly warrant additional comment. Yet, to call RVA an evangelical institution prior to WWII would have been inaccurate. For early on these evangelical characteristics were wedded to the strict biblical literalism and an ardently "other worldly" perspective more accurately described as "fundamentalist". And while fundamentalism certainly continued to be strong within AIM and RVA, after WWII both institutions began to display hints of the more ecumenical perspective characteristic of the "new evangelicalism".

The increasing influence of the more open, evangelical perspective did not mean that there was a decline in the disciplined spiritual life of the campus. Daily chapels were followed up by various optional prayer meetings in the evenings and mandatory group devotional times in the dormitories before "lights out". The required Bible classes and the Bible memory competitions that made up part of the Livingstone and Stanley House Games complimented these non-academic religious duties. Sundays were, of course, entirely devoted to worship, with the community taking part in up to three lengthy religious services in the day.[65] What had changed was not the earnestness of the community, but subtleties in the message behind the earnestness. RVA remained dogmatically committed to the essential doctrines of historical Christianity as exemplified by the school motto of 1957 "Omnes Christo" (All for Christ).[66] But unlike their strictly fundamentalist predecessors, whose perspective had been shaped by the modernist controversy, the post-war generation of RVA faculty were more willing to accept other Protestants who shared Bebbington's definitively evangelical characteristics. In an article published in the 1946 September/October edition of Inland Africa entitled, "Inter-mission Relationships in Kenya Colony" the writer gave evidence of this new

---

[64] Bebbington paraphrased from Noll's, *The Scandal of the Evangelical Mind*, p. 8.

[65] Sources include the 1958 *RVA Student Handbook* and an interview with Wilfred Danielson and Lois (Danielson) Carlson at the Buck Creek Camp, May 29, 1999 by the author.

[66] As first printed in the 1957 RVA yearbook *Kiambogo* under the heading "Information Please" on page 7.

evangelical spirit stating, "Many feel a need for an evangelical union which would embrace believers of every denomination who had the true evangelical position". Even with regards to the liberal Christian Council of Kenya the writer conceded, "We recognize much good that this organization is trying to do, yet we feel the emphasis is in the wrong place".[67] This growing openness is best reflected in AIM's willingness in the 1950's to accept funds from the Lutheran National Council hoping to secure a place for its students at RVA.[68] Even more significant evidence of AIM's evolving perspective was the decision, after considerable internal struggle, to open the school to the children of any protestant mission group working in Africa – provided the parents were willing to accept the doctrinal positions of the school.[69]

The "new evangelical" perspective that began to appear at RVA after WWII did not mean an immediate end to the religious exclusivism that had existed on a social level. Children of the mainline Lutheran denominations who were students at RVA during this time consistently commented on an unspoken (and at times spoken) message that Lutherans, because of their "catholic" theology, might not be saved.[70] And unquestionably the school encouraged a homogeneous orthodoxy. At the same time, the increasingly tolerant AIM perspective was an implicit acknowledgment by the mission of the unified purpose being pursued by the diverse body of evangelical mission groups active in Africa; as well as an indication of AIM's willingness, through RVA, to aid in the work of these groups.

Through the all-encompassing nature of the evangelical message at RVA in the post-war period, the school exemplified the Biblically based, Christ-centered message of evangelicalism as defined by Bebbington. In their choice of behavior guidelines RVA also displayed the evangelical belief that conversion to Christianity also meant a new life transformed by God. At times, such as the rules governing the interaction of the

---

[67] *Inland Africa* "Inter-mission Relationships in Kenya Colony", Sept./Oct. 1946.

[68] Entwistle, Roy, M.Ed. Thesis, pgs. 36-37. Other mission groups also tried to follow the Lutherans in securing special consideration from RVA for the children of their missionaries.

[69] Interview with Glen Downing by the author at Buck Creek Camp, WA on May 29, 1999. The taped interview is available at the BGC Archives at Wheaton College, IL under "the Papers and Materials of Phil Dow".

[70] Interview with Will Danielson and Lois (Danielson) Carlson by the author at Buck Creek Camp, WA on May 29, 1999. The interview is in the possession of the author.

sexes, this belief led to the imposition of extreme and unhealthy moral codes. Yet it is important to note that most of the rules governing the students at the time were marked by their concern for character development and proper social decorum. Even in the case of social relations between the sexes, the excessive measures instituted by RVA were nevertheless in the pursuit of developing a, "wide sphere of friendship...between (the) boys and girls".[71] In the pursuit of character development and social decorum, the 1958 Student Handbook states, "When visitors enter a room, students will stand until they are told to be seated". And further, "Students are expected to ... assist (visitors) in any way possible."[72] The entire aim of the school's behavior guidelines in the post-war period can be summed up in the words of the Student Handbook (1958); "A sincere desire to be Christ-like should govern the general conduct of every student".[73] In sum, while some rules were unintentionally detrimental to the students, most (even apparently legalistic ones) were created with a mind for the larger and positive goal of Christian character development.

As we have already seen the "new evangelicalism" that was now influencing AIM and RVA had its origins in the spiritual renewal taking place in America in the 1940's and 1950's. As a result of the bitter conflict fundamentalism had had with the liberal mainline denominations in the 1920's, a group of fundamentalists had reevaluated their perspective and had consciously discarded non-essential doctrines which were either intellectually untenable or unnecessarily divisive. The result was a more intellectually sound and culturally open brand of orthodox Protestantism. Yet, with regards to AIM and RVA, the emphasis on the unifying power of "Mere Christianity" was not entirely a product of the American experience.

THE INTIMATE INVOLVEMENT of AIM with African culture had also transformed the perspective of the mission in subtle but significant ways. Time and experience had forced many missionaries to reconsider their blanket condemnations of African culture. Between 1900 and 1950 there was a noticeable change in the language used to describe African culture, as well as the subject matter of AIM materials. The mission's official history published in 1903 spoke of Kenyans as

---

[71] *Student Handbook: Junior-Senior High School of Rift Valley Academy* – 1958, p. 4.
[72] Ibid., p. 3.
[73] Ibid., p.4.

"totally uncivilized…black creatures…(and) degraded".[74] By the 1940's, however, these sensationalistic and derogatory terms had disappeared being replaced by articles centered on, "training (Africa's) youth for leadership".[75] An increasing number of articles also took a noticeably sympathetic view towards African culture. The official AIM position on female circumcision had softened as a result of the traumatic events of the late 1920's to a point where, although many still felt the practice abhorrent, it was seen as an issue irrelevant to the critical essentials of orthodox Christianity. In short, experience with African culture and people had complemented the egalitarian worldview of the AIM missionaries to produce a perspective that was increasingly open to the validity of African culture and customs. In this way the missionaries had not just changed Africa, but Africa had changed them.

THE POST-WAR PERIOD in Kenya is best described as one of profound and rapid change and nothing illustrates this truth better than the sudden and violent upheaval of Mau Mau. The result of long simmering political and cultural tensions, and the rapidly evolving realities of the post-war period, Mau Mau shattered the illusion of tranquility that had settled over the colony in the mid 1940's. In order to understand RVA and AIM's relationship to the movement is it important to first look at Mau Mau in a more general context.

The causes behind Mau Mau are myriad, but the question of land is certainly central to any discussion of the movement. When the first Europeans arrived in the late 19th Century an already sparsely populated Kenya had just come through a debilitating famine. Land, relatively speaking, was available. Yet by the 1920's the combination of an increasing number of European settlers and a rapidly expanding African population meant an increase in tension over land rights. The on-the-spot colonial government, acting independently from the British colonial offices at Whitehall, had often blatantly favored the interests of the settler over that of the African – granting settlers large tracts of land and restricting some Africans to native reserves.[76] To the Africans who had been removed from their ancestral lands, the economic loss, immense as it was, was secondary to the cultural and spiritual devastation created by

---

[74] *A Short History of AIM,* written in 1903, author is unknown. This document can be found at the AIM headquarters in Pearl River, NY., pgs. 15-19.
[75] Nixon, Harmon S., "Inter-mission Relations in Kenya Colony", in the Sept./Oct., 1946 edition of *Inland Africa,* p. 6.
[76] Murray-Brown, Jeremy. *Kenyatta,* George Allen & Unwin, London: 1979, pgs. 88-89.

their separation from the land. The effect of this on the Kikuyu population was especially profound. The pain and alienation of the Kikuyu were poignantly expressed through the Kenyan novelist Ngugi's words, "Where O' Creator, went our promised land? At times I wanted to cry or harm my body to drive away the curse that removed us from the ancestral lands. I ask, have you left your children naked O' Murungu (God)?"[77]

But the anger of the Kikuyu population often went unnoticed by the settler community who had been its cause. The ignorance of the settlers concerning the African perspective was a necessary result of their unapologetically racist attitude. Even many of the sophisticated and educated Europeans did not escape the bigotry of their class. Elsepth Huxley, author of *The Flame Trees of Thika* wrote, "(African brains have) a shorter growing period (and thus possess) less well-formed, less cunningly arranged cells than the brains of Europeans... there is a fundamental disparity between the capabilities of his brain and ours."[78] As late as 1955 a common settler myth implying African barbarity was that the Africans had, "no words for love, gratitude and loyalty".[79] Regarding this ignorant arrogance, Sir Philip Mitchell, governor of the colony until 1952, wrote, "the greatest danger for Kenya lay not in Mau Mau but in its color bar, prejudice and rudeness".[80] Not surprisingly, his warning went unheeded until it was too late. Many settlers were simply oblivious to the anger eating away at the hearts and minds of even their own workers because they believed the African's concerns to be of no consequence.

The missionaries were also central players in the development of the Mau Mau movement, but for quite different reasons. As we have seen, missionaries (AIM certainly included) were not immune to the racism that had pervaded much of Western Civilization before the mid 20th Century. That racism did at times act to antagonize the very people they had come to work with. The bitter controversy surrounding female circumcision in the 1920's is only one of the many examples of the strife the missionaries instigated by their well-intentioned ethnocentrism. However, the nature of their missionizing project necessitated intimate involvement with African individuals and culture; and over time the

---

[77] Ngugi wa Thiong'o, *Weep Not, Child*, Heinemenn, Oxford: 1964, p. 25.
[78] Huxley, Elsepth. *White Man's Country: Lord Delamere & the Making of Kenya*, Vol. 1, Macmillan, London: 1935, p. 221.
[79] Brockway, F., *African Journey*, Gellancz, London: 1955, p. 144.
[80] As quoted in Robert Edgerton's, *Mau Mau: An African Crucible*, The Free Press, NY: 1989, p. 31.

result was a growing regard for African ability and culture to the degree that, quite early on, the missionaries consciously began to train Africans for leadership positions in a post-colonial system. Further, unlike the settler community who had little concern for the day-to-day economic and material struggles of the Africans, missionaries not only knew of these difficulties, but responded to them. Due in part to AIM's focus on strictly spiritual issues, this could not be said of all of their missionaries. Still, several members of the RVA faculty such as the Lehrers and Roy and Betty Schaeffer made repeated calls for increasing the wages of the school's African staff during the inflationary crisis that preceded Mau Mau.

Yet intimate involvement alone did not lead the missionaries to initiate the program of educational empowerment that they did. Lying beneath the ubiquitous racism of their culture, the Christian message the missionaries internalized and taught was inherently egalitarian. The entire missionary movement was premised on the belief that all peoples were equally loved by God and equally worthy of the Christian message. Of course, when combined with the missionary experience of educational and technological superiority, these egalitarian presuppositions still produced a form of paternalism. And yet significantly, missionary paternalism was of an inherently temporary sort. Through the development of African education and leadership, missionary paternalism assumed its own death.

In addition, by translating the unwritten African languages for the purpose of creating vernacular Scriptures, the missionaries gave those languages (and thus the cultures) both prestige and staying power for the coming battle with the dominating culture of Anglo-American modernity.[81] Regarding language translation, AIM was on the cutting edge. By 1913 AIM missionaries had already translated significant portions of the Bible into Kikamba, Kikuyu, Masai and Dholuo – and in many instances the work of translation was continued by these missionaries' RVA-educated children.[82]

Therefore, whereas the settler's influence on the call for African self-determination was almost entirely negative, the significant missionary influence was generally positive. By taking the African language and culture seriously the missionaries had, both intentionally and

---

[81] This argument is convincingly made on a general level by Yale historian Lamin Sanneh in "Mission and the Modern Imperative – Retrospect and Prospect: Charting a Course" in *Earthen Vessels*.
[82] The reference to AIM's translation work by 1913 is found in *Hearing and Doing*, April-June, 1914, p.5

unintentionally, confirmed the value of Africans as individuals and African culture generally. Further, in translating the Bible into the vernacular, the missionaries had empowered the African Christian to apply the Truths of Scripture to their cultural context, opening new vistas for Christianity and leading to an increasingly full-bodied and universally applicable faith – a faith that was becoming history's first genuinely world religion.[83] Finally, the education provided by the missionaries had given Africans an eloquent and increasingly confident voice – one that would not accept the indignities of the settler-colonial system.

Ideally, the British colonial administration was to serve as an arbitrator between the often-conflicting settler and missionary influences. Thanks to missionary pressure, the colonial office at Whitehall had, from the early 1920's, been a consistent supporter of the African interests in the colony. The local colonial administrators, however, had more often than not ignored the home office in favor of the settler interest. And these interests almost invariably meant a further exploitation of the African population.[84] As a result, the British colonial government came to be seen by most as a defender of the settler-dominated status quo. By refusing to act until it was too late, the British government played a significant role in seeing the Mau Mau revolt into reality.

Global affairs also played a part in the evolution of Mau Mau as well. In the two world wars well over 100,000 Kenyans had served under the British flag. During WWI their role had been little more than manual laborers, carrying supplies and weapons around the rugged East African terrain. In thanks for their efforts, many of the Africans returned to find their lands taken by a new wave of British settlers. In the Second World War things were somewhat different. Kenyans fought and died alongside the English in the battle against Fascism. These soldiers fought admirably, traveled widely and lived the life of a British soldier with most of the rights and responsibilities this entailed. They had seen white soldiers die by their bullets and had slept with white prostitutes. In short, the war fundamentally undermined the illusion of superiority the settler community had created. Kenyan chief Koinange, in a 1952 speech put into words the sentiments of many of his African peers. The venerable chief said,

---

[83] This argument is made with far more power and support by Lamin Sanneh in, *Translating the Message*, Orbis Books, NY: 1989.
[84] Murray-Brown, Jeremy, *Kenyatta*, pgs. 88-89.

I can remember when the first Europeans came to Kenya... In the First World War you asked our young men to go and fight against the Germans and many were killed. In the Second World War you came again...Now there are Germans and Italians in Kenya and they can live and own lands in the highlands from which we are banned, because they are white and we are black. What are we to think? I have known this country for eighty-four years. I have worked on it. I have never been able to find a piece of white land.[85]

Added to those causes already mentioned (the cultural/spiritual significance of the land to Kenyans, settler racism, missionary education and Christian egalitarianism, the colonial administration's commitment to the pro-settler status quo, and the role of the world wars) was the wildcard of economic circumstance. For the Africans, the loss of their lands had economic as well as spiritual and cultural significance. Thousands of them had been forced to become "squatters" (semi-regular laborers) on the vast European farms or had moved into Nairobi looking for the non-existent jobs rumored to exist there. Their plight was a direct result of economic exploitation and after WWII things went from bad to worse.

Kenya's industrialization during WWII had brought the colony fully into the global economy and as a result, those in positions of financial strength (the settler community) benefited tremendously. The rapidly expanding economy brought with it an equally dramatic rate of inflation that hit the African population with unjust force. Between 1939 and 1952 the price of maize, the staple crop, rose anywhere from 600 to 800 percent. Yet, because of the high number of unemployed Kenyans, the settler community was not forced to raise wages in step with the skyrocketing inflation.[86] Therefore, the privileged settler class (often hardworking as they were) grew increasingly wealthy and arrogant, while the disenfranchised African community grew desperate. Thousands of these despairing Africans flooded Nairobi and by 1952 over 100,000 lived in a congested section of the once tiny colonial outpost. Forced into designated "African locations" – which often packed 10-12 people into filthy one room tin shacks – discontent turned to rage.[87]

---

[85] As quoted in Edgerton, Robert, *Mau Mau: An African Crucible*, The Free Press, NY: 1989, p. 63.
[86] Ibid. pgs. 31-32.
[87] Ibid. pgs. 32-33.

At first it was an individual here and there who snapped under the long-rising pressure, but by the early 1950's these angry individuals had begun to come together in what was to be called Mau Mau. As early as 1948 groups began to meet secretly, taking sacred oaths to fight until they had taken back their lands.[88] Almost without exception, those involved in Mau Mau were the young Kikuyu, Meru, and Embu who had been displaced from the "white highlands" that spread north and west from Nairobi up to Mt. Kenya a couple hundred miles away. A few of their leaders had been missionary educated, but most were the uneducated and desperately poor who felt increasingly out of step with the modernization of their country.

Before 1952 Mau Mau seemed to be little more than rumors of clandestine oaths and stolen weapons. Still, the widespread murmurings were having an effect. Spreading quickly and developing a life of their own, the rumors were enough that by 1950 the government, believing them to be hothouses for discontent, closed over 300 schools that had broken away from missionary and colonial influence. The oaths grew more radical, as did the ceremonies surrounding them. One common oath went, "I will always try to trick a white man... I swear that I will kill, if necessary... any opposed to this organization."[89] The ceremonies always included blood in some capacity – usually from a butchered goat or a menstruating woman – which was spread across the chest of the initiate and ingested as they took the oath. Yet, tales of sexually bizarre ceremonies also abounded causing the government to dismiss the oaths as "mumbo jumbo" or "sexual orgies".[90]

It was not until October 9, 1952 that the mysterious oaths of Mau Mau were translated into violence. In what became a defining characteristic of the movement, it was a fellow African who first fell victim to Mau Mau. A Kikuyu chief loyal to the British government driving just outside of Nairobi was stopped by three men dressed as policemen. The men, citing official business, asked for Chief Waruhiu, who upon identifying himself, was shot four times at point blank range.[91] Many in the settler community dismissed the murder as nothing more than some inter-tribal squabble. However, three weeks later, on October 28, the settlers were forced to stand up and take notice. On this night a lone settler on an isolated farm was hacked to death along with two loyal

---

[88] Barnett, Erik, "The Political Situation in Kenya", in the March/April, 1953 edition of *Inland Africa*, pgs. 9-10.
[89] Edgerton, p. 61.
[90] Ibid., p. 54.
[91] MacPhee, Marshall, *Kenya*, Praeger, NY: 1968, p. 110.

workers. Hardly two months later a trusted servant lured a much loved settler couple and their young child out of their home where they too were brutally dismembered and murdered.[92] By February of 1953 Mau Mau rebels had killed a total of nine Europeans, three Indians and one hundred seventy-seven Kikuyu.[93]

The responses to Mau Mau were many and serve to highlight the complex political situation in Kenya. The uneducated Kikuyu, and those most marginalized from the benefits of the colonial economy and culture, either joined the Mau Mau or were vocal supporters of the movement. This group was by no means a majority, but due to the violence, their defiant call for self-determination gained a widespread hearing. It was this group who created songs like the one celebrating Chief Waruhiu's assassination. The Kikuyu song translated into English went,

> I will never sell out my country,
> Or love money more than my country,
> Waruhiu sold out his country for money,
> But he died and left the money.[94]

Those Kenyans who had either been educated in missionary schools, converted to Christianity or both, made up a second general grouping that rejected the violence of Mau Mau. Some like the AIM initiated African Inland Church (AIC) were outspoken in their loyalty to the colonial government, believing the political leadership of the colony to be God ordained. The AIC and other Christian Africans endured the period in the face of continual threats and physical intimidation. Indeed, many of the nearly 200 Kikuyu who had been killed by the Mau Mau before 1953 were Christians. Writing in *Inland Africa*, Erik Barnett observed that, "missions have become a target of the Mau Mau because of their teaching that one should obey the powers that be, for they are ordained by God."[95] Unlike the "wholesale walkouts from the church" that had occurred during the female circumcision controversy in 1929-30, this time (under even greater pressure) the African church not only stood firm, but displayed a deep-seated conviction that surprised even the missionaries. Barnett noted with excitement,

---

[92] Ibid. pgs. 128-130.
[93] Edgerton, p. 77.
[94] Ibid. pgs. 65-66.
[95] Barnett, Erik, "The Political Situation in Kenya", in the March/April 1953 edition of *Inland Africa*, p. 10.

There has been a definite increase in attendance at services... Many are making professions of faith. Above all, the church leaders are standing true. In every way they are bearing a testimony which is having a dynamic effect on those who are unstable and fearful. The Kijabe church has nearly doubled in its attendance.[96]

While most of those converted or educated by AIM adopted the apolitical perspective of their parent mission, many supported a move towards self-determination. Several of AIM's African Christian leadership, such as Daniel Moi, Robert Ouko and Jean Marie Seroney, while supporting the colonial government in its battle against the violence of Mau Mau, nevertheless were calling for an independent and African Kenya.[97] They were joined by many of the African leaders educated by the more politically involved missions. Under the leadership of Jomo Kenyatta, this group called for a peaceful transition to an independent African nation. Although the settler community and many colonial officials often tried to link Kenyatta and the mission educated moderates to the violence of Mau Mau, this group consistently spoke out against the movement. In a strongly worded speech made even before the worst of the Mau Mau violence, Kenyatta declared, "Mau Mau has spoiled this country. Let Mau Mau perish forever."[98] Also speaking out against Mau Mau at this rally was the very symbol of Kenyan self-determination – the mission educated Harry Thuku.[99]

The response of the colonial government betrayed an ignorance of the dynamics taking place within the African community. Taking their cue from the settler community, the colonial authorities under governor Baring chose to treat the entire African population as Mau Mau or Mau Mau sympathizers. Over 100,000 people were forced out of the white highlands, where they had worked on settler farms, and onto Kikuyu reserves.[100] Many of the Kikuyu had been either uninvolved or loyal to the government prior to the "squatter evacuation", but actions like these began to erode African loyalty to the colonial government, even as the African community remained true to the Christian church.

---

[96] Ibid. p. 10.

[97] The ties of Jean Marie Serony to AIM are shown in Morton, Andrew, *Moi*, p. 48. Robert Ouko was a childhood friend of RVA student Charles Skoda. This information is found in an interview with Skoda by the author in May of 1999. The tape is available at the BGC Archives.

[98] Edgerton, p. 63.

[99] Ibid.

[100] Ibid., p. 77.

For a number of reasons, the Rift Valley Academy was a central player in the turbulent years of the Mau Mau Emergency. If for no other reason, the location of the school meant that RVA would not be able to ignore the volatile political realities engulfing the colony. The town of Kijabe was located right in the heart of Kikuyu territory. In fact, during the uprising many of the major catastrophes were to take place within a twenty-mile radius of the school.[101] In addition, the dense forests that blanketed the Rift Valley Escarpment and surrounded RVA acted as a perfect shelter for the bands of renegade Mau Mau fighters fleeing the colonial forces.[102]

But geography was not the only reason RVA was a focal point during the emergency. As has already been shown, the Christian missionary project had from its onset created divisions in African culture. Whether it was through western education, Christian ideals or both, the missionaries and their message had profoundly shaken the status quo of each tribe they had come into contact with – and none more so than the Kikuyu. AIM's early repudiation of almost everything linked to African traditional culture as "unchristian" had exacerbated the already destabilizing message of Christianity, and had made AIM the focus of some of the earliest anti-missionary anger. In fact, the first act of violence that can be directly linked to the culture war initiated by the missionary movement in Kenya was the murder of AIM missionary Hulda Stumpf.[103] And while AIM's view of African culture had warmed in the years prior to Mau Mau, in the minds of the most ardent defenders of traditional African culture, and the uneducated young turks of Mau Mau, the mission remained an antagonizing symbol of western cultural imperialism. The large number of Kikuyu that had embraced Christianity in the Kijabe area only made matters worse. Thus, to the degree that Mau Mau was a movement intent on returning Kenya to African cultural purity, there could not have been a better target than the island of Western Christianity that was the Rift Valley Academy. Indeed, the school was not only a symbol of the cultural war's roots, but also a threat of a continuing and growing missionary presence in Kenya.

---

[101] The Naivasha raid (20 miles), the Lari Massacre (less than 5 miles), the Murder of Chief Waruhui (less than 20 miles) and several other major attacks occurred close to the campus.

[102] A picture of one of the multiple Mau Mau caves hidden underneath the forests surrounding the school can be found on page 40 of the 1957 edition of *Kiambogo*.

[103] For all the sources on the Hulda Stumpf murder please see the chapter entitled, "Wandering in the Wilderness".

Shortly before the murder of Chief Wahuriu, the Kijabe area experienced a series of small incidents that foreshadowed the eruption of the violence ahead. In September of 1952 three RVA students had snuck off campus for a trip to the dukas near the railroad station a couple miles from the school.[104] After buying candy from the Asian merchants at the station, the three students looked up to see RVA's principal, Herb Downing, coming down the road towards them. In an attempt to avoid being caught, the three fled out the back of the duka and took "the usual shortcut" back to campus, which passed through some of the densely wooded areas near Kijabe. About a mile from campus the path turned abruptly and the three boys came face to face with four Africans armed with pangas[105] and a gun. The Africans were clearly startled and threatened to kill the boys, who were able to escape into the bushes and managed to get back to campus.[106] Incidents like this confirmed the rumors of local Mau Mau activity that staff and students had begun hearing from the school's Kenyan staff and the local African Christians. Scarcely a month later both Chief Wahuriu and the settler Mr. Bowker were dead and a state of emergency was declared.

There was immediately talk amongst the school's faculty and administration of closing RVA during the emergency; but as no major violence had yet broken out, it was decided that the school was safe enough to stay in session.[107] Nevertheless, as rumors of Mau Mau oaths and atrocities continued to trickle in, the school began to implement significant security measures. A detachment of African Home Guard under a young British officer nicknamed "Chipps" took up residence on campus and lines of barbed wire soon surrounded the Kiambogo building.[108] Paul "Junky" Teasdale and several of the older students were enlisted as scouts because of their intimate knowledge of the

---

[104] "dukas" are small shops or tea ("chai") houses that are often the favored meeting spots for the local community.

[105] "panga" is the Swahili term for a machete.

[106] Letter from Art Davis to the author dated June, 3 1997. The letter remains in the possession of the author.

[107] Interview with John Morris conducted by the author in May of 1999. The tape remains in the possession of the author, but should become available at the BGC in the future.

[108] Separate interviews with Charles Skoda and John Morris conducted by the author in May of 1999. The interview with Charles Skoda is available on tape at the BGC Archives, Wheaton College under "the Papers and Materials of Phil Dow". The interview with John Morris should become a part of the same collection in the future.

forested hills surrounding the school.[109]   Finally, a bell system was initiated, whereby the various houses spread out across the sprawling campus could communicate in the event of an emergency. A bell at the center of campus was rung to which each building would, in its turn, answer to confirm "all's well". If the chain of bells fell silent before all had chimed in, it meant that that house or dormitory was in danger and prearranged defense procedures were initiated.[110]

For some of the more fearless students the whole thing took on an air of adventure. Others, however, were all too conscious of the very real dangers that faced them. In the midst of it all, the frightened staff regularly assured the students that there was no immediate danger. Their paternal deception was uncovered one afternoon when several students decided to explore the catacombs underneath the Kiambogo building. Deep under the building in near pitch-blackness the students overheard a frightened faculty discuss reports of an imminent Mau Mau attack. Shaken, the nervous students returned to tell their peers of the situation.[111] From this point, the school community began to share the collective fear that Mau Mau had unleashed. But still nothing happened.

In the next several months the colony began to descend into an abyss of fear and violence. By March of 1953 the situation was almost unbearable. The Mau Mau had killed several hundred people and there were reports of equal atrocities being committed by the colonial forces in their attempt to quell the rebellion. Jomo Kenyatta, whose outspoken anti-Mau Mau rhetoric had been seen as a hopeful sign by many in the missionary community, was put on trial by the colonial government, further exacerbating the divisions in the colony. Then on the night of Thursday, March 26, 1953 it looked as if the RVA community's worst fears were to be realized.

---

[109] Letter from Paul Teasdale to the author dated April 1, 1998. The letter remains in the possession of the author. Interviews with Joyce Baker, Charles Skoda, Stan Barnett and others conducted by the author in May of 1999 all confirm in detail the Teasdale letter.

[110] Several sources describe the warning bell system established during the emergency. Among these are: a letter from "Judy" to her parents from RVA dated April 1, 1953; and an interview with Joyce Baker in May of 1999 (tape available at the BGC Archives under "the Papers and Materials of Phil Dow").

[111] A letter from Lois (Danielson) Carlson to the author received during the summer of 1997. The letter remains in the possession of the author but may become part of "the Papers and Materials of Phil Dow" at the BGC Archives, Wheaton IL.

In a flawlessly planned raid 80 Mau Mau fighters broke into the Naivasha police station armory well after dark and stole 18 submachine guns, 27 rifles, and "a truck load of ammunition". They then freed 173 Mau Mau prisoners before escaping into the night.[112] Only a half an hour after this raid at Naivasha the town of Lari, less than five miles from RVA, was attacked. Estimates of anywhere from 1,000-3,000 Mau Mau descended on the ardently Christian Kikuyu community, burning homes and hacking people to death as they tried to escape.[113] As one RVA student remembered, "through the night the hills above Kijabe glowed red from the fires of the burning huts of Lari."[114] The carnage lasted for several hours and when the dawn came 97 Kikuyu villagers were dead, 32 wounded and almost 1,000 cattle had been maimed.[115]

On Friday, a group of Kenyan Home Guards captured some Mau Mau near RVA and took them to the Kijabe police station. A lone policeman, reasonably anxious after the previous night's atrocities, was on duty. When he heard the sounds of a truck approaching and saw a group of Africans with guns he panicked and began firing into the truck. By the time he realized what had happened two Home Guards were dead and several others were injured. As a symbol of the growing solidarity between the European and African Christians at Kijabe, staff and students at RVA took part in the funeral service.[116] The RVA campus itself, by employing African Christians, became something of a refuge for those fleeing Mau Mau intimidation.[117] By Saturday the nerves of the Christian community around Kijabe were ragged.

---

[112] The quote is from Edgerton's *Mau Mau: An African Crucible*, p. 78. The numbers of weapons and other details of the raid are found in both Edgerton and the speech of Shel Arensen to the RVA community during the 1996-97 school year. That speech can be found in the BGC Archives under "the Papers and Materials of Phil Dow".

[113] Edgerton, p. 79.

[114] See Shel Arensen's speech referred to above.

[115] Edgerton, p. 79.

[116] Letter from RVA student "Judy" to her parents, dated April 1, 1953 and confirmed in Shel Arensen's speech to the RVA community during the 1996-97 school year (available on tape at the BGC Archives).

[117] It should be noted that a large number of Kikuyu staff at RVA were also dismissed during the emergency under suspicion of having taken the Mau Mau oath under pressure. Indeed Glen Downing acknowledged that the man who had been selling vegetables to his family at Kijabe for years was being forced to monitor the family's activities (see Glen Downing interview at the BGC Archives).

The sun rose Saturday morning accompanied by a host of rumors that confirmed an impending Mau Mau raid on RVA. Convinced that they would be attacked, several high school girls took time in the afternoon to write letters they hoped would be read by their parents if they were to be killed. That night the students went to bed under a star-filled sky fully clothed and expecting to be awakened by the sounds of gunfire and angry voices.[118] Soon after the students had gone to their beds the alarm did sound and shots were heard in the distance. Suddenly wide awake, the students watched as the African Home Guards and some men from the mission station hurried up the hill in the direction of the gunfire. Then all went quiet. Several minutes later the "all clear" bell sounded and the defenders of the campus were seen coming back down the hill. It was not immediately evident what had happened.[119] Indeed, to this day there is considerable speculation surrounding the events of Saturday, March 28, 1953. By far the most widespread explanation is simply miraculous.

Less than a month later a band of Mau Mau hiding in the caves above the school were caught by a group of Home Guards that included RVA student Paul Teasdale. While being questioned the men did admit to a planned attack on the school, but claimed it had been abandoned because the Mau Mau could not penetrate the lines of British soldiers surrounding the campus. It is at this point that the story takes its miraculous turn, because in March of 1953 there were no British soldiers at Kijabe.[120] Whatever did happen that night, the Christian community at RVA was convinced that they had been kept safe by supernatural intervention. Indeed, the night's events continue to be remembered as an example of God's provision for the devoutly Christian community.[121]

---

[118] This picture is found in many places but most poignantly in the author's interview with Joyce Baker in May of 1999 available on tape at the BGC Archives.

[119] Multiple sources confirm this telling of the night's events including: the second chapter of Roy Entwistle's M.Ed. Thesis at Seattle Pacific College (1968) entitled "Years of Expansion: The Rift Valley Academy After WWII", p. 25; the interview with Joyce Baker; the letter from "Judy" to her parents from RVA dated April 1, 1953; among others.

[120] That is of course, with the exception of the young officer "Chipps" referred to earlier.

[121] Again, multiple sources confirm this interpretation of the night's events including, most importantly, a letter from Paul Teasdale to the author dated, April 1, 1998. Paul was among the group that captured and questioned the Mau Mau caught near RVA. (The letter remains in the possession of the author).

In early April, with Jomo Kenyatta's trial coming to a close and tensions likely to escalate further, Herb Downing cut the academic term short and sent the students to their homes.[122] Over the extended school break the campus's appearance changed drastically. Acknowledging that the Kijabe missionary community would be a desired Mau Mau target, the colonial government now stepped forward with protection of the very worldly kind. A group of Lancaster Fusiliers, newly arrived from England, moved into the rooms under the Kiambogo porch. With the British soldiers came a seven-foot wall of tangled barbed wire surrounding Kiambogo that was interrupted only by guard posts and mounted machine guns. If this was not enough, bamboo shoots were cut from the forest surrounding the school and fashioned into a second wall of spikes.[123] The sense of relief felt by the school community as it reassembled was palpable. The emergency was by no means over, but for the community at Kijabe the worst had passed.

While the immediate threat of Mau Mau had dissipated, the psychological and emotional affects of those events lingered, burrowing deep into the psyche of the school's extended community. For helpless parents, separated from their endangered children by hundreds of miles, the anxiety must have been unbearable. Letters home filled with their children's innocent sense of adventure could only have had a chilling effect. One such letter from a student named Judy to her parents dated April 1, 1953 reads:

> Boy there sure is a lot of excitement around here. Last week, sometime in the middle of the night, the whole station was alerted because Mau Maus had escaped from prison in Naivasha and were said to be coming this way. The big bell here started ringing as a signal and cars were whizzing around like a racetrack. Every night the men of the station patrol. One of the policemen killed two of our Home Guard by mistake. I went to their funeral Sunday.... I suppose you've read in the paper about people being killed. They killed the chief's wife by laying her on a table and cutting her into pieces, throwing each piece in the

---

[122] Interview with John Morris by the author in May of 1999. The tape is in the possession of the author.

[123] The defenses set up around the school are mentioned in multiple sources but can be viewed in pictures in Edith Devitt's self–published memoir entitled, *On the Edge of the Rift* (available through AIM headquarters in Pearl River, NY) and in the RVA annual, *Kiambogo* in 1957 & 1959.

fire. That was about a mile or two from here…. They're expecting things to happen around here. Last night there was some trouble…[124]

As the violence of Mau Mau dragged on, the sense of adventure felt by some began to fade and a very real fear confronted the children at the school. In ways unfathomable to their peers in America and Europe, the students at RVA during Mau Mau were forced to confront their own mortality and the darkest recesses of human depravity. It seemed at times that every atrocity committed by Mau Mau was answered in kind by forces loyal to the colonial government. In the alleged Kayahwe River Massacre, 94-captured Mau Mau were stripped of their clothing and possessions and machine-gunned to death as white officers looked on.[125]

For many, the harsh realities of life in Mau Mau Kenya acted as an anvil for the formation of a deep and lifelong spirituality. Several of the girls, in particular, made religious commitments under the pressures of their circumstances that translated into a lifetime of Christian service. Wrote Lois (Danielson) Carlson, "I can remember lying in my bed night after night praying to be kept safe until morning, and promising God almost anything if He wouldn't let me die."[126] Joyce Baker, likewise, prayed, "Lord, if I live, my life is yours".[127]

The traumatic events of Mau Mau also forced both the mission and school communities to examine their part in the movement's origins. In this way, Mau Mau betrayed the deep differences that continued within the missionary community concerning African culture and Africans. Almost no one attempted to defend the atrocities committed by either side. Yet to many at RVA the Mau Mau were simply barbaric, anti-Christian terrorists that deserved whatever consequences their actions drew. From here the jump to an all-inclusive prejudice against Africans and African culture was an easy one to make. And, in light of the hysteria that engulfed the missionary community at the peak of the emergency, it is surprising more of the children at RVA did not adopt this perspective.

---

[124] Judy's last name is not on the letter dated April 1, 1953 - Kijabe. The handwritten letter is in the possession of the author.

[125] Edgerton, p. 166.

[126] A letter from Lois Carlson to the author received in the summer of 1997. The letter is in the possession of the author.

[127] Interview with Joyce Baker by the author in May of 1999. The taped interview is available at the BGC Archives.

Sadly, this sort of prejudice did exist as was shown by the words and actions of some of the children. Will Danielson remembered with regret his participation with five other RVA schoolboys in a mock raid on some Kikuyu women gathering wood in a ravine near the campus. With hunting knives in hand, the screaming boys charged down the hill towards women hoping to at least frighten them. Such a game played on white adults would have never been tolerated, but in the boy's minds, these were just Africans. Danielson continued, "the only one who stayed at the top of the ravine was David Dibbens, who was the only non-missionary kid among us."[128] The children were punished by the school for the action, but like other similar events, it displayed an underlying disdain for the African culture and people that a few of the missionary children had brought with them from their homes. Because RVA remained an all white school at the time, and because most of the Africans the children came into contact with were there to serve the student's needs, the institution served to reinforce whatever homespun bigotry that already existed.[129]

However, if the institution acted to bolster prejudice, many of the faculty served to undermine that bigotry. Easily the most popular faculty members at the school during the Mau Mau years were Roy and Betty Schaeffer. Young, enthusiastic and intellectually sharp, Roy was revered by many of the boys. Stan Barnett was not alone when he said; "I modeled myself after Roy".[130] Schaeffer was a second generation AIM missionary. Like many of these men and women, he had developed a deep respect for African culture and counted many of the Africans in the Kijabe community as close friends. It was quite common for Schaeffer to bring students along when he went to drink chai at the African shops or attended an African church service in the valley below the school.[131]

---

[128] Letter from Wilfred Danielson to the author dated, June 18, 1997. The letter remains in the possession of the author. It should be remembered that David Dibbens was the Eurasian boy who had been the subject of some race-based controversy earlier and from his personal experience seems to have been more sensitive to the question of racial equality and the necessity of treating all people with dignity and kindness.

[129] In interviews, both Charles Skoda and John Morris observed the unspoken racism that the separate spheres of white and black in Kenya had on the European children growing up in Kenya. The interview with John Morris is in the possession of the author and the interview with Charles Skoda can be found in the BGC Archives, Wheaton, IL.

[130] Interview with Stan Barnett by the author in May of 1999. The taped interview is available at the BGC Archives, Wheaton, IL.

[131] See the interviews of Charles Skoda, Stan Barnett and John Morris.

Herb Downing, too, modeled a respect for the Kikuyu both by seeking out his African peers and by treating the African school staff with dignity and respect. The Downing children adopted this perspective of their parents referring to the African staff or Home Guards as "rafiki" (Swahili for "friend").[132] As a balance to the blanket racism of the colonial culture, these second-generation AIM missionaries forced the children at RVA to look past skin color. Yet, the complex, contradictory and ultimately ambiguous racial perspective that existed at RVA during the Mau Mau era is captured in Stan Barnett's final moments in Kenya. As his car drove off the campus and toward the plane that would take him to America, Barnett saw two prisoners being interrogated and beaten. Said Barnett, "I have never been able to explain to myself why, when I saw these prisoners being beaten, my reaction was to laugh."[133]

In 1954 additional British troops descended upon the colony and effectively, sometimes ruthlessly, destroyed Mau Mau strength in Nairobi and began to gain control over portions of the forested highlands. For all intents and purposes, by 1956 the emergency was over. In the meantime missionary-educated progressives had been working with the colonial government and the Home Office to develop the foundation for a free and multi-racial republic. By the time Kenyatta was finally released from detention in 1961, independence was a foregone conclusion. Mau Mau had forced the British to count the economic and moral costs of retaining the Kenya colony. It had also given rise to all of the deep-seated anger that had been building for generations. But in doing so, Mau Mau had torn the African community apart. Divisions between the progressive Africans, who had embraced the Western influences of education and Christianity, and the increasingly marginalized traditionalists became apparently insurmountable. When independence came on December 12, 1963, the new nation looked to

---

[132] Letter from Wilfred Danielson to the author, dated June 18, 1997.

[133] Interview with Stan Barnett in May of 1999. The taped interview is available at the BGC Archives, Wheaton, IL. While Stan was quick to find fault with himself, it was pointed out to me by one insightful reviewer of this book that laughing in uncomfortable situations is accepted and quite common among many people groups in Kenya. Therefore, Barnett's response, while disconcerting to an American might have actually reflected a deep, and perhaps unconscious, connection to the culture and worldview of the people he had grown up amongst.

Kenyatta, "the black Moses"[134] as the best hope for national unity and reconciliation.

DURING THE POST-WAR period rapid changes confronted both RVA and the colony it was a part of. On a global level the United States had assumed center stage and with it came considerable American cultural influence on the rest of the world. An increasingly significant part of that American culture was the new and evolving sub-culture of evangelical Protestantism. Because conservative Protestantism was intimately connected to the Christian missionary enterprise, changes in its outlook necessarily meant changes in the missionary movement; and in this case that translated into more Protestant Americans considering involvement in the missionary movement. Hoping to facilitate this potential growth, the Rift Valley Academy under Herb Downing made a concerted effort to expand its facilities and improve the quality of its faculty. Between 1946 and 1963 the student population rose from 38 to 168.[135] This growth implied correctly that the American evangelical missionary influence in Kenya was on the rise. The school produced its first high school graduate in 1949 (Paul "Shorty" Smith) and its first graduating class in 1950 that included Harold LaFonte, Gloria Kitts, Kate Downing and Esther Schaeffer.[136] Indeed, the school's importance to the larger missionary movement became undeniable as more and more families in remote locations of East and Central Africa relied on the school for the education of their children. Finally, the prominent visits of evangelical heroes Corrie Ten Boom and Billy Graham to the school in 1960 also point to the growing appreciation of the schools' essential role in the future of evangelical missions by the larger American Evangelical community.[137]

But it was the school's role prior to WWII that was most critical to the dramatic changes that occurred in Kenya from 1946-1963. The existence of RVA had been critical to the consistency and growth of AIM prior to 1946. That consistency had meant the development of a significant educational and evangelistic program which profoundly influenced the colony's future course. By introducing Christianity and

[134] Ngugi, *Weep Not, Child*, p. 43. Though a fictionalized account, Ngugi's works are representative of the Kikuyu experience. In this case the use of Biblical imagery by the Kikuyu towards Kenyatta was widespread.
[135] Entwistle, Roy. M.Ed. Thesis at Seattle Pacific College (1968), p. 49.
[136] See interview of Glen Downing by the author in May of 1999, available at the BGC Archives, Wheaton, IL.
[137] See RVA yearbook, *Kiambogo* (60' p. 56 and 61' p. 53).

education, and then nurturing it over the years through the presence of second and third generation missionaries, AIM helped plant the seeds of Kenyan independence. Missionary educated leaders were at the forefront of the peaceful demand for self-determination that matured during the post-war period. The marginalized and angry traditionalists that fueled Mau Mau also derived much of their passion, albeit negatively, from the influence of the missionaries.

When combined with the racism and land seizures of the settler community, the complacency of the colonial government and the crippling economy, the effect of the missionary movement in Kenya was to help spark a dynamic struggle for African self-determination. By 1963 the Christian progressives and the traditionalist Mau Mau had combined to make Kenya an independent African republic. But what the future held was anyone's guess.

For the missionary movement especially, the future in Kenya appeared tenuous at best. Now that the Kenyan people were out from under colonial rule, how would they and their leadership react to the presence of Christian missions? The answer would speak volumes about how the Kenyans viewed both Christianity and western-style education. If the missionary movement was nothing more than an unwanted advance by an overpowering suitor, as many historians have claimed, the Kenyan people would have ample opportunity to say so. As the British flag was lowered over parliament and the flag of the new Kenyan republic ascended, the missionary community awaited the verdict.

CHAPTER 5

AN UNEXPECTED EXPLOSION: RVA AND THE MISSIONARY EXPANSION IN KENYATTA'S POSTCOLONIAL KENYA FROM 1963-1976

JANUARY OF 1964 FOUND CHILDREN FROM THROUGHOUT East Africa following well-worn tracks back to RVA. As they went, they were met by the same dusty roads and the same railroad stations that had greeted generations of missionary children before them. On the railway platforms, the children exchanged with their parents the familiar bittersweet farewells that had been shared by the first RVA families almost sixty years before them. As the trains of the E.A.R.&H. pulled away from the stations and into the African night, little appeared to have changed.[1]

Beneath this placid veneer, however, everything was being turned upside down. After over seventy-five years of British rule, Kenya's African population had risen up to claim its political birthright. The colonial era was over and with it the sense of security the expatriate

---

[1]Many of the students who boarded at RVA up to this period came by train. For many, these train trips had an almost mystical quality and have remained firmly planted in their memories of Africa and RVA. Folk singer, Roger Whittaker, who grew up in Kenya and experienced the same train trips to and from boarding school (although he did not attend RVA) has captured the sense of adventure and mystery these train trips held for the school children in a song entitled, "The Good Old E.A.R & H".

community enjoyed under the British. Violence and anti-European rhetoric had accompanied the struggle for African self-determination and remained fresh in the minds of many. As a result, thousands of settler families continued to flee the colony convinced that their land, if not their lives, would be endangered under African rule. The fears of the settler community were not without foundation. Much of the wealth their community had amassed was a result of generous land grants doled out years before by the colonial government at the expense of the now exploding African population. Therefore when the government changed hands, and the legal and political legitimacy of their wealth dissolved, it left the settler community entirely vulnerable to the political redistribution of land many felt was sure to come.[2]

Yet, the settler community also represented the majority of the foreign capital that had poured into the colony making it the economic success story of East and Central Africa. Kenyatta's young government understood this and as a result made every effort to reassure the settlers that their lands and investments were safe. In a speech given just months before Independence, Kenyatta reached out to the settlers in a spirit of reconciliation. Said Kenyatta, "You have something to forgive just as I have... many of you are as Kenyan as myself... We want you to stay and farm well in this country, that is the policy of this government".[3] Kenyatta's appeal was met by thunderous applause and succeeded in pacifying most of the remaining settlers.

Like the settler community, missionaries had benefited under the colonial system, often garnering huge plots of land upon which were built schools, clinics, churches and missionary compounds. AIM's one hundred acre plot at Kijabe was just one of many such land grants that now were in jeopardy. The angry anti-missionary rhetoric that poured from some branches of the nationalist movement led the expatriate Christian community to believe that their days in Kenya were numbered. Further, unlike the settler community, the missionaries did not represent a decisive portion of the Kenyan economy, making them economically expendable.[4] Fully cognizant of these realities, the missionary

---

[2] One only has to look at the Zimbabwe of 2000-01 to get a picture of the very real fears that swept through the settler community in Kenya during the early 1960's.

[3] Edgerton, Robert, *Mau Mau: An African Crucible*, p. 217.

[4] As the number of missionaries in Kenya grew, their economic importance increased – not so much because of their personal wealth, but due to the funds they represented to Kenya by way of development and job creation for the national population.

community waited to hear what, if any, role they were to have in the new Kenya. In many ways the African government's policy on foreign missionaries would be a referendum of the Kenyan people on the missionary enterprise to date. If the missionary community had been viewed as exploitive or coercive (as many in the Western academy believed), the people would have their chance to say so.

From the onset of Kenyatta's presidency it became evident that the Kenyan government and its people did not generally share the sentiments of the Western intelligentsia regarding Christian missionaries. Tolerated under the British colonial system, missionaries were now actively sought out. Shortly after independence Kenyatta's Minister of Education, the Honorable Jeremiah Nyagah acknowledged both the new government's endorsement of the missionary movement and the centrality of RVA to the effectiveness and future growth of the movement stating, "the value of the Rift Valley Academy is not only for its products (its graduates) but (for its role) in the organization of … missionary society".[5] With regard to RVA's role in producing future missionaries, Nyagah was just as clear. Speaking directly to the academy's students he stated, "You students who were born and trained here are the ones that we would like to see come back and help us (build a new country), for we know the value of second-generation missionaries".[6] Minister Nyagah's words were not empty political rhetoric. Of Kenyatta's original cabinet, three-quarters had been educated at the Protestant missionary run Alliance High School.[7] In addition, many other key political figures in the new republic, like the young Daniel arap Moi, had received their training in upcountry schools, established and run by missionaries and the Kenyan Christian faculty they had trained. But it was not just through education that the missionary movement had touched the new Kenyan government. The churches they went to, the hospitals they had seen their children born in, and the many agricultural projects that were transforming their rural communities – most of these were the result of missionary efforts.

Kenyatta's encouragement of the missionary enterprise was both direct and indirect, formal and informal. In 1966, on one of several similar instances, Kenyatta invited RVA's choir to his home for a private performance. The one hour engagement turned into an afternoon of

---

[5] The address of the Honorable Jeremiah Nyagah at the RVA Commencement Exercises on Tuesday, July 25, 1967 – Handwritten notes of the speech are available in the archives of RVA, Kijabe, Kenya.

[6] Ibid.

[7] Kipkorir, B.E., "Carey Francis at Alliance High School, Kikuyu – 1940-1962" in Kipkorir, p. 113.

singing and sharing, concluding with the president giving the choir an extensive tour of his home and an invitation to return.[8] The sentiment seemed to flow in both directions. Whether out of gratefulness or political necessity, RVA had begun accepting a small number of national students during the 1964-65 school year, despite the fact that the school no longer could adequately house the number of missionary children requesting admission.[9] Evidences of mutual goodwill such as the private concert and the government's pro-missionary rhetoric were abundant in the Kenyatta years (1963-1978).

SIGNIFICANTLY, THE KENYAN government's encouragement of the Christian missionary movement coincided with an outpouring of idealism in American culture. The young and charismatic John F. Kennedy helped spark and nurture the waves of optimism that washed over America's youth in the early 1960's. In 1961 Kennedy initiated a program that epitomized the spirit of the age. The Peace Corps, as a secular missionary phenomena, not only sent thousands of young Americans around the world on humanitarian projects, but also acted to fuel Christian missionary zeal at home among a growing number of young, college-educated, evangelical Christians. The tragic assassination of JFK just weeks before Kenyan independence only inflamed the idealistic spirit of the day – as millions swore to carry JFK's legacy of American altruism to the corners of the globe.[10]

Simultaneous with the idealism of Camelot came the onset of the greatest economic boom in U.S. history to date. The combination of Kennedy altruism and increasing wealth turned missionary zeal into missionary enterprise as both the Peace Corps and traditional Christian missions swelled in both numbers and financial resources. At its peak in 1966 over 15,000 Peace Corps volunteers were working in 52 countries worldwide.[11] The number of American Protestant missionaries working

---

[8] *Inland Africa*, "RVA Choir Sings for President Kenyatta", Nov./Dec. 1966.

[9] Entwistle, Roy, "Year of Expansion" from his M.Ed. Thesis, Seattle Pacific College, 1966, p.52.

[10] For an excellent synopsis of the Kennedy era and the effects of the assassination see James T. Patterson's, *Grand Expectations*, Oxford University Press, NY: 1996, chapters 16&17.

[11] "Peace Corps 1961" *Life Magazine*, "The 100 Events that Shaped America", (1975), p. 38. The missionary movement utilized the Peace Corps phenomenon, by remodeling some of their longstanding humanitarian efforts along the lines of the American program. Campus Crusade for Christ is noteworthy here, setting

overseas more than doubled this figure. Estimates put the number of American missionaries working overseas during the same period at somewhere between thirty and fifty thousand.[12]

In most cases, the explosion of missionary zeal flowed along the paths of least resistance and thus into those nations that both welcomed missionaries and could meet their most pressing personal need – namely an education capable of preparing their children for entrance into American colleges. Due to the presence of RVA and the national government's explicitly pro-missionary stance, East and Central Africa was inundated with missionaries, with Kenya receiving the bulk of the number. As the number of missionaries increased, so did RVA's student population. It had taken the school fifty-two years to surpass the one hundred-student mark. In contrast, in just four years (between 1962 and 1966) enrollment at the school exploded from 155 to 305.[13] And by 1974 the school's student body had pushed above the 400 mark.[14]

As WE MIGHT expect, growth of this kind brought with it dramatic changes. Perhaps the most significant change to the life of the school was a decreasing adult presence. In contrast to the exponential growth of the student body, the size of the faculty and staff grew only

---

up the Agape Movement in East Africa under the direction of Stewart Dow in the early 1970's.

[12] According to Patrick Johnstone's research in *Operation World*, in 1978 there were 56,600 "Western Protestant missionaries" of which approximately sixty percent were North American (the vast majority of those being American). If we estimate that the numbers of missionaries increased between 1966 and 1978 at approximately the same rate as the change between 1978 and 1991 (1.24) then we can estimate that in 1966 there were approximately 45,000 Western Protestant missionaries of which at least 27,000 were Americans (approximately sixty percent).

[13] By this time RVA was, with only a couple exceptions to be discussed later, accepting only missionary children. Therefore this dramatic increase in enrollment must point directly to the influx of missionaries to Africa. Some have suggested that a portion of the increase also could be attributed to missionaries already in the region who no longer felt that the British schools under African leadership were preparing their children for post-secondary studies. However, most missionaries by this time were American and had for some time sought out American style education – namely RVA. Thus it would be erroneous to attribute any significant part of the rise in enrollment to those families opting out of formerly British schools.

[14] The statistics cited here can be found in several places: "RVA Enrollment" (Graph), available at the Billy Graham Center, Wheaton College under CN 34-18; or Roy Entwistle's MA thesis, p. 49.

slightly in the 1960's. In 1962 the student to staff ratio was 5.5 to 1. Just four years later that ratio had fallen to 8.2 students for every staff member.[15] Granted, outside of its first years, RVA had never enjoyed adequate adult supervision – at least by standards acceptable to 21st Century boarding schools.[16] As a result, RVA had a history of over-burdened staff and relatively unrestrained students. With a small, homogenous and responsible student body such overextensions of personnel usually did not have a significant impact on the quality of the school. However, when the student/staff ratio almost doubled between 1962 and 1966 even the most dedicated of faculty could not stand in every gap that had been created. So acute was the adult shortage that in one case, when the school had completely outrun its available staff, two senior boys were forced to act as dorm parents.[17]

As staff supervision declined, RVA's British heritage came to the forefront. Student prefects began to wield tremendous authority and the school began to take on the tone of a quintessential British boarding school, complete with a *Lord of the Flies*-like code of student behavior. During this time all dormitories had unofficially defined boundaries through which only those with special permission could pass. Deference to elder students was demanded, with harsh penalties doled out by upper classmen for even perceived disrespect.[18] For those students in positions of either *dejure* or *defacto* authority life was an intoxicating blend of power and freedom. However, for those willing to question the pecking

---

[15] The calculations were made by the author based on the number of students at the school in 1962 and 1966 (as found in the aforementioned sources); and the number of faculty in these same years (as found in a personal interview with former principal Roy Entwistle at Kijabe, Jan.1, 1998). A recording of the interview is available at the Billy Graham Center under "The Papers and Materials of Phil Dow".

[16] The significance of these numbers only sinks in when we see them within a larger context. The Bear Creek School in Redmond is a school with similar goals. Its student to adult ratio in 2001-2002 was 5.2 to 1. This number is reflects a greater adult presence than existed at RVA in 1962 and a dramatically more healthy ratio than existed at RVA in 1966. But here is the critical point – TBCS is strictly a day school and RVA is a boarding school where adults are responsible not just for running the school and teaching, but for parenting as well. The adults at RVA are on duty twenty-four hours a day.

[17] Personal interview of Roy Entwistle by the author at Kijabe on Jan. 1, 1998.

[18] Personal Interview with Tim Cook by the author at Kijabe, Dec. 20, 1997. Tim Cook was a student during this time and is now the school's superintendent. This interview is available on tape at the Billy Graham Center, Wheaton College, under "The Papers and Materials of Phil Dow".

order or who happened to be disliked by the Alpha Male, life often became a nightmare.

With so much power resting in the hands of the students, the quality of a given school year often rested on the character of the student leaders. In good years, the considerable freedom students enjoyed translated into usually harmless adventures and rites-of-passage such as unsupervised hikes across the valley to Mt. Longonot or skinny dipping parties at the waterfalls, hidden high in the hills above the school. In bad years this freedom could mean the emotional, or even physical, abuse of frightened underclassmen, and any number of less healthy adventures. Without enough adult mentors, the cruelty of peers and the challenges common to boarding schools at times left already vulnerable children emotionally scarred. Looking back on her experience at RVA during these years a now successful writer recalled, "My time there was lonely, depressing and miserable. The food was appalling. I weighed 98 Ibs. when I graduated and I'm 5'7''. There were no adult role models... depression still haunts me, and when I have my worst nightmares they are of RVA".[19]

Yet, for many the early and mid-sixties at RVA were good years. There was a sense of excitement about both the school and the missionary enterprise due to the blossoming influence of Christianity in Kenya and fueled by an abundance of fresh and idealistic missionary families. Long viewed by those in Kenya with muted admiration as an isolated but decent American missionary school, RVA suddenly garnered an international reputation. Success in sports was one reason for the school's apparently sudden stardom.

Several factors came together to produce excellence in sports at RVA. First, the growing size of the school meant that RVA could now field several interscholastic teams per sport, creating a sort of farm system for young student athletes. Without access to the idle distractions of urban life, the adolescent energy of the students was funneled either out into the surrounding natural habitat, in the form of uniquely African escapades, or into sports. During the considerable free time the students enjoyed, the school's athletic fields and basketball courts rarely saw rest. These casual games that developed spontaneously naturally functioned as the informal training grounds for the school's increasingly skilled teams. Running for hours in the crisp highland air did not hurt either, as it

---

[19] A letter to the author from an RVA graduate of this period. The writer of the letter wished to remain anonymous – the letter remains in the possession of the author.

produced in the school's athlete's legendary stamina.[20]   Finally, the countless hours spent together, not just playing sports, but in classes, at meals, in dorm rooms, and the like, created in the RVA student a sense of camaraderie that translated on the playing fields into a remarkably high level of team work and mutual self-sacrifice.

Not surprisingly, RVA dominated its schoolboy competition in boy's basketball, having introduced the game to Kenyan interscholastic sports just years earlier.   What was surprising are the competitive teams the school fielded during the early and mid 1960's in boys soccer and girls field hockey – both traditionally non-American sports.[21]   However, these sports notwithstanding, it was in the quintessentially British sport of rugby under South African coach Dave Reynolds that the school made a name for itself.   With realistically low expectations, RVA began playing rugby in 1963 against the second and third teams from rival schools. However, in just three years the school's team had risen to be the top schoolboy side in East Africa, with seven of its players representing Kenya internationally.[22]   Almost immediately rugby at RVA took on a significance that transcended sport.   Like a varsity boys basketball game between rival Indiana towns or a high school football game in Texas, rugby games at RVA developed into community events complete with pomp and circumstance and proverbial Monday morning quarterbacks. It was during these early years that the storied rivalries with Nairobi School (Prince of Wales), Lenana (Duke of York) and St. Mary's began in earnest.[23]

---

[20] During the late 1980's the Nation wrote a story on former RVA student Paul Obwa (then a rugby star for one of the Nairobi schools) in which it implied that the school's sports teams ate meals that included performance enhancing nutritional supplements.

[21] The best story of the school's sporting success is found in the pages of the school's annual, Kiambogo during these years.   A complete collection resides in RVA's graphic arts room, Kijabe.

[22] RVA annual, *Kiambogo*, 1966-67, pgs. 90-100.

[23] A brief tangential anecdote illustrates the role Rugby has come to have at RVA.   In the late 1990's Tim Bannister, a veteran English teacher at RVA and the author of an alumni e-newsletter, sent out a letter in which he described the decision by the school's administration and board to end its rugby program in favor of an expanded intramural program.   The reaction among RVA's alumni was vitriolic.   Angry letters poured into Bannister and the school demanding that the tradition of Rugby be retained.   Even some who felt little emotional tie to their alma mater reacted as though life as they had known it would be over.   Of course, no one had bothered to check the date of the email – April 1st – and so Bannister was forced to write a second letter to assure the school's hysterical

But sports were not the only thing that put RVA on the map during the early and mid-sixties. Under the remarkable leadership of Don Fonseca the school's choir rose to receive widespread acclaim. By 1966 the choir's concerts were fixture highlights in the Nairobi arts schedule, with RVA usually being picked to present the annual Christmas concert in the National Theatre. Beyond weekly performances at RVA, a private concert for the President, and the "cutting" of a record on Diadem records, the choir was regularly sought out to perform on national television, at official US Embassy functions and at various ceremonies for the Kenyan government.[24] Explicitly Christian in their message, the choir bolstered RVA's reputation as a hothouse for future missionaries and reinforced its image as an island of wholesome American evangelicalism. The music program also rightly kept outside observers from seeing the school strictly as a sports machine. The drama program, though less storied, was active as well, putting on classic period plays such as *The Comedy of Errors* and *The Winslow Boy,* and combining with Kijabe High to produce *Cry The Beloved Country.* Not to be ignored, instrumental music also flourished during the early and mid-sixties with over thirty percent of the student body actively involved in piano lessons.[25]

With so much emphasis being devoted to extracurricular activities it seems logical that the academic calibre of the school – never particularly stellar to that point – would have suffered, but this was not the case. In many regards the academic progress the school achieved during this period was a culmination of the consistent scholarly push by longtime principal Herbert Downing since his return to RVA in 1948. Credit must also be given to several key additions to the faculty in the early 1960's such as that of future principal Roy Entwistle and his wife Judy.

And yet strong leadership and important faculty additions were only part of the story behind RVA's significant academic progress. Dramatic changes were also afoot in American education that had a forceful influence on the school's academic culture.   In the midst of the peaking tensions of the late 1950's Cold War, America had suffered a startling defeat that had far reaching consequences. In the form of the first unmanned satellite Sputnik, the Soviet Union had provided convincing

---

alumni that it had all been a joke. The moral of the story – at RVA there are some things that you don't joke about.

[24] Entwistle, Roy, M.A. Thesis, pgs. 61-61.

[25] RVA Newsletter, May 1966; RVA annual, *Kiambogo* 1969-70, p.77; RVA Newsletter 1965, under "Music". Both newsletters can be found in the archives at RVA, Kijabe.

evidence that the quality of education in the Communist Bloc had surpassed that of the free world. Education experts and schools around America responded in force by raising standards and introducing numerous reforms. The young faculty who arrived at RVA during this time were coming out of an American context obsessed with academic standards due to Russia's successful Sputnik launch. The resulting combination of Downing's pro-intellectual bent and this new wave of academic concern produced several scholastic initiatives at RVA. In 1965 the school created a National Honor Society chapter named, "Elimu Bora" to encourage and reward academic excellence.[26] Standardized testing also took on increased importance with the school adopting mandatory testing in the 1960's, including the college entrance exams: PSAT, SAT and ACT. RVA had good reason to be pleased with the results of these tests as at least a quarter of its students ranked in the top ten percent on the exams in any given year - a group regularly including several National Merit Scholarship Semi-finalists. The push for academic excellence appeared to be succeeding. Although RVA published the figure that ninety percent of its graduates were going on to higher education, the number in most of these years was closer to ninety-five percent.[27]

Yet, for all the added academic flavor that the National Honor Society and the standardized tests gave, the real boon to academic quality at the school was the push for accreditation that came during the mid-1960's. The grueling accreditation process required RVA to outline and justify all of its academic programs. Previously accountable only to its families and its own fluctuating standards, RVA had been subject to occasional bouts of academic incoherence. In 1966-67, with Roy Entwistle in charge, the entire faculty sat down and completed a comprehensive self-appraisal. The process did not lead to radical changes in the curriculum or pedagogy, but it did highlight some of the school's enduring weaknesses such as a generally under-qualified and numerically insufficient faculty. When the accreditation committee arrived from the Middle States Association of Colleges and Secondary Schools, RVA was able to present a sound and coherent enough educational program to become the first school in Africa to receive American accreditation.[28] By 1968 they could state with confidence that,

---

[26] RVA annual, *Kiambogo* 1967-68, p. 76; Entwistle, M.A. Thesis, p64.

[27] RVA Newsletter, dated May, 1966. Available in the RVA archives, Kijabe. The RVA Student Handbook of 1968 does claim the 95% figure as going "on to further education".

[28] RVA Newsletter, dated June 1988. Available in the RVA archives, Kijabe.

"RVA has a high academic standard and a good reputation among the various colleges and universities in the USA where our graduates have established the honor of the school".[29]

In the final analysis, the golden years of the sixties can be attributed largely to the robust health of the school's culture to date. As we have seen, that school culture did not develop easily, but instead was a product of the six, well intentioned but haphazard decades that had preceded it. When this healthy school culture combined with the idealism and wealth of post-WWII America and the pro-missionary stance of the Kenyan government, RVA grew and blossomed. For the school, however, the golden years were not to last. Quite simply, the school's growth had been too fast and the expectations too lofty. By 1968 the school was thriving, but on borrowed time. Indeed, by the late 1960's it was not hope but anxiety that best characterized the missionary community in East Africa.

FOR BETTER OR worse, the influx of new missionaries from America tied the missionary community ever more closely to the ebb and flow of American culture and by the mid to late sixties this culture was in turmoil. Politicians caught up in the euphoria of the early sixties had also exploited that idealism for political gain – promising the world to a hopeful American public. Said Lyndon B. Johnson, "Hell, we're the richest country in the world, the most powerful. We can do it all".[30] In addition, the extravagant promises and programs of the politicians were exponentially exacerbated by the spread of image-based media – namely television. As early as 1961, the historian and cultural critic Daniel Boorstin had foreseen the ability of television to divorce culture from reality. Said Boorstin, "(America) suffers primarily not from our vices or our weaknesses, but from our illusions. We are haunted, not by reality, but by those images we have put in place of reality".[31] The key result of the image-media's ability to manufacture an alternate ideal universe was, in Boorstin's opinion, the growth of extravagant expectations about the world. Americans began not just to believe that murder, racism, dishonesty and every other evil could be erased, but that

---

[29] RVA, *Student Handbook* 1968. Available in the RVA archives, Kijabe.

[30] As quoted in Robert Collins, "Growth Liberalism in the Sixties: Great Societies at Home and Grand Designs Abroad," in David Faber, ed., *The Sixties: From Memory to History*, UNC Press, Chapel Hill, 1994, p. 19.

[31] Boorstin, Daniel, *The Image: A Guide to Pseudo-Events in America*, 25th Anniversary Edition, Macmillan, NY: 1987, p. 6.

these things could and should happen immediately, and without any real costs.

Of course, high hopes were nothing new to Americans. Indeed, the country had defined itself from the onset as an attempt to create a "more perfect union" where the ideals of "life, liberty and the pursuit of happiness" would be accessible to every citizen. What was new was the growing belief that these ideals could be fully realized without Churchill's "blood, sweat and tears". And as Boorstin wryly noted, "when the gods wish to punish us they make us believe our own advertising".[32] Thus, when the American government and consumer culture could not deliver the heaven on earth it had promised, the country grew increasingly frustrated.

American frustration had two forms. One form reflected the enduring quest in America for greater social justice. Fueled by righteous indignation, African Americans, and other previously marginalized groups, stepped up the call for equality. When the non-violent civil disobedience of Martin Luther King and the moderate Civil Rights leaders did not immediately produce the dramatic results the young militants believed were possible, frustration turned to anger and anger turned to violence. Despite the groundbreaking Civil Rights Acts of 1964 and 1965, race related riots on a massive scale broke out across the country. Between the infamous Watts riot of 1965 and the end of 1966 there were 38 major race riots across America. The assassinations of Martin Luther King and Robert F. Kennedy in 1968 further fanned the flames of racial militancy. In addition, the same moral energy that was poured into the civil rights movement was also funneled into protests over American involvement in Viet Nam and the women's liberation movement. By 1970 America seemed to be unraveling faster than it could be patched back together.[33]

But there was a second kind of frustration that was just as influential in the evolution of American culture at this time. This second form of frustration was born, not of injustice or want, but out of privilege and plenty. The first form of frustration was focused outward and its fruits were external – riots, demonstrations and strikes. The second form, with its more basic needs met, turned expectations inward and demanded immediate gratification and self-actualization. Thanks in part to the human potential movement and pop psychology, pleasure became a

---

[32] Boorstin, Daniel, *The Image*, Macmillan, NY: 1987, p. 239.
[33] Patterson, James T., *Grand Expectations*, Oxford University Press, NY: 1996, p. 662 and themes covered in chapters 19-22.

sacred right and the effect of this "right" on the culture was not long in coming. When the value previously given to duty and responsibility was placed on immediate gratification, the divorce rate shot through the roof. The Moynihan Report of 1965 was only the first of several reports confirming the rapidly declining American family. The cultural endorsement of pleasure also produced a measurable increase in the number of Americans engaging in premarital sex, experimenting with illegal drugs and abusing alcohol.[34] Yet despite these warning signs the "culture of the self" made deeper inroads into the soul of American culture. Popular culture reflected this development as Hollywood championed the American pursuit of pleasure. Among the many films that touted self-gratification was 1969's *Easy Rider*, starring Peter Fonda, Dennis Hopper and Jack Nicholson, which unapologetically glorified recreational drug use, free love and self-indulgence.[35]

It did not happen immediately, but it was only a matter of time before the growing number of new missionary families would unconsciously bring with them the seeds of this cultural revolution.[36] However unaware of the influence on them of American culture, the new missionaries often acted as carriers of the American cultural virus. And as we will see shortly when the values of the cultural revolution did come to RVA, the combination of an overextended faculty and the necessity of student self-supervision were not enough to maintain the school's wholesome culture.

Accentuating the anxiety felt by the missionary community over the imploding American culture was the uncertain future of the Kenyan political arena. Much like the turbulent early years of the American republic, during its early decades Kenya experienced a series of significant challenges to its political stability. Within three years of Kenyan independence (1963) there had already been one coup attempt and rumors of several more. In 1969 popular Kenyan politician Tom Mboya was assassinated. And shortly thereafter yet another coup attempt was put down with the help of British forces.[37]

The vague anxiety felt by the missionary community over the turbulent political climate could often be boiled down to a very real

---

[34] Patterson, James T. *Grand Expectations*, Oxford, NY: 1996, pgs. 670-674.

[35] Patterson, James, T. *Grand Expectations*, Oxford, NY: 1996, pgs. 710-713.

[36] Ironically, many of the new missionaries were acutely anxious over the decline of American virtue, in some cases considering missions, in part, as an attempt to flee American hedonism.

[37] Edgerton, Robert, *Mau Mau: An African Crucible*, p. 231.

concern for personal safety.[38]   In 1969 this vague anxiety at RVA became acute when a young student at the school was kidnapped – apparently by young Kenyan discontents. In retrospect the Keith Baker incident looks like an episode of the Keystone Cops. However, at the time Keith's disappearance was the realization of the community's worst fears and, as such, represented a genuine safety crisis.

The kidnapping happened in 1969 during the elementary school's lunch break. Keith's family were AIM missionaries stationed at Kijabe and so instead of eating in the cafeteria with the rest of his peers, Keith walked home for lunch. Returning to school after lunch he was abducted by two Kenyan men and spirited away to one of the caves in the hills above the school. Because Keith was known for his fondness for mealtime, his tardiness that afternoon did not initially concern his teacher. Yet when it was discovered that he was neither at home nor in school, warning bells were sounded around campus and search parties were frantically organized. On the second day of his disappearance an inept ransom note was found on campus. In the note the kidnappers made clear their demand for money but on where or how the money was to exchange hands the note was silent. Frustrated but hopeful, the search parties continued while prayer groups met hoping for God's miraculous intervention. As the saying goes, "God works in mysterious ways" and two days later Keith meandered onto campus with culinary demands of his own. Unable to procure the ransom they had sought and tired of the Baker boy's endless complaints about the food, the kidnappers had simply let him go. The debacle was over, but it left in its place a sense of vulnerability that exaggerated the anxiety that had been spreading through the campus now for several years.[39]

The revolution in American culture and the political tension that remained in the new republic were not the only causes of stress that were

---

[38] Just one of many examples of this sense of vulnerability during the late sixties and early seventies is a comment made by Karen Rispin in a letter to the author, dated, June, 2, 2000. The letter remains in the author's possession. In this letter Rispin remarks, "I remember the whole junior high girls dorm being very nervous during the ugly 'oathing' time as Kenyatta's party made sure all the Kikuyu voted onside in '68".

[39] Personal interview with Jack Wilson Sr., longtime staff member at RVA, on Dec. 19, 1997. The tape of this interview is in the archives of the BGC at Wheaton College, under "the Papers and Materials of Phil Dow". Also corroborating the details of this story is an address given to the RVA during the 1996-97 school year by RVA graduate of the class of 1974 and longtime AIM missionary Shel Arensen.

present at this time. While the Kenyan government was enthusiastically pro-missions that did not mean that they were enthusiastically in favor of the status quo. Perhaps more than some of the missionaries themselves, the Kenyan people understood that the goal of the missionary enterprise was to help build an indigenous church and a Christian body politic that at some point would take the reins of leadership from their Western mentors. Thus, with the dawning of independence there was a parallel push within the African church for African leadership. This movement for nationalization brought with it considerable tensions as, in some instances, career missionaries were abruptly, and without ceremony, removed from important leadership roles.[40]

The shift in church power from American and British missionaries to Kenyan leaders was uneven and at times descended into an all too worldly struggle – with both groups losing sight of their sacred calling in a single-minded pursuit of secular power. The tensions between AIM and its Kenyan church (AIC) boiled over at times. Yet, eventually AIM turned over governing authority for almost all of its ministries to AIC with the result that AIM missionaries were now to serve under Kenyan national leadership.

IN THIS EVOLVING power-shift, the future of RVA was anything but certain. As the number of American missionaries skyrocketed in the sixties and early seventies, and the need for a school for their children was more pressing than ever, the status of the school grew less and less secure. For starters, the land on which the school sat was colonial grant land. The fact that over the years AIM and RVA had built up the land with an impressive conglomeration of buildings did not help matters. Indeed, the beautiful campus was now of considerable value to any Kenyans who might seek to use the nationalization push for personal gain. Finally, even if the land could be kept as church land, with AIM now under AIC, what was to stop AIC from turning RVA into a national school and thereby destroying the school's mission to adequately prepare missionary children for life in the North American context.

In retrospect, it is surprising that RVA did continue to be run by AIM. More startling still is the fact that it continued to exist primarily for the purpose of educating the children of missionaries. Even with the introduction of a limited number of Kenyan students directly after

---

[40] Mark Shaw in *The Kingdom of God* in Africa relates a story in which the son of Charles Hurlburt was forcibly removed from his pulpit by the African leadership of his congregation. Shaw, p. 233.

independence, the makeup of the school's student body remained overwhelmingly American.[41] The fact that RVA remained, more or less, as it was gives us important clues, not just to the role RVA played in the larger protestant missionary enterprise, but to the nature of the complex relationship that had developed over the years between AIM, the national church and its African context.

To begin with, the national protestant church in Kenya understood (again better than some of the missionaries) the centrality of RVA to the size and success of the missionary enterprise in Kenya. They saw that to dissolve or to nationalize RVA would almost certainly translate into a significant decline of the American missionary presence in Kenya. Of course, this begs the question: if the indigenous church was already firmly in leadership by the early seventies, what value did they see in such a continued, even growing, missionary presence?

On an entirely pragmatic level, American missionaries meant American money; and the national church, to adequately fulfill its mission, needed that money. Thus money was certainly a motive. Of course, relatively speaking, AIM was not a wealthy mission and its "faith basis" philosophy did not translate into a reliable source of financial assistance for the national church. Nevertheless, in the context of third world poverty even a poor American mission had financial resources that all but the wealthiest Kenyans lacked. Therefore the allure of American money certainly played a part in keeping the missionary community firmly established at Kijabe and around Kenya; but it also complicated that missionary enterprise. In fact, as some have suggested, the relative affluence of the American mission at times created very real obstacles to the spread of the authentic Christian message. For to what degree did the average Kenyan see inclusion in the missionary endorsed church primarily in terms of a ticket to prosperity and opportunity? As former Kijabe High student and senior pastor at the influential Nairobi Baptist Church has remarked concerning the Kijabe of the sixties, "If you were a good boy and played by the rules you would get incorporated … and perhaps become wealthy, (you would) have your education and your children's education (taken care of). (Some of these people even)

---

[41] RVA School Board Minutes of March 24, 1964 outlines the extensive criteria that would govern the acceptance of national students at RVA. At that time the number of national students admitted per year was to be limited to four – two boys and two girls. The SBM are available at RVA, Kijabe.

managed to get scholarships into America... so a lot of people played by those rules because it was a (ticket) to opportunity".[42]

But if money had, in however a limited and ambiguous way, preserved a place for AIM at Kijabe, it also acted to undermine that place. Despite the fact that many of the AIM missionaries had chosen to live at a standard significantly lower than the one they would have enjoyed in their home country, the reality was that economically and educationally they remained far above the average Kenyan. And while few believed that the missionaries should voluntarily adopt abject poverty, the socioeconomic disparity between them and their African peers was painfully obvious. As one Kenyan argued, "the (socioeconomic) curtain (separating the missionary from the African) was so solid and so clear that it cause(d) resentment."[43] Therefore, those Kenyans who either remained on the fringes or did not get the perks they expected from their AIM missionary ties often became bitter and noticeably opposed to Christianity. As Rev. Gichinga concludes, "For (that reason) Kijabe had some of the hardened people against Christianity. (Yet) there are no easy answers... If I was a missionary at Kijabe and the one with the gospel I am not sure how else I would have done it... and (so) we are not trying to attach blame; but the reality is that it (the disparity) hindered the gospel".[44] Thus while money must be included as a factor in the continuing presence of AIM and RVA at Kijabe, it also acted to alienate and embitter substantial numbers of local Kenyans to the extent that one must conclude that money alone cannot explain the significant cooperation that continued between the Kenyan church and the missionary community. There needed to be something more.

Despite the tensions caused by unchristian Christians on both sides of the missionary/indigenous church divide, the reality was that the generations of missionary activity in Kenya had also created a considerable level of mutual respect and concern between the two groups. Human failings aside, the values of the Faith that the missionaries and the national church shared did result in a slowly developing picture of a genuinely global Christian church. That is not to say that the soft racism of the earlier generations of missionaries had

---

[42] Personal Interview with Rev. John Gichinga, pastor of the influential Nairobi Baptist Church, conducted on Aug. 11, 2001 in his Nairobi office. The tape of the interview remains in the possession of the author.
[43] Interview with Rev. John Gichinga.
[44] Ibid.

evaporated. In fact, in some cases the old patterns of white privilege and black subservience continued to be perpetuated.

Nevertheless, generally speaking, the missionary enterprise had been an education for both the Western Christians and their national counterparts. Experience had given the missionaries tangible proof of the Biblical truth – often previously held only in the abstract – that all people are God's creation, and as such equally capable and worthy of dignity. One prominent Kenyan church leader acknowledged the education the western Christians had received through the missionary movement saying, "(After) Lausanne (1974) there was a tremendous sense of awareness within evangelical circles of the need to …recognize other cultures in a much more healthy way".[45]

Curiously, the growing awareness of equality before God encouraged, not discouraged, the missionary project. In reconceptualizing the model of the global church all Christians, regardless of their nationality, education or talents were now seen as having an equally important role to play in the Church, thus beginning to free the missionary movement from the taint of imperialism. Years later Mutava Musyemi, the head of the National Council of Churches of Kenya (NCCK), articulated this budding vision in its matured form. Said Musyemi,

> There is always room for missionary work in any country and Kenya is no exception. There should always be room for a healthy cross-pollenization… (The Christian community) is a family, it is a global family. It spans borders. It spans race. It spans generations and … it is important that it sees itself as one family, prepared to receive and give to each other in a dignified and genuine way.[46]

The respect many of the missionaries had developed for their Kenyan peers was in large part due to their personal experience. The relationships that they had been forced to develop in order to carry out their work had, in many cases, encouraged the missionaries to reconsider their preconceived stereotypes. The same relationships often acted in a similarly constructive fashion to alter the Kenyan perception of the

---

[45] Interview with Mutava Musyemi (Head of the NCCK) at his home in Nairobi, Kenya, January 3, 2000. The tape of this interview remains in the author's possession. The Lausanne Conference was a meeting of Evangelicals from around the world that met in Switzerland with the purpose of exploring the present state, and the future of, Evangelical missions.
[46] Ibid.

missionary. Yet, just as significant to the Kenyan perception of the missionary community was the reality that the missions had so obviously and tangibly brought positive good to Kenya. To this effect, John Gichinga states,

> There is no question that the mission (AIM) was doing a good work...Kijabe provided one of the best hospitals in the area and we were happy about that. I was happy to go to Kijabe High School (which was started and then run by AIM). In fact, a lot of the people who went to school with me are doing well. Here at Nairobi Baptist there is a military general and a number of medical doctors (from Kijabe High). We have made it because we had the opportunity at Kijabe High.[47]

In short, the generations of personal interaction between AIM missionaries and Kenyan Christians, when combined with the Biblical message of human equality and dignity, and the many tangible fruits of missionary effort, had produced within the Kenyan church and people an appreciation for the positive role missionaries had had in their society. And that was in spite of the taint of an ambiguously racist past and the significant tensions that the socioeconomic disparity between the mission and the Kenyan people had caused. That said, in the late sixties and early seventies, socioeconomic tensions and racial prejudice between the two groups remained a significant part of their relationship – always smoldering just beneath the surface. In such a world any significant shift in the breeze was capable of stirring up the fires of resentment and fundamentally altering the status quo that had allowed RVA to prosper.

As WE HAVE seen, the rapidly changing world of the missionary community in independent Kenya included several significant threats to this religious and political status quo. Among these the following were noteworthy: (a) threats to the status of the missionary in the African church; (b) the threat of personal harm and; (c) a powerful but almost subconscious moral anxiety rooted in the American cultural revolution. Yet, it was not until there was a perceived threat to the moral and spiritual well being of their children in the early seventies that the fears

---

[47] Personal Interview with Rev. John Gichinga of Nairobi Baptist Church, Nairobi, Kenya. The interview took place on Aug. 11, 2001 at NBC and was conducted by the author. The recording of the interview is in the possession of the author.

of the missionary community burst through the surface. At this time, rumors of student drug use and sexual indiscretions at RVA that had begun circulating through missionary circles in the late sixties appeared to be confirmed as the number of students being suspended or expelled abruptly increased. At the peak of the crisis the school board expressed the belief that "twenty-five to thirty-five students (were) using drugs, possibly including some girls".[48]   Based on student testimony and confiscations the board added that, "seven or eight different types of drugs, including opium, (are) apparently being used".[49]   Added up, this number meant that anywhere from ten to twenty percent of the High School students were experimenting extensively with drugs – a shocking figure at any school, let alone this isolated and seemingly pristine missionary school.   The fears of the school board and parents were confirmed when between December of 1973 and January of 1974 thirteen boys were expelled or suspended indefinitely for drug use or sale; and several more were suspended for either drunkenness or tobacco use.[50]   Like an air-borne virus, the American cultural revolution had infected even this biosphere of innocence hidden half a world away. As it did the glow that had surrounded this "school in the clouds" seemed to dim.[51]

The response of the missionary parents to this rash of bad behavior was at once expected and ironic. At the core of the orthodox Protestant belief system is the conviction that human nature is fallen. Translated into practical terms this means that bad decisions are not primarily the result of environmental conditions but the free choice of a sinful will – a will that must be converted and over a lifetime, with God's help, made pure.   Thus, in the final analysis, it is the individual who is to bear primary responsibility for his or her actions.   Yet, when missionary children began to make bad decisions, parental affection often overwhelmed parental theology. Common to parents everywhere, this chosen blindness meant that because "my child is basically good" the cause of the bad behavior must be found outside of the child. But if it

---

[48] RVA School Board Minutes – special meeting of Dec. 3, 1973. Board Minutes were made available to the author by permission of the administration at RVA during Dec. of 1999.
[49] Ibid.
[50] RVA School Board Minutes – special meetings of Dec. 14, 1973 and Dec. 17, 1973. Board Minutes were made available to the author by permission of the administration at RVA during December of 1999.
[51] Okie, Susan, "School in the clouds" is the title of Ms. Okie's Washington Post article on RVA of Feb. 2, 1993.

was someone else's fault, whose was it? Ironically, although they were keenly aware of the disturbing trends in American culture, when those trends began to show themselves in their African haven of evangelicalism (RVA), most parents failed to see the connection. To be sure, geographically and culturally America was half a world away, but that world was shrinking faster than anyone was aware – least of all the agents of that change, the missionaries themselves. Thus, with the two most likely suspects exempted from blame (the children themselves and the American cultural revolution) many drew the next natural conclusion. The school was to blame.

Not surprisingly, the complaints that poured into AIM's Kenya Field Council were full of blanket condemnations and bordered on hysteria. Yet, as we have already seen, what made the hysteria so powerful was the legitimacy of some of the concerns. For one, the school was grossly overcrowded. Students were being packed into dormitories meant for half their number. Blaikie dorm, for instance, with its twelve, 10" by 10", rooms was housing forty-eight boys in the early 1970's.[52] The newly built Kedong dorm had girls sleeping on the floor in almost every room because all the beds were full.[53] As a result, the survival-of-the-fittest student culture that had developed at RVA after independence, when combined with the influence of the American cultural revolution, did permit some unsupervised students to nurture personal demons. Beyond the growing drug problem, pornography began to surface in the boy's dormitories and thievery became more common.[54] The unofficial code of student behavior previously overseen by prefects and other student leaders turned ugly. So desperate did some underclassmen become that at times they united to fight back for survival. On one occasion a senior boy, whose antics had made him universally feared among the student body, was returning alone one evening to his dormitory. As he passed under an overhanging branch, five ninth grade boys fell from the tree, dropping a burlap bag over his head and torso. With the senior boy blinded and immobilized the five boys proceeded to

---

[52] This translates into four high school boys sharing a 10x10 room. Personal interview with Glendan Rae at Kijabe, Dec. 19, 1997. The tape of this interview is available at the BGC, Wheaton College, IL under "The Papers and Materials of Phil Dow".

[53] A letter from "Rod and Jane" to Acting Field Secretary and then school board member Rusty Baker, dated Sept. 26, 1971. Available at the Billy Graham Center, Wheaton College under "CN 81 30-12".

[54] A letter from Arnold Egeler to Rusty Baker, dated Oct. 22, 1971. Available at the BGC, Wheaton under "CN 81; 30-12".

level a barrage of fists and feet to his head and chest, all the time issuing threats of more to come for any other senior who continued to harass the younger students.[55] But for every student who fought back there were several more who lived in loneliness or fear. Said one student from the era, "I can remember my first day at RVA, scared, intimidated... being put into the 'hatchery' with twenty-four other girls in bunk beds, never accepted but trying to get attention. It was all a bad scene and never got better. No one tried to help me".[56]

Yet it was not the emotional stress or lack of sufficient adult mentors that inspired the greatest vitriol from parents. What triggered the most urgent letters was the appearance of worldly rebellion. Because they appeared to be condoned by the school, an occasionally irreverent student newspaper, short skirts, long hair, and of course rumors of dancing, were all seen as evidence of RVA's moral decline.

In very real terms the years from 1969-1975 were difficult. There were real problems that the school needed to address – and quickly. That said, generally speaking, the hysteria exceeded the reality. Even in the darkest hour, when perhaps one-fourth of the senior class was experimenting with drugs, the vast majority of the school's students were not using drugs or having sex, let alone dancing or indulging in any of the cosmetic misdemeanors that were so offensive to some within the missionary community. Nevertheless, the hysteria did force RVA and AIM to take a serious look at the state of the school and its future.

IN 1971, EVEN before the peak of the crisis, two sides began to form in a fight for the school's soul. On one side stood the Kenya Field Council and many of the more conservative AIM missionaries. Opposing them were many of the school's faculty, and parents from some of the less rigid missions. Despite the desire of both sides to act in a spirit of Christian charity and love, the debate, which extended over the next five years, was not a pleasant one – occasionally degenerating into petty name-calling and not so subtle forms of character assassination.

It was a grassroots movement of parents during the fall of 1971 that initiated the push for significant changes at RVA. The length of the choirgirl's skirts was the first symptom of decline to draw attention from

---

[55] E-Interview with Greg Bakke, then student at RVA and a participant in the attack.
[56] Email from Debbie Becker to the author, Jan. 13, 1998.

parents for the "rather worldly impression" given.[57] Soon letters were being discreetly circulated among concerned parents filled with second-hand evidence of serious behavioral improprieties among the students. For instance, it became common knowledge that "Room 15" in the high school boys dorm had been used as a "rendezvous for boys and girls where they had danced together".[58] In addition, rumors were passed along on authority, that choir trips were regularly accompanied by student drinking and smoking – and not just by the misfits and scoundrels, but also by "class officers and team captains".[59]

But it was not the student rebellion that frightened the parents so much as the impression that had developed that this behavior went on without interference from the RVA staff. Wrote one missionary couple, "The thing that disturbed us most is that staff members tell us that it is not possible to enforce certain standards".[60] Not only did many parents believe that staff were turning a blind eye to student indiscretions, but some began accusing the school's staff of actually encouraging student rebellion. The popular teacher Don Fonseca was singled out by some for undisclosed, "escapades, sarcasm and tearing apart of spiritual messages".[61] Not surprisingly, mistrust soon dominated the relationship between this growing circle of disgruntled parents and the school's faculty. So poisonous had the environment become that some parents believed that if their accusations became public their children would suffer at the hands of those staff accused. Said one parent in a letter to a school board member, "The source of the information (my name) you should keep confidential. The reason you no doubt know. It is to safeguard my own children at RVA against bitter reactions of the staff who might turn against them for what I say. This has happened".[62]

It was within this environment of hysteria and mistrust that the battle for the school's soul was fought. Between 1971 and 1973 the two sides

---

[57] Letter from what appears to be "Klaus" to Rusty Baker – School Board Member, dated Oct. 21, 1971. The letter is available at the BGC, Wheaton, under "CN 81; 30-12".

[58] Letter from Arnold Egeler to Rusty Baker – School Board Member, dated Oct. 22, 1971. The letter is available at the BGC, Wheaton, under "CN 81; 30-12".

[59] Ibid.

[60] Letter from Jim and Gloria to Mr. Russel Baker – School Board Representative, dated Nov. 6, 1971. The letter is available at the BGC, Wheaton under "CN 81; 30-12".

[61] Letter from Arnold Egeler to Rusty Baker – School Board Member, dated Oct. 22, 1971. The letter is available at the BGC, Wheaton under "CN 81; 30-12.

[62] Ibid.

Plate 1 – The Nairobi that Hurlburt found when he arrived in 1901.

Plate 2 – A Saturday picnic near Kijabe in 1913.
Courtesy of Rift Valley Academy

Plate 3 – The Stauffachers on route to RVA at the beginning of the school year in the 1920's. *Courtesy of Rift Valley Academy*

Plate 4 – By the mid 1920's Nairobi was the bustling and raucous hub of the British colony in East Africa – a far cry from the tented camp Hurlburt had found just twenty years previously. *Courtesy of Rift Valley Academy*

Plate 5 – The Westervelt Home (1923). Mrs. Westervelt (Hope) established a home in America for RVA students needing to finish their secondary education. Almost every one of these young men returned to Africa as missionaries. *Courtesy of Rift Valley Academy*

Plate 6 – The Barnett family (1920's). A part of the third generation of Barnetts continue to work at Kijabe, while members of the fourth and fifth generation of the Barnett family live elsewhere in Africa as missionaries and MKs.
Courtesy of John and Elaine Barnett

Plate 7 – A young Herb Downing with RVA's first orchestra during the 1930's.
Courtesy of John and Elaine Barnett

Plate 8 –"Pa" Lehrer and Paul "Shorty" Smith (RVA's first graduate) stand next to a leopard they shot at Kijabe in the late 1940's. Hunting was done for a variety of reasons during this period in the school's history – food, recreation, and (in this case) self-preservation. *Courtesy of John and Elaine Barnett*

Plate 9 – Mr. Devitt and "Pa" Lehrer after shooting an elephant that had been destroying farms in the valley (1940's). *Courtesy of Rift Valley Academy*

Plate 10 – Freshman initiation in the 1940's complete with "chamber pots" as hats and burlap bag cloaks. The student with the toothbrush pipe (top left) is David Dibbens, the school's first mixed-race student.
Courtesy of John and Elaine Barnett

Plate 11 – Piling in the "lorries" for a school picnic just before the Mau Mau Emergency was declared. Notice the Thomsons gazelle to the bottom right. "Bambi" was a wounded orphan that was found and nursed back to health at RVA. She became something of a fixture in the fifties as the school pet.
Courtesy of John and Elaine Barnett

Plate 12 – Putting on a brave face. A school photo taken with an African Home Guard member and a British Officer (a.k.a. Chipps) in front of the barbed wire encased Kiambogo building in 1952. *Courtesy of John and Elaine Barnett*

Plate 13 – Evidence of the continuing British influence at RVA during the 1950's – celebration of the Queen's birthday near Kijabe High School. *Courtesy of John and Elaine Barnett*

Plate 14 – RVA students during an outreach program to distribute the Kamba Bible completed by AIM missionaries in the 1950's. All but one returned to Africa as missionaries. *Courtesy of John and Elaine Barnett*

Plate 15 – The visit of American Evangelicalism's standard-bearer, Billy Graham, in 1960 highlighted the importance of RVA to the growing American missionary movement. *Courtesy of Rift Valley Academy*

Plate 16 – The Makers of Tradition. The First XV rugby squad in 1966. By the late 1980's, RVA and rugby were virtually synonymous terms in Kenya. *Courtesy of Rift Valley Academy*

Plate 17 – Symbolic of a healthy relationship. RVA's choir poses with President Kenyatta after a command performance at his home in 1966. *Courtesy of Rift Valley Academy*

Plate 18 – A regular on the nation's arts calendar, RVA's choir sings for VOK (Voice of Kenya) TV in 1968. *Courtesy of Rift Valley Academy*

Plate 19 – The Entwistles and Beverlys (1973). *Courtesy of RVA*

Plate 20 – The Entwistle Boys Hunting (1970's). Hunting continued to be legal in Kenya until the mid 1970's. *Courtesy of Rift Valley Academy*

Plate 21 – "An Island of Americana"? Homecoming (1980). *Courtesy of RVA.*

Plate 22 – RVA's First XV (1988) – The Keepers of Tradition. The best ever?
This RVA team went through the entire season without a try being scored
against it while winning every major trophy available including the Blackrock
Tournament, both schoolboy "sevens" tournaments and, most importantly, the
prestigious Prescott Cup. *Courtesy of Rift Valley Academy*

Plate 23 – Still young. The Entwistles retire (1998). *Courtesy of RVA*

Plate 24 – The Kitchen Staff in front of Kiambogo (2000).
Courtesy of Rift Valley Academy

Plate 25 – The Tradition of Junior-Senior Banquet. The Juniors of 2003 put on
the Gilbert and Sullivan light opera, *The Pirates of Penzance*.
Courtesy of Rift Valley Academy

Plate 26 – Hello Dolly. (2003). *Courtesy of Rift Valley Academy*

Plate 27 – A once-in-a-lifetime experience. RVA students conquer Mt. Kenya during the Interim week (2000). *Courtesy of Rift Valley Academy*

Plate 28 – Part of the view from the porch on Kiambogo (Mt. Longonot).
Courtesy of Rift Valley Academy

Plate 29 – The Administrative Team (2003)
From left to right: Mark Kinzer, Tim Hall, Jim Long (departing Superintendent),
Tim Cook (arriving Superintendent), Mr. Buhler.
Courtesy of Rift Valley Academy

Plate 30 – Flag raising chapel during the 2003-2004 school year.
Courtesy of Dale Linton

Plate 31 – Multicultural Day in 2003. Each of the thirty-some flags signifies a nationality represented in the student body. A Third Culture nestled alongside the Kijabe Escarpment. *Courtesy of Dale Linton*

Plate 32 – Children of a common mother reunited. Multicultural Day (2003).
Courtesy of Dale Linton

Plate 33 – Winning Blackrock (2002-2003). *Courtesy of Rift Valley Academy*

Plate 34 – Following a path forged by generations before him. A student on Leaving Day at RVA at the dawn of the 21st century. *Courtesy of Dale Linton*

wrestled for control of the school board – submitting competing visions for the school that betrayed a deep theological and philosophical split in the mission community. One champion of the more conservative camp was AIM missionary Arnold Egeler. In a series of letters to School Board and Field Council personnel, Egeler made the case for fundamentalism at RVA. He spoke for many when he argued that a philosophy of "permissive broadmindedness" had infected RVA that was not based on the Word of God but on "modern intellectual psychologies".[63] This philosophy of broadmindedness encouraged "exposure to evil" in the form of worldly "films, books, magazines, suggestive music, etc" which are "poison to the mind and to the spirit".[64] Egeler conceded that,

> The Christian should not be an uninformed 'stick in the mud'. But his study should be made with the same precaution as a soldier would take when going into enemy territory. For worldly philosophies and psychologies and carnality are in fact anti-scriptural and hence anti-Christian.[65]

In Egeler's mind, it was the liberal educational philosophies of the RVA faculty that were behind the decline of virtue at the school.

The culmination of Egeler's efforts was a redraft of an "RVA Philosophy Paper" which was brought to the Kenya Field Council for consideration in 1973. In this redraft, the Egeler camp laid out their plans for reform at RVA. Their goal, that under AIM's governance, RVA must reestablish a community environment of Christian discipleship, was heartily applauded by both sides of the debate. However, it quickly became apparent that the two sides had significantly different conceptions of what a "community environment of Christian discipleship" should look like. To Egeler such an environment, "necessarily exclude(d) the modern education philosophy of permissiveness with extreme freedom of choice even to rebel against authority. The staff shall enforce this Christian discipline in every area of student life".[66] In the area of music he gave an example of how this

---

[63] Letter from Arnold Egeler to the Chairman of RVA School Board, dated May 14, 1973. The letter is available at the BGC, Wheaton, under "CN 81; 30-12".

[64] Ibid.

[65] Ibid.

[66] Egeler, Arnold, "Notes on Revision of RVA Philosophy Paper" available at the BGC, Wheaton, under "CN 81; 30-12". The "Notes" are undated, but almost certainly were written either late in 1972 or early in 1973.

might look. States Egeler, "I would like to see control over music played everywhere at RVA – not merely in the student center. Stereo music from the dorms is as much public as that played in the student center, and is often bothersome to other students".[67] With regards to literature, Egeler claimed, "the staff revision (of the philosophy paper) allows for any and all reading material – as long as the student can critically evaluate it". Continued Egeler, "I disagree strongly with this 'exposure need' philosophy".[68]

As the Egeler camp's criticisms gained support among the members of the School Board and the Kenya Field Council, vice-principal Roy Entwistle stepped forward to vigorously defend the perspective of the school's faculty, being completely aware that doing so could mean the end of his work at RVA. In an open letter to the Board Entwistle said as much acknowledging, "there may be a conflict between what I feel my responsibility is towards the school and its students and what the governing bodies feel my obligation is".[69] Yet, trying to achieve some sense of perspective he stressed that concerning the overarching goals of the school, the two camps were in agreement. It was only on the means best able to achieve the shared end that there was disagreement. As the letter went on it became obvious just how profound the disagreement was. Said Entwistle,

> In my opinion these goals can only be realized if students are given a great deal of opportunity in personal choice. I reject the philosophy of protection that argues for complete parental or administrative control...
> I believe that a forced conformity on the outside often heightens tensions on the inside. Originality should be allowed and even encouraged.[70]

It goes without saying that Entwistle did little to ease the fears of the fundamentalist camp. Indeed, the conflicting visions for the school could not have been more clear.

THE FIRST CASUALTY of this battle was long time principal Herbert Downing. Unwilling to implement the more stringent disciplinarianism called for by the Field Council and surrounded by

---

[67] Ibid.
[68] Ibid.
[69] Letter from Roy Entwistle to the School Board of RVA, dated, May 16, 1973. The letter is available at the BGC, Wheaton, under "CN 81; 30-12".
[70] Ibid.

increasing criticism, the aging Downing was encouraged to step aside for a new generation of leaders.[71] Thus, having been the driving force behind RVA's rise from a relatively small and haphazard school to one with a worldwide reputation, Downing was abruptly discarded. Many in the faculty feared that Downing's removal was just the first stage in an impending bloodless coup.

With Downing's significant presence fading, the Field Council began looking for someone to replace him – someone who they hoped would "re-establish the moral and spiritual standards which had made RVA great in the past".[72] Over the objections of Downing and the school's faculty; and despite the fact that he had neither college degree, nor educational experience, the Board chose Paul Beverly, a well respected, longtime AIM missionary from Tanzania to be RVA's next leader.

In spite of the nearly universal respect Beverly enjoyed among the missionary community as a committed and heart-felt Christian, doubts immediately surfaced regarding the wisdom of the Board's choice. The philosophical divide and spirit of suspicion that separated the two camps was by this point common knowledge and many felt this choice of a close friend and ally of Arnold Egeler would only further antagonize the school's faculty. Because of the "bitterness...coming from various people concerning the absurdity ... of putting a man in charge of RVA who has no degrees nor experience in running a school" Beverly's own friends counseled him against accepting the post.[73] But Beverly's inexperience and close ties to Egeler were only the tip of the iceberg.

In choosing Beverly the board had rejected Downing's personal choice of successor. It was not a secret that Downing had enthusiastically endorsed Roy Entwistle as the best person to follow him.[74] Entwistle was not only extremely popular among the school's faculty, but was eminently qualified for the position, having been both a teacher and an administrator in his twelve years at RVA.[75] In addition, Entwistle held both a Master of Education degree and an administrator's credential. In short, it would have been difficult to find a better candidate. Yet, Entwistle's philosophy of education was at odds with

---

[71] Beverly, Paul. Unpublished manuscript, "Years at Rift Valley Academy (1974-1976)", "R-1". Mr. Beverly was kind enough to send me this work in progress on Feb. 4, 2000. The manuscript remains in the possession of the author.

[72] Ibid. "R-1".

[73] Ibid. "R-1" and "R-2".

[74] Ibid. "R-2".

[75] Ibid. "R-2" and Entwistle interview of Jan. 1, 1998.

that of the Field Council who were convinced that only increased discipline and a purified curriculum could save the increasingly worldly academy. Thus when the board chose Beverly it made a statement that Egeler and his band of fundamentalists were, for the time being, calling the shots.

Having no experience and little popular support, Beverly began his duties at RVA in 1974 a condemned man. Yet despite his precarious mandate, Beverly was convinced of the divine origins of his calling. As a result, he wasted little time in enforcing a more rigid disciplinary system at the school in the hopes of arresting the school's moral decay. Not surprisingly, student complaints began surfacing immediately. Making matters worse was the fact that many among the staff were at least partially sympathetic to the student perspective – believing some of the rules petty, if not harmful. Still, not every faculty member opposed Beverly's appointment. In fact, while the school's faculty was generally less conservative than the Field Council, their loyalties nevertheless closely reflected the split sentiments of the larger missionary community.[76]

With the odds stacked heavily against him, it should come as no surprise that Beverly's arrival on the scene did not immediately cure the school's maladies. Yet, many felt that there were significant signs of hope. In 1975 a group of young missionaries from Life Ministry came to lead the school's annual spiritual emphasis week. The theme was "Sharing Your Faith" and the enthusiastic response of the student body gave evidence that perhaps the school's spiritual climate was on the mend. Teams of RVA students poured into Nairobi speaking to whomever would listen about Christianity. Although several Kenyans did convert to Christianity, the brief movement did not noticeably affect Nairobi. It did, however, leave a deep impression on many of the students who took part. Whether the evangelistic experience had forced them to reconsider the meaning and extent of their own faith, or if it had simply forced them to look outside of their comfortable community, the result was a modest revival as evidenced by student-initiated prayer meetings and an apparent drop in the use of drugs and alcohol.[77]

However, in the end, despite several similar successes, Beverly was unable to escape the criticisms that most threatened to undermine his leadership at the school. Because Beverly lacked the credentials of an

---

[76] Ibid. "R-4".
[77] Beverly, Paul. Unpublished Manuscript, "Years at Rift Valley Academy (1974-1976)", "R-5".

educator, resistance to his leadership seemed inevitable. When that resistance came, it did so in several forms. Least harmful to his position was the active and vocal antagonism displayed by members of both the student body and the faculty towards his strict conservativism. In one of several similar incidents, a satirical essay entitled, "the Parable of the Green House" was circulated among the school's faculty. Because they struck moderates as malicious and personal, attacks like "the Parable of the Green House" actually created sympathy for the new School administrator by setting him up as a persecuted prophet of righteousness.[78]

Yet, the sympathy such attacks created was still just sympathy. For while most were disturbed by the tone of the satire, they did acknowledge the substance at the root of the essay. The reality was that Beverly was not qualified. In addition, as an outsider, he had no real context for understanding the school's unique culture and aspirations – that is outside of the moral hysteria that had thrust him onto the school in the first place. Thus, quietly another form of resistance began to surface. Quite naturally when the faculty had concerns or questions about the academic program they consulted Roy Entwistle. Just as naturally, Entwistle as the Academic Principal would make a recommendation and life would go on. In much the same way questions and circumstances that were rooted in the past were directed towards the administrator that best understood that historical context and in whom the faculty felt most comfortable approaching. Again, this meant that the faculty actively sought out Entwistle and not Beverly. It goes without saying, that had Beverly's personality been any less strong he might have become entirely invisible in time. As it was, although he did his best to stay near the center, more and more often Beverly was bypassed in the school's chain of communication. When he did confront the mounting instances of exclusion, the offending parties inevitably would claim that there had been an oversight and make their apologies.[79]

In retrospect there are only two explanations for Beverly's marginalization. Either Beverly was consciously being ostracized or he was being innocently overlooked. The first explanation, which implies at least some degree of malicious intent, was certainly the case in a few instances. However, the second explanation – the one that appears to be applicable in most cases and the one which appears to be the least

---

[78] Ibid.
[79] Beverly, Paul. Unpublished Manuscript, "Years at Rift Valley Academy (1974-1976)".

personally critical – was actually the one that prophesied the demise of the Beverly administration. For it was not his commitment to a more rigid, otherworldly culture at RVA that ultimately ended his tenure at the school.

In fact, when Beverly was encouraged to resign, the school's spiritual and moral compass seemed to have been largely stabilized, not to mention realigned in a fundamentalist-friendly direction. As long as an impassioned moral battle waged for the school's soul, Beverly was needed. But with the moral crisis slipping into the past, all eyes turned to the task of running the school and for this Beverly was seen to be irrelevant at best. In short, his success had made him expendable. With the accreditation committee returning to re-evaluate the school's status, the Field Council and School Board that had been instrumental in placing Beverly at RVA now agreed that his presence at the school might jeopardize its academic credibility. In a tense meeting early in the fall of 1976 the school board unceremoniously asked Beverly to resign. With his characteristic candor Beverly pressed the board for an explanation. Believing his task unfinished Beverly asked point blank if, "my presence...at RVA would be an embarrassment and a hindrance to you when this (accreditation) team arrives". By simply replying "Yes" the Field Secretary ended the shortest but perhaps one of the more consequential administrations in RVA history.[80] Little more than a footnote in the school's collective memory, the Beverly era was nonetheless a watershed for the school. For while moderate evangelicalism had won the day, the Beverly/Egeler fundamentalist coterie, to a large extent, did succeed in setting the moral and spiritual agenda for the incoming Entwistle administration.

LIKE THEY HAD been across the ocean in the United States, the sixties in Kenya and at RVA had been tumultuous. Change had come at a dizzying pace that left many nauseous. Independence and the nationalization of the Church in Kenya had begun to fundamentally alter the role of the western missionary. A few old-timer missionaries unable to adapt to the new paradigm, and incapable of seeing Christianity as anything more than a composite of western values, bowed out or were forced out. Yet, counter-intuitively the new era of national leadership actually led to an increased demand for western missionaries in Kenya.

---

[80] Beverly, Paul. Unpublished Manuscript, "Years at Rift Valley Academy (1974-1976)".

Of this new generation of western missionaries, the vast majority were American; and of these Americans a disproportional percentage were second, third or even fourth generation missionaries. Of these multi-generational missionaries almost all were the products of the now well-known greenhouse of evangelical missionary zeal – RVA. Granted, the legacy of these multi-generational missionaries was not unequivocally positive. For while personal experience had developed in some of these former missionary children a deep respect for the culture and people of Africa, for others that personal experience had been uncritically interpreted through the lenses of a fundamentally racist colonial culture. As a result, instead of growing a more biblical conception of race, for some missionary children experience had acted to perpetuate the racist assumptions of their parents. At best, for these individuals the mission field represented a place of paternalistic condescension. At worst, they saw a return to Africa as an opportunity to rule the private kingdoms their parents had established before independence.[81] Yet, on the whole the missionaries who had themselves grown up as children of missionaries were generally more culturally sensitive and less parochial than their parents and grandparents. As a result, this new generation of missionaries continued, together with their African brothers and sisters, to forge a new conception of Christianity as a truly global and egalitarian religion.

Accompanying this latest generation of RVA graduates were a new and highly idealistic wave of missionaries. This group brought to the field almost unlimited zeal and optimism, but they also carried with them the seeds of the cultural revolution that had begun to turn America upside down. The combination of the exploding number of students and the revolt against traditional values in America threw RVA into a period of both real and imagined moral crisis that came close to destroying the school. Before the hysteria was over the more conservative members of the community had pushed out some of the school's most dedicated and talented faculty. In a relatively short period the ousted Downing family was joined by Don and Ruth Fonseca, Judy Oulund and Faye Leitch (the Elementary Principal). Thus, in the process of satisfying the moral demands of fundamentalists, the Field Council had jeopardized the

---

[81] Stan Barnett in an interview with the author made an observation that has been made regularly concerning some RVA graduates. It was Barnett's conviction that during the Vietnam conflict some of his classmates intentionally escaped the draft by returning to Africa as missionaries. In addition, it has often been observed that some people seem to return to Africa primarily because they cannot adapt to life in their "home cultures".

school as a place of learning. In the end, it was the moderate Roy Entwistle that returned to the school a sense of perspective, but not without having accepted significant elements of the agenda championed by the fundamentalists.

At the end of the day, in spite of the turmoil that wracked the school during the late sixties and early seventies, RVA did continue to provide a quality education for the children of missionaries to East and Central Africa. By weathering a storm that had threatened the school's existence RVA played an important role in encouraging the unexpected explosion of American missionaries to the newly independent republic. Perhaps as much as any of the previous generations of missionaries to East Africa, the post-independence swell of missionaries had a significant influence on the young republic. While many of the new missionaries did take on roles in support of the new national Church leadership, others continued the traditional pioneering task of bringing the Christian faith to "unreached people groups". Between the evolving role being played by the second or third generation missionaries, the efforts of the national Church and the zealous new wave of pioneering missionaries, Christianity exploded in Kenya growing from 30% of the population in 1948 to almost 70% by 1975.[82] Thanks in part to the existence of RVA, AIM and AIC had a disproportionate influence on the cultural and political development of Kenya. By the mid-seventies AIC was the largest Protestant denomination in Kenya. With this new high profile came some unexpected challenges. Most significantly, the religious success of AIM/AIC had ironically brought it increasingly close to those corridors of political power that AIM had so painstakingly avoided during the colonial era. Thus, in 1976 as the sun began to rise over the Kedong Valley and a new era, the school found itself looking at an entirely new set of obstacles, linked at least in part to the school's newly acquired position of political privilege.

---

[82] Barrett, David, The Encyclopedia of World Christianity, "Kenya", Oxford University Press, Nairobi, 1982.

CHAPTER 6

THE ENTWISTLE YEARS AND BEYOND: RVA FROM 1976 TO THE PRESENT

AS FOREIGN DIGNITARIES AND PROMINENT KENYANS mingled with the American community on the grounds of Nairobi's Jamhuri Park, the RVA choir was making the almost routine hour-long trip from Kijabe to Nairobi. By this time it had become something of a tradition in Kenya that RVA students would play a prominent role in significant American or Missionary community events. And this day, July 4, 1976, was about as significant as it got for both communities. Two hundred years earlier the dream of forming a constitutional republic based on the ideal of God-given universal human rights had been mocked by the world community as the stuff of children's fairy tales. Yet, the American Bicentennial found that the great experiment based on these values had more than survived. Beyond conquering some imposing internal demons and a wide array of external challenges, the once fledgling republic had grown into the wealthiest and most powerful nation in the history of the world. There was much to celebrate.

As RVA's choir began their selection of Christian and patriotic anthems the celebratory mood was infused with a shot of adrenaline. A rumor ricocheted through the crowd with the news that the Israelis had done it again. Early that morning, under the cover of darkness, a group of Israeli commandos had flown into Idi Amin's Uganda and rescued a hijacked plane full of hostages from the hands of Anti-Semitic terrorists being harbored by the Muslim Amin. For the staunchly pro-Israeli American and missionary communities, the mix of excitement and patriotism was intoxicating.[1]

But in the midst of the American triumphalism, there was also a sense of ambiguity in the celebrations – a moral uncertainty that many expatriate Americans had begun to assume during the turmoil of the sixties and early seventies. The American image of high-minded democratic idealism that had received widespread international praise after WWII had not just begun to mellow, but had taken on the taste of milk past its prime. To be sure, American wealth and power were admired, even if resented. But the moral authority America had enjoyed through much of its history had been dealt a crippling blow by the Vietnam War and by domestic and international policies that many in the world community saw as hypocritical.

IT WAS INTO this larger context of American moral uncertainty and waning self-confidence that Roy Entwistle assumed the principalship of RVA in 1976. The crisis of values that had torn American culture apart in the late sixties and early seventies had been mirrored in this once apparently idyllic missionary station, almost destroying it. Indeed, when the dust stirred up by the school's own internal conflict had settled, Roy Entwistle was among the few that remained standing – and even he did not look quite the same. Gone were the most brash of the fundamentalists, but gone also were some of the school's most dynamic (and less conservative) faculty.[2] The turbulent period had shaken the campus and undermined the stability that had defined the Downing years. It is safe to say that when Entwistle began to sift through the ashes of his strife-torn campus no one could guarantee what type of school would rise up from them.

Originally a clear voice for a less rigid and more dynamic school culture, a guarded Entwistle now walked a slightly more conservative

---

[1] The mood and circumstances of the day were related to the author by his parents who were part of the group of Americans that met at Jamhuri Park that day. However, I remember the day quite clearly in terms that only a six-year-old can, which are not significantly different from the story above.

[2] In saying "less conservative" here it is important to remember that relatively speaking the "liberals" among the RVA faculty were still far more conservative in their theology and lifestyle than the average American Christian. As one of these "less conservative" faculty members correctly pointed out to me, they considered themselves within the category of "conservative evangelicals".

path. Having been burnt both by some of the fundamentalists he originally opposed and a few of the more progressive faculty with whom he had enjoyed a warm relationship, Entwistle began his term as Principal as a moderate progressive. To be sure, there were to be no major changes in the school's rules or philosophy. Nevertheless, an assortment of new programs did begin to pop up, quietly signaling the arrival of fresh growth and the beginning of a new day.

Almost immediately Entwistle began to look for ways by which RVA might be able to rediscover the warmth and family atmosphere that had defined the school when he had first arrived in 1962. But this was to be no small task. The school he now led was nearly three times the size of the school he had come to as a young elementary teacher just fourteen years before. And, unfortunately, as the size of the school had mushroomed in pace with the massive growth in the number of American missionaries to East Africa, it had started to take on some of the negative characteristics to be expected of any overpopulated and understaffed institution.

Entwistle and his team of teachers saw in cinderblock and mortar one part of the solution – more, but smaller, dormitories. As the school population had exploded RVA had sought to manage the influx by either forcing more children into an existing dorm or by building larger "super-dorms" like Kedong or Westervelt, both of which held upwards of seventy students. The result was a loss of contact between the student and his or her dorm parent and an apparently related increase in student misbehavior. With little accountability, and relatively little quality contact between students and faculty, a hostile "us" versus "them" mentality easily developed. Entwistle believed that if smaller dorms could be built, the increased accountability and quality interpersonal contact would necessarily create a more healthy community ethos.[3] The idea was simple and sound, but the implementation would take a generation. Nevertheless, by the late 1970's the school had begun a building program that would aid in a qualitative increase in the school's community dynamic.

At the same time, the new school head began looking for ways that the school's faculty might compliment the renewed family emphasis being encouraged by the improvements in the facilities. To this end, Entwistle approached new faculty member Dave Pollack and asked him

---

[3] Personal interview with Roy Entwistle by the author at his home in Kijabe, Kenya Jan 1, 1998. A recording of the interview is available at the BGC Archives under the "Papers and Materials of Phil Dow".

if he would adapt and lead a program being used at The Stony Brook School in New York. The result was an evening every month called "Caring Community" during which small groups of students would meet in a faculty home for treats, games and a time to relax in an intentionally safe and nurturing environment.[4] Between smaller dormitories and programs like Caring Community the hope was that there would be an increase in the number of healthy and meaningful relationships between students and faculty. These relationships would not simply humanize the institution, but would begin to develop a foundation of mutual trust and affection upon which a rejuvenated school culture could emerge.

Of course, an increase in the number of both dormitories and programs demanded a larger faculty to house and run the new, more family-oriented campus. As a result, Entwistle and his team began an aggressive recruitment program with the hopes of increasing the number of faculty at RVA. By 1985 the school had gained some ground, decreasing its staff to student ratio from 6.3 to 1 in 1975 to 5.2 to 1 in 1985. Nevertheless, even then RVA was open to the criticism of being understaffed. To this effect, Dr. Aho, of the Middle States Association's accreditation committee said in 1985, "In my sum of 15 years associated with the visiting evaluation committee, I don't think I have ever seen a staff more dedicated...and more concerned with the welfare of kids than I have seen here... It's a shame in a way, that such a dedicated staff... are so overextended".[5]

In time the efforts towards developing a healthy, family-like, atmosphere even extended to the way discipline was meted out. By the late seventies and early eighties the rigid paranoia that had defined discipline at RVA early in the seventies had begun to develop a human face. Two examples may help to illustrate this trend. One night, dorm parent Dave Pollack was awakened by the sound of students sneaking out the Blaikie dormitory windows. Dressing frantically, Pollack jumped out of his window and joined the boys as they ran into the night toward some unknown destination. One by one the students realized they had a jogging partner. As they slowed to a stop Pollack cheerfully asked, "So where are we going?" To which the leader replied, "Back to the dorm I guess". The next day, and likely for many days afterwards, the boys

---

[4] Letter from Dave Pollack to the author, dated April 24, 1998. The letter is in the possession of the author. More details on the initiation of "Caring Community" at RVA came from discussions between the author and Roy Entwistle on Jan. 1, 1998.

[5] Dr. Aho as quoted in a paper presented to the RVA School Board in 1985 entitled, "Staffing at RVA".

waited for the inevitable call into the office. It never came.[6] This example stands out not to illustrate a sudden laxity in enforcing the rules, but rather a budding environment of flexibility in which grace and relationship-building were becoming as important as swift and clear justice.

On another occasion two students got a hold of several stink bombs in Nairobi and decided to unleash their pungent powers in the class of Miss Winterberg, the loved but feared teacher of Senior English. The plan went off with only one hitch. As a result of a car accident some years previous Miss Winterberg had lost her sense of smell and so as the smoke and stifling sulfur odor filled the room, Miss Winterberg obliviously continued to lecture in front of her wilting students. For the two deviants however, the worst was to come. After figuring out who was behind the episode, Mr. Entwistle confiscated the remaining stink bombs. He then put the boys into the tiny, windowless French room, had them break open one of the bombs, shut the door and told them they would be allowed out in thirty minutes time. No demerits or D-Halls were handed out, no grim letters were sent home. Nevertheless, in the process the students learned their lesson, healthy relationships were established and the faculty and administration came out smelling like roses.[7]

Along with the attempt to create a more family-like atmosphere came some relatively dramatic changes designed to develop mature, independent and healthy decision-making skills among the student body. Reversing more than fifty years of tradition, in 1981 Entwistle and the RVA school board eliminated the school uniform in favor of a limited dress code.[8] After five years as principal it now looked like Entwistle was trying to realize the vision he had stated in a letter to the board in 1973. Entwistle had written then, "I am basically much more interested in what is happening inside the child than what the outside appearance is. I believe that a forced conformity on the outside often heightens tensions on the inside. Originality should be allowed and even encouraged."[9] It looked as if moderate progressivism had arrived.

---

[6] Letter from Dave Pollack to the author, dated April 24, 1998.

[7] Personal interview with Roy Entwistle by the author at Kijabe, Jan. 1, 1998.

[8] Letter from Art Davis, school board member at the time of the uniform decision, to the author, June 3, 1997. The letter remains in the possession of the author.

[9] Letter from Roy Entwistle to the RVA School Board, dated May 16, 1973. The letter is available at the BGC Archives under CN 81; 30-12.

But the move away from uniforms was riddled with unforeseen consequences. The simple uniform was replaced by an excessively detailed, and in some senses more restrictive, dress code – one that was every bit as susceptible to the complaints of rigidity and conformity that had ended the reign of the uniform. In addition, with the advent of free dress came the inevitable concern with fashion. And with fashion came the wedded vices of materialism and vanity. Ironically, Entwistle's intended concern with the inner life of the child seemed to create an atmosphere that fostered an emphasis on the externals. But the decision had been made and most soon acknowledged that a return to the uniform was virtually impossible. In the end, Entwistle's ultimate aim of providing the students with more freedom was served – even if they used this freedom to choose a new vanity-inspired conformity.[10]

The attempt at RVA to create an atmosphere where students could develop healthy and independent decision-making skills also extended to the sensitive area of dating. Early on the missionary community had been so concerned with the sexual purity of their children that the school's rules concerning boy-girl relationships had produced a genuinely distorted, and unbiblical, perspective on sex in the minds of many of the children. As recently as the late fifties there had been a line across campus separating the boys and girls. Stan Barnett was not alone in saying that because of the school's, "rigid rules…a lot of us grew up with a sort of guilt complex about girls."[11] The infamous line was gone by the time Entwistle took over but strong elements of the earlier unhealthy atmosphere remained. Without bowing to the equally unhealthy direction of contemporary American culture, Entwistle hoped to further liberalize the atmosphere in which relationships between the sexes at RVA took place. Physical displays of affection became acceptable but only in their most chaste forms. Holding hands was permitted but contact beyond that (including kissing) was officially forbidden. In addition, Entwistle did achieve for the upperclassmen the freedom to take dates into Nairobi once a term.[12] This was not exactly the earth-shaking step that some might have liked to see, but it was just one more example of Entwistle's revolution by increments.

This quiet revolution did have results. When compared to the early seventies, and even many of the school's earlier eras, there can be little

---

[10] Interview with Roy Entwistle, Jan. 1, 1998 and June 3, 1997 letter from Art Davis.

[11] Personal interview with Stan Barnett by the author at Buck Creek Camp, WA May 29, 1999. The recorded interview remains in the possession of the author.

[12] Personal interview with Roy Entwistle, Jan. 1, 1998.

question that under Entwistle RVA had begun to develop a genuinely healthy and thriving family culture. It is therefore supremely ironic that, during the Entwistle years, the most profound challenge to the school's existence came from an American evangelical community increasingly convinced that boarding was inherently damaging to both a child's psyche and the health of the nuclear family. By the mid-eighties the boarding school phenomenon, so central to the explosion of evangelical influence around the world, was under serious attack in the church.

THE ROOTS OF the anti-boarding movement can be found in the culture war taking place in America. During the massive cultural upheaval of the sixties and early seventies the disintegration of the American family, rumored to have been coming on since the fifties, became a reality. The divorce rate in America skyrocketed and the carnage produced by broken homes laid waste the American moral landscape.[13] Indeed by the mid-eighties the crisis of the family was so great that the secular academic Allan Bloom called divorce, "America's most urgent social problem".[14] In response to this cultural crisis, evangelicalism's traditional defense of the family went into high gear. As it did, the healthy impulse to protect the family became, for some Christians, a mission of almost idolatrous proportions. It was one thing to say, as one evangelical leader did, that, "the home is an island of serenity and support... in a hectic, pluralistic and often avaricious world".[15] It is quite another to suggest, as other contemporary evangelicals did, that, "*only* through the family can we hope to achieve serenity, a sense of well being and belonging".[16] Or again, that "the home is the *last bastion* against depersonalization and dehumanization".[17] Clearly for some, the family had begun to take on the place of God in the life of the Christian. With this sort of rising allegiance to the nuclear family it is no wonder that institutions such as boarding schools, which necessitated a separation of family, became objects of suspicion. It mattered little that the studies done to date had overwhelmingly supported the health of the boarding school and missionary child experience.

---

[13] Bloom, Allan, *The Closing of the American Mind*, Simon and Schuster: 1997, p. 118.
[14] Bloom, Allan, *The Closing of the American Mind*, pgs. 118-122.
[15] Evangelical leadership as quoted in *Gender and Grace*.
[16] Evangelical leadership as quoted in *Gender and Grace* (Italics mine).
[17] Evangelical leadership as quoted in *Gender and Grace* (Italics mine).

As an important aside, in the following pages we will be analyzing the MK boarding experience typified by RVA. It is critical to note that some of the statistics being referred to include all MKs – not only those at boarding schools. However, because MK boarding schools are the most efficient place to do studies on MKs, most research on MKs is necessarily weighted heavily towards the boarding experience. In addition, because boarding schools have amounted for the bulk of MKs worldwide, the statistics that include all MKs can still be used with a high level of confidence as expressive of the experience of the MK boarder. And the message of that research supported the health of MK boarding experience.

The Sprinkle study of 1976, for instance, found that an overwhelming number of missionary kids (MKs) would choose to relive the experience if given a chance – ninety-five percent in fact.[18] In another well-respected book written during the controversy, Edward Danielson cited his and other studies to show further that MK boarders developed essentially the same positive personality traits as non-boarders.[19] In 1988 Larry Sharp summarized the findings of these and other studies, concluding, "research continues to debunk the common myths about MKs and shows MKs to be intelligent, moral, well adjusted and privileged."[20]

Yet in the face of the academic studies many remained suspicious and continued to question the parenting of those who would send their children away to boarding schools. In 1987 missions expert Marjory Foyle confirmed this animosity amongst evangelical Christians towards boarding schools stating that, "over the last six years I (have been) surprised at the hostility towards the idea of missionary boarding schools".[21] While not based on empirical research, this increasingly negative sentiment was not simply hysterical and reactionary ranting. Indeed, this position had some evidence of its own. For starters, even the advocates of boarding were willing to admit that not all children (and

---

[18] Sprinkle, L. "Survey: Missionary Kids share their feelings about being MK's, Unpublished manuscript, Carson Newman College: 1976.

[19] Danielson, Edward E., *Missionary Kid – MK*, William Carey Library, Pasadena: 1984, p. 66.

[20] Sharp, Larry, "Towards a Greater Understanding of the Real MK: A review of recent research" as quoted in Kelly O'Donnell's, *Helping Missionaries Grow*, William Carey Library: 1988, p.219.

[21] Foyle, Marjory F., *Overcoming Missionary Stress*, MARC Europe, Kent UK: 1987, p. 58.

families) were suited for the boarding experience. Perhaps no book did more to highlight this reality than Ruth Van Reken's, *Letters Never Sent*.

In this moving book Van Reken's painful MK childhood is relived through a series of fictional letters to her parents. At its core, the message of the letters is that the long periods of family separation experienced by the boarding MK necessarily lead to deep and lasting emotional wounds.[22] In the increasingly nurturing culture of American evangelicalism the book sold extremely well. Part of what made Van Reken's book so successful was the fact that MKs and non-MKs alike could identify with her story of loneliness and separation. In expressing the pain of her experience she had given voice to other MKs whose experience was equally difficult, opening up what seemed to be a chorus of anti-boarding feeling. As a result, a moral stigma was placed on the shoulders of those perceived to be responsible for the MK's pain – the missionary parents and the boarding schools. Fairly or not, the evangelical perception of missionary parents began to slip from being heroes of the faith to people of questionable character. Likewise, the perception of missionary schools slid easily from havens of moral and spiritual health to cold institutions of emotional isolation.

This mounting antagonism was compounded by the fact that by the eighties there were an increasing number of attractive educational options for North American MKs. For one, the home-school movement had by this period grown and developed to a point where, academically, it was capable of providing isolated missionary families with a curriculum of considerable substance. Of course, this option had significant social and extra-curricular drawbacks. For the increasing number of urban missionaries, the International School system provided generally outstanding, if secular, academic training – if one could afford it. Unfortunately, most missionary families did not have the salary necessary to send their children to an international school. Finally, in some locations (Nairobi being one of them) day schools for MKs like Rosslyn Academy were developing.

Between the intense devotion to the family, the emotional scars of a few MKs and the availability of alternatives to boarding, those opposed to boarding school education began to enthusiastically prophesy a post-boarding era. Yet against this backdrop of evangelical criticism, many missionary parents in Africa continued to choose RVA over the other available options. In fact, they did this to such an extent that by the mid-

---

[22] Van Reken Ruth, *Letters Never Sent*, Self-Published: 1988. (Originally published as "Letters I Never Wrote" in 1986.)

eighties AIM was forced to consider building a sister school near Mt. Kenya.[23]

WHY DID THE demand for an RVA education continue in the face of American evangelical pressure to the contrary? Assuming that these parents were loving and conscientious, our only conclusion must be that for them the positives of boarding schools continued to outweigh the negatives. But were they right? Were all the attacks on missionary boarding schools without merit? For RVA, those missionaries on the field, and for those many evangelical families considering the African mission field, these questions needed to be addressed. Indeed, no one involved in Christian missions could afford to push them under the carpet.

Unfortunately, the debate over MK boarding schools was muddled from the beginning. For starters, the sheer number of issues involved necessarily complicated matters. When discussing MK education, was one primarily concerned with academic performance? Emotional and psychological health? Spiritual growth? Cultural adjustment? Or some assortment of all of these – prioritized to each individual MK? And, assuming one could come to some agreed upon definition of MK education, how could one best go about objectively evaluating the merits and failings of boarding specifically?

Even historians sympathetic to Evangelicalism have conceded that intellectual complexity has never been its strong suit. Unfortunately the issue of the effects of missionary boarding schools proved no exception as many chose to jump to the conclusion that Van Reken's experience was universal and that separation was inherently debilitating.[24] But was it really fair to pin any and all MK issues on the separation from family inherent in boarding? What of the parent-child relationship? What of the child's genetic make up? And what of the child's own responsibility for their choices – choices that are at least partially responsible for their emotional or spiritual health? Finally, when analyzing holistic health, to whom are MK's to be compared? What group should act as the control? Are we to pretend that American or British children grow up free of

---

[23] Letter from Roy Entwistle to Peter Stam of April 25, 1985; AIM International Council Minutes, May 1985; RVA School Board Minutes, Oct. 11, 1985.

[24] The most widely respected evangelical historians today have consistently lambasted their own faith community for lacking the intellectual character that allows one to consider fairly and honestly wrestle with intellectual complexity. The most well known example is Mark Noll's *The Scandal of the Evangelical Mind*, Eerdmans.

emotional struggles or spiritual crises? In short, to what degree is the boarding school experience responsible for a child's overall health – and, to the degree it is responsible, has that influence been primarily positive or negative?

The logical place to begin any evaluation of the quality of an educational experience is with the academic standards. Because it is easy to quantify, academic education also happens to be the portion of the overall MK educational experience that is most capable of producing a sense of objectivity. If we are to believe the numbers, the academic training MK's have received over the years has been outstanding. The "sterling record" MK's have amassed may be attributable in part to their uniquely mind-stretching life experiences.[25] Indeed, there seems to be no better explanation for the fact that historically, MK IQ scores have been between fifteen and twenty percent higher than the national average.[26] However, the quality of one's education is not determined by the quality of the student who arrives at the school but the degree to which the school develops that student's raw ability.

There can be little question that by the eighties the quality of education available at RVA had improved considerably from the school's haphazard pre-war past. Because AIM missionaries staffed RVA, the school had been able to use its modest financial surpluses to considerably improve its facilities. In fact, by the early nineties the facilities had improved to such a degree that the Washington Post, in a feature article on RVA stated that the school, "offer(ed) facilities that would be the envy of most private schools anywhere (including)... a state of the art science and computer complex and well equipped studios (for the arts)."[27]

But education is never primarily about the facilities and even in the eighties RVA was notoriously inconsistent in the quality of its faculty. Said one student, "because RVA accepts most of the teachers 'called' to the school, we got the extremes – from the most capable and talented faculty to those who couldn't get a job anywhere else".[28] To be sure, thanks to the efforts of the Entwistle administration, the level of

---

[25] Pollock, Dave and Ruth Van Reken, *The Third Culture Kid Experience: Growing Up among Worlds*, Intercultural Press, Maine: 1999, pgs. 79-80. Also see the study by Krajewski as quoted in O'Donnell's *Helping Missionaries Grow*, p. 220.

[26] Danielson, Edward, *Missionary Kids-MK*, p. 73.

[27] *Washington Post*, Feb. 2, 1993 – Susan Okie, "School in the Clouds".

[28] Personal interview with Christy Dow Murray by the author. (Christy was a student at RVA from 1987-1990).

professionalism at RVA had increased considerably from the early days. As late as the mid-sixties students experienced classes where, "each student – one after the other – read in front of the class one or two pages out of the history book, until the bell rang and until the school year ended".[29] Yet, by the late eighties a survey of the school's forty-four high school teachers found all with college degrees (most in the fields they were teaching) and fourteen holding graduate degrees.[30] Perhaps even more critical was the self-conscious push by the school's administration to formalize the curriculum in the high school. As late as the mid-eighties the curriculum was essentially dependent on the individual teacher. When a given teacher left, so did the curriculum; and the next teacher (competent or not) was forced to create their own course virtually from scratch. By the nineties this casualness had been replaced by a systematic approach whereby course plans and units were stored from year to year, allowing each new teacher to utilize, and add to, an already well-developed course.[31] In short, despite a legacy of inconsistency, by the time the boarding school debate had reached its zenith, RVA seemed to be offering its students an excellent opportunity for academic growth. But what of the results of the MK boarding schools? To what degree did this improving academic lead to tangibly improved results?

A study by Roy Entwistle covering the years 1974-1984 found that MK boarders scored on average 100 points above the American average on the SAT test. By 1983 the gap between MK and American achievement had actually increased to 120 points.[32] While these numbers are impressive, even more startling is the percentage of MK boarders who went on for higher education. Towards this end, study after study has revealed that between ninety and ninety-five percent of MK boarding school graduates went on to higher education.[33] During the eighties RVA was no exception to this rule. Indeed, at the turn of the

---

[29] Letter from Christof Puttfarken to the author, dated, Nov. 4, 2001 (Christof was a student at RVA from 1964-67).

[30] Survey by the author, based on information in the 1988 RVA annual "Kiambogo".

[31] Personal interview with longtime RVA faculty member Tim Bannister at Kijabe on Dec. 19, 1997. Tapes of the interview are available at the Billy Graham Center under the "Papers and Materials of Phil Dow".

[32] Entwistle, Roy, "Developing a Strong Academic Curriculum in an MK School" found in the *Compendium of the International Conference on Missionary Kids*, Manila, page 276, ICMK, 1986.

[33] Danielson, Edward, *Missionary Kid-MK*, p. 24.

21st Century RVA continues to send at least that number on to colleges and universities around the world.[34] When put alongside the American population as a whole, the contrast is particularly dramatic. In two of the largest studies to date of adult MKs it was found that of the ninety to ninety-five percent that went on to university, between seventy-four and eighty-one percent respectively actually graduated. To put this into perspective, that is compared with a university graduation rate of twenty-one percent in the population as a whole. More remarkable still is the finding that approximately forty percent of Adult Third Culture Kids (ATCK) achieve a graduate degree of some kind.[35] While that number does include children of American businesspeople and military and diplomatic personnel, there is no reason to believe that the MK is underrepresented in that statistic. Indeed the opposite is likely the case. For in the only study to date specifically comparing the relative academic merits of these groups, MKs placed first in academic achievement.[36] In short, the education provided at RVA during the Entwistle years was commendable. Thus, it is difficult to imagine how anyone would make their case against missionary boarding schools based on academic achievement.

BUT ACADEMIC ACHIEVEMENT was often not even near the center of the debate. Critics of missionary boarding schools were far more concerned with the emotional, psychological and spiritual health of the missionary children. The two hubs around which most of the controversy raged were: (a) the perceived emotional cost resulting from the separation inherent in the boarding experience; and (b) the psychological trauma created by the intense cross-cultural experience of the MK. Of these two, the issue most directly related to boarding schools and the one most potentially damaging for RVA and schools like it was the experience of separation.

It is not necessary to have read Van Reken's book for one to sympathize with the potential pain the MK might have to endure due to

---

[34] Personal interview with Tim Cook, Academic Vice-Principal of RVA, Dec. 20, 1997 at RVA.

[35] Unseem, Ruth Hill, "ATCKs maintain global dimensions throughout their lives", *Newslink* 1994; Vol. XIII, No. 4, Princeton, NJ. Also see MK CART/CORE survey of 1995.

[36] Krajewski study of 1969 as quoted in Danielson, p. 33. It is important to note that in 1969 MKs, almost to a person, went to boarding schools, as few other options existed at the time. Therefore, this study is speaking directly to the issue of MK boarding and not simply MKs in general.

the separation intrinsic to boarding. Anyone who has gone to camp for the first time knows the sadness, fear, and perhaps even anger, that can accompany that separation from family. The fact that so many evangelicals could point to Van Reken's story, or better yet to an embittered adult MK, only confirmed their instinctive condemnation of the boarding school concept. The fact that many well-intentioned evangelicals were quick to assume that the boarding experience was necessarily a harmful one is, therefore, not surprising.

Among the research and missionary communities however, boarding schools continued to be viewed in a generally favorable light. Significantly, most of the studies that continued to come out during this period seemed to argue that the separation caused by boarding, when experienced within the context of a loving family and a healthy school environment, yielded mostly positive results. In fact, the doctoral dissertation of David Schipper of Rosemead Graduate School of Psychology concluded that the separation during the teen years even seemed to enhance the student's self-concept.[37] Other studies suggested that the separation consistently and positively influenced the parent-child relationship. Unpublished dissertation research by Jack Taylor in 1998 revealed an extraordinarily healthy parent-child relationship within the missionary community – relative to that experienced by their North American peers. When asked if their relationship with their father was a source of enjoyment for them, 93% of MKs answered yes – compared to 58% of their North American peers. While not as dramatic, the same pattern also applied to the MK's relationship with their mother, siblings and grandparents – again, relative to the same relationships experienced by their North American peers.[38] If separation, in and of itself, was harmful it seemed that these critical relationships would have suffered, but that appeared not to be the case. This research seemed to confirm the conclusion reached by Dr. Raymond Chester in 1984 when he said, "Family unity is based on something deeper than geographical location. I know of no study that would support the idea that sending a child away to school is, by itself, detrimental to the child. In fact, studies indicate

---

[37] Schipper, David, "Self-concept differences between early, late and non-boarding missionary children", Unpublished dissertation, Rosemead Graduate School of Psychology, CA: 1977.
[38] Jack Taylor, "Synopsis of MK's Staying Aware in Today's World", Unpublished dissertation, Azuza Pacific University. Given by Taylor to the author in 1998.

that if parents (families) are having troubles, it will not matter how the child is educated – the problems will probably transfer (to the child)".[39]

However, in 1986 David Pollack and Ruth Van Reken produced a study that appeared to condemn the boarding school concept. Based on the data compiled from 282 adult MK respondents, Pollack and VanReken concluded that the separation inherent in the boarding experience had had a profoundly negative impact on the emotional and psychological development of over forty percent of MKs. By implication, virtually every other student who attended an MK boarding school was likely to end up emotionally scarred by the experience. Because the study was done by two highly respected authorities in the field and had been one of the largest to date, many assumed that they had heard the final word on the effects of separation and boarding on MKs. The study did, however, have several fatal flaws. Most significantly, it lumped every generation of MKs into two large groupings and thus did not take into account the radically different circumstances experienced by each successive generation of MK boarders – circumstances which had a profound impact on the way the MKs of that generation viewed separation. In fact, a close look at the numbers revealed that of those MKs born after 1961, approximately ninety percent reported that separation had had either neutral or a positive impact in their emotional development.[40]

These numbers support the conclusions of Dr. Larry Sharp, whose 1990 study of 286 adult MK products of boarding schools found that well over 90% said that, if given a choice, they would grow up, "just as they did".[41] In other words, the hasty condemnation by evangelicalism of boarding school education, based on the belief that separation from parents – in and of itself – is damaging, seemed to be misguided. In retrospect, the debate over the health of boarding had more than its share of irony. For at the very moment the boarding school experience was enduring its most intense criticism, it was reaching a new zenith as a place of academic, personal and spiritual development.[42]

---

[39] As quoted in Dan Harrison's, "Causes and Effects of Changing Attitudes Towards Boarding Schools" found in, *The Compendium of ICMK* Manila, 1984, page 306, ICMK 1986.

[40] For a much more in depth analysis of Pollock and Van Reken's study please see Appendix D.

[41] Sharp, Larry, *Evangelical Missions Quarterly*, Jan. 1990.

[42] The connection between the MK boarder's experience and the quality of their family relationships prior to, and during, boarding is one that is paramount to the controversy surrounding boarding schools. What the research seems to

WHILE MOST OF the controversy surrounding MKs during the eighties and nineties revolved around the separation issue, a second issue complicated matters further and added to the tensions surrounding MK education. That issue was the considerable trauma of the cross-cultural experience. Some argued that the mission field was responsible for producing socially dysfunctional adults who, according to both themselves and their Western peers, never really fit in their "home" cultures. As early as Rudyard Kipling's 19th Century fictionalized character, *Kim*, Third Culture Kids (TCKs) had developed a reputation as fascinatingly odd misfits. And more than any other group of TCKs, MKs were especially vulnerable to this judgment. The nature of their parent's work often meant total immersion in a culture that was almost completely "other". In a way that risked making them strangers to even their own parents, the young impressionable bush MKs of the 20th Century took on the language, mannerisms, and even thought processes, of the alien culture their parents had chosen to live amongst. Thus, in colonial terms, the RVA MK could, and often times did, "go native".

For Rudyard Kipling the exoticism was romantic and full of adventure. However, when the real-life Kims returned to their home cultures for university the shock was considerable. Despite the fact that on the surface they looked like everyone else, they were aliens. They knew it, and worse yet, in short order, so did their social acquaintances. Not surprisingly, stories of social ostracism, loneliness and cultural confusion have been a part of the MK story from the beginning.[43]

For good reason, during the Entwistle years this social pain became a second major area of concern to the psychologists who had attached themselves to the plight of the MK. Some were quick to point out that the potential for emotional and psychological scars resulting from the MK experience and the trauma of "re-entry" was too great for loving parents to take. Others believed that the advantages of the MK's cross-cultural experience outweighed the potential risks. Pollack and Van Reken, in their groundbreaking book, *The TCK Experience*, summarized the potential affects of the cross-cultural experience by setting up the following opportunity/risk categories:

---

consistently reveal is that children from families with a significant level of dysfunctionality are far more likely to struggle in boarding schools because they tend to interpret boarding as a rejection or abandonment by their parents. What is unfortunate is that the boarding schools often times get blamed by both the parents and the children for problems that were first and foremost their own.
[43] *The TCK Experience* includes myriad stories of MKs being misunderstood, ostracized, isolated and the like.

Opportunity	**vs.**	**Risk**
Expanded Worldview	vs.	Confused loyalties
Cross-cultural enrichment	vs.	Ignorance of home culture
Adaptability	vs.	Cultural schizophrenia
Less prejudice	vs.	More prejudice
Concern for human rights	vs.	Cultural relativism[44]

The work of Pollack and Van Reken made two things clear. First, the effects of the cross-cultural experience on children were profound. And second, these effects varied significantly from family to family and child to child. In short, regardless of the family or specific child, the cross-cultural experience should be taken seriously.

With this sort of daunting uncertainty, missionary parents were left to ask, how could the considerable risks linked to the cross-cultural experience be minimized and the opportunities maximized? Central to this issue, of course, was the nature of the child's education. Concerning that education, what situation would provide the greatest potential for developing in the MK of a clear and healthy sense of personal and cultural identity (that quality so often lacking in the MK historically). Further, which situation might be best suited to encourage in the MK both a deep appreciation of all the cultures competing for their allegiance and the social skills necessary to succeed in the Western world?[45]

RVA'S ANSWER FROM the beginning was the creation of a bridge between the cultures that would allow the MK to view every culture in a healthy way, while ultimately preparing the students academically and socially for a return to a university education in North

---

[44] Compiled from Pollack and VanReken, *The TCK Experience.*

[45] By the late 1970's there were several available options for the missionary family living outside cosmopolitan urban centers – home schooling, local national schools, boarding schools and leaving the mission field. The academic success of home schooling was largely dependent on having a parent with a deep and wide knowledge base and an ability to communicate that well. Home schooling also had the massive drawbacks of a lack of social interaction and tremendous extracurricular opportunities often available during the critical high school years. Local national schools had the two significant drawbacks of lacking a curriculum capable of preparation for a North American university education; and often times an educational and disciplinary philosophy significantly different than the North American equivalents.

America. The goal was admirable but was complicated to say the least. What sort of balance between the cultures would allow the MK to exploit the many advantages of their rich multicultural heritage while still providing them with the social and cultural tools necessary to thrive in their home cultures?

Being almost entirely immersed in African culture, many of the earliest missionaries had hoped that RVA might balance out the cultural scales and gradually come to resemble a mini-England or America. And with the swell of American missionaries after WWII, the school did increasingly take on the feel of a self-contained American town. This pattern continued so much so that by 1993 the *Washington Post* observed that the community, "looks and feels like a small Midwestern town". While the *Post* did not mean this disparagingly, others were less sanguine, believing that RVA had intentionally isolated itself from its African surroundings. Said one prominent Kenyan, "It never struck me that the school was ever set up to be part of Kenyan society. It was set up to be an island and it succeeded in that... you made sorties from time to time (but) then went back to the island".[46]

Those who saw Entwistle's RVA as nothing more than a little America did so with some cause. In earlier generations the influence of American culture at RVA had been muted by the long shadow of the British Empire. However, by 1980 it seemed that everything about the place was screaming "America". American history and literature were graduation requirements within a fundamentally American curriculum taught primarily by American teachers. Each year a new batch of anxious juniors took the American SAT and ACT tests in the hopes of getting into their American college of choice. On Tuesdays the school's cafeteria would turn out burgers and fries for freckle-faced boys and girls wearing blue jeans and the latest Nike sneakers. Sundays found the school choir singing to the community faithful songs from the latest Continental Singers tour. And home basketball games in the school's gym regularly took on the feel of a Friday night in Indiana, complete with mini-skirted cheerleaders and gum-chomping, gangly players. In fact, to the non-American observer the uniquely American fervor surrounding the high school's athletic teams must have seemed entirely out of proportion to their importance in the grand scheme of things.[47]

---

[46] Personal Interview with Mutava Musyemi at his home, January 3, 2000. The tape of the interview remains in the possession of the author.

[47] These comments are the result of the personal experience of the author as a student-athlete at RVA during the late 1980's.

Of course, the American enthusiasm for high school sports was not the only thing responsible for the community's frenzied attention to sports during these years. The teams also happened to be extremely good. In 1988 the boy's varsity teams won virtually every trophy available. In soccer they won the Nairobi Schools Cup and in basketball the team compiled an undefeated record of 32-0, winning three major tournaments. Not to be outdone, the year's Rugby team won the Blackrock tournament, as well as the highly sought after Prescott Cup. In fact, the rugby team managed to go the entire season without a single try being scored against them. At first glance, it would have been easy to assume that the school's goal of preparing their students for a return to the sports-crazed American culture had been a little too successful – at the cost of missing out on the tremendous benefits of living within the African culture and context.[48] Indeed, by the 1970's both the missionary community and its increasingly vocal opponents were of the opinion that the re-creation of a little America was distasteful, if not morally dubious.[49]

Yet, on one level, even if RVA had intended to become an isolated island of American culture, that was never a legitimate option. Beyond the obvious fact that the school was in Africa and was surrounded by the African community, the school's whole reason for being was to support the missionary movement – a movement whose basic goals encouraged substantial and meaningful interaction with the African culture. The school's faculty was in Africa because they believed that the Christian message needed to be heard by the people of Africa; and the school's students came from families whose life mission was to share that message with real people in the real African context. As a result, the vast majority of the school's students came from homes in rural or semi-rural East Africa where they were entirely immersed in African culture. In short, while some degree of isolationism was inherent in the school's mission, neither the school's faculty nor its students could accept total isolation without feeling hypocritical.

---

[48] Ibid. For further verification see the 1988 version of the RVA Annual "Kiambogo".

[49] It should be noted here that by the sixties and seventies (partly because of "American Imperialism" and partly because of the rise of postmodern cultural relativism due to the cultural crisis in America and the West generally) the Western world had begun to see claims of absolutism – either cultural or religious – as immoral. Therefore the entire missionary enterprise, seen as the vanguard of virtue earlier in the century, had become blacklisted and continued under a cloud of moral suspicion – even in the Church.

Thus when the school's blossoming American family atmosphere began to lead to an increasing isolationism it should surprise no one that internally-driven criticism followed in short order. Indeed, early on in Entwistle's tenure as Principal one frustrated student came to him with the complaint that, "I have lived in Kenya much of my life and all I know of Kenya is Nairobi and RVA".[50] While the parents of the missionary child were equally culpable, the legitimacy of this potential criticism of RVA was growing and Entwistle began looking for a remedy. It was true that the school now offered Swahili, accepted a limited number of Kenyan students and had a narrow outreach program through its choir and sports teams, but the criticism seemed to be increasingly true that the overall experience of the RVA student was one of isolation in an almost entirely American bubble – untouched by the lives and concerns of the people surrounding it.

During a trip to the Good Shepherd School of Ethiopia in 1976, Entwistle came across what he felt was the beginning of a solution to the problem of isolationism at RVA. Good Shepherd School had begun to set aside a period of time during the school year to take extended field trips around Ethiopia. The goal was to create in their students an appreciation of the rich culture they had become apart of. From this appreciation it was hoped a deep respect would develop that would break down the barriers of race, culture and language that separated the mostly American students from their Ethiopian peers.[51]

Calling the program Interim, Entwistle and a team of RVA faculty set aside a week during the second term in which juniors and seniors could travel in small groups to various select spots in East Africa. Like Good Shepherd School, the goal was cultural enrichment and, despite some early hurdles, in many respects the program succeeded admirably.[52] But programs like Interim had one significant drawback – they were based on the assumption that interaction with African culture was something you went away to do when the real potential for cultural growth lay at the very heart of RVA's community. The real question was, to what degree did the rejuvenated community at RVA interact with the African community in and around it? And, to the extent that there was interaction, how healthy was that interaction?

---

[50] Interview of Roy Entwistle at his Kijabe home on Jan. 1, 1998.
[51] RVA Newsletter dated Jan. 1976 available at RVA. Also, see Entwistle interview of Jan. 1, 1998.
[52] Ibid.

ON ONE LEVEL, over the years the community at RVA had developed a generally friendly rapport with the African community at Kijabe. Some of these relationships brought levity to the formal relationship between the two communities. Several Kenyans stand out in this way during the Entwistle years. One was Mugo Scout.

As the story goes, during the Mau Mau era Mugo's wife had tried to kill him by poisoning his tea. Although he survived the poison, Mugo was never entirely rational again. A walking contradiction, during the seventies and eighties Mugo religiously attended the Friday Kenyan flag raising ceremony while constantly carrying a circa 1950's photo of Queen Elizabeth – whom he called, "my queen".[53] One of the many similar examples of Mugo's contradictory eccentricity occurred during the Gulf War. Convinced that this new conflict was just a flare-up in the continuing battle against the British Empire, Mugo came onto the school campus and attempted to recruit RVA boys for an imminent attack on the American and British invaders. Evidently he eventually saw the conflict of interest that the mostly American schoolboys would have had in attacking their countrymen because nothing ever came of the plan beyond his promise of commando training in the forests above the school.[54] Episodes like this one allowed both communities to take each other less seriously, breaking the cross-cultural tension and creating space for a more relaxed and healthy relationship between the communities.

While relationships with the likes of Mugo brought levity to the dialogue between the communities at Kijabe, other relationships had the potential for more substantial interaction. The hospital at Kijabe served the African population almost exclusively and was run by missionary doctors, many of whom had children at RVA who volunteered as "candy-stripers" in the hospital wards. Moffat Bible College, Kijabe Press and other AIM ministries at Kijabe also acted as a bridge between RVA and the African community surrounding it. In addition, missionary wives met regularly with the their African counterparts. While these relationships usually began when the African women came to the missionary homes in the hopes of selling vegetables from their gardens, it was not uncommon for these relationships to spawn Bible studies where these casual relationships would develop further, breaking down the etiquette of reserved interaction that existed between the two

---

[53] Several personal interviews conducted in Seattle with RVA graduates verified this anecdote.

[54] Personal interview with Tim Bannister at Kijabe Jan. 1, 1998.

communities and acting as a living example of human brotherhood to the school's students.

Yet beyond the biblical message of human equality and dignity, by far the most powerful antidote to racism in existence at RVA was the presence of Kenyans in the student body. As scholars of antebellum America have shown in the case of the black abolitionists like Fredrick Douglass – there is nothing that destroys prejudice like the power of significant personal experience with the objects of potential prejudice. Some of the most ardent white abolitionists only began to fight against slavery and racism after meeting and developing relationships with Douglass, Tubman and others.[55] The same principle was certainly at work among the student body at RVA, where American and European MKs shared classrooms, dinner tables, dorm rooms and playing fields with their Kenyan peers.

Nevertheless, despite the power of personal experience and the generally positive nature of these relationships, it is important to remember that these interactions still took place against a backdrop that, while not intentionally so, was less healthy. As we have seen, despite the biblical message of equality that fueled the movement their missionary parents were a part of, Kenya's colonial history and the economic realities of life in developing Africa created circumstances such that the missionary child often inhabited a world of privilege unimaginable by all but the wealthiest of their American peers. In this world, middle-class American children could easily take for granted a reality of African servitude. The complex historical and economic circumstances that had caused this disparity were not directly the fault of the missionary or their children, but this reality nonetheless did send a message, easily perpetuated, that human worth and ability could be measured by the color of one's skin.

DURING THE ENTWISTLE years at RVA the story was no different. African cooks served the meals, African dishwashers cleaned up the mess, African gardeners landscaped the grounds and African guards kept the community safe. Indeed, the key characteristic every African at RVA had in common was one of subservience to the white missionaries and the school's mainly white student body. In this unintentional, but very real, master-servant world it was understandably rare that real and substantial relationships between the students and the

---

[55] For an excellent example of this well established argument see Paul Goodman's, *Of One Blood*, University of California Press, Berkeley: 1999.

African adult staff developed. And thus, without any substantive relationships to destroy potential prejudice, students at RVA were left to develop their view of Africans against a ubiquitous backdrop of African subservience.[56]

Of course, every boarding school needs a trained support staff to function and it is hard to imagine a scenario in which strong and substantial relationships between the students and the support staff at any school would develop. In fact, such relationships would likely be looked on with suspicion in most schools, for what do adult support staff have in common with school children? Yet in most similar situations the students and staff are of the same race and nationality and so the question of race is a non-issue. At RVA it was impossible to miss the fact that a black staff served a primarily white student body and therefore, unintentionally or not, the school's system remained a potential object lesson to its students – Africans must be inferior.

For this reason it is easy to self-righteously condemn the school as a greenhouse for unconsciously racist students. But things are rarely that simple. Despite its image as Africa's golden child, by the Entwistle era the post-colonial Kenyan economy was beginning to wrestle with a massive population explosion that had begun to balloon the nation's unemployment and threatened to plunge the country into deep and long term economic crisis.[57] Fearful of perpetuating racism, RVA could have tried to find within the AIM missionary community the people necessary to carry out the duties that African workers filled in 1976, but this would have meant the elimination of a large number of jobs for local Kenyans otherwise without work. Believing that it was their responsibility to provide quality work for the community, RVA chose to continue their practice of hiring Africans to fill the blue-collar tasks requisite for maintaining the school.[58] Under the economic circumstances it is nearly impossible to criticize the school for the choice. Indeed, almost to a person those Kenyans employed at RVA considered themselves lucky to have secured as position at RVA where they were paid considerably more than the average income available in the local economy.[59] Yet the problem of perpetuating the image of Africans as subservient, and

---

[56] Observations of the author based on personal experience as a student at RVA from 1985 to 1988.

[57] Edgerton, Robert. *Mau Mau: An African Crucible*, p. 231.

[58] Letter from Entwistle to Dick Anderson dated, May 29, 1984. Letter is available at the BGC Archives under CN81; 34-18.

[59] This point is based on multiple interviews with RVA's African support staff during my research trips there between 1997 and 2002.

intellectually bound to menial labor, remained. The stark reality was that there was not one African adult at RVA in a position of authority. There was not one adult who, in that regard, could act to dispel any unconscious notions of a racial hierarchy latent in the school's system.[60]

In the mid-eighties someone noticed. Dick Anderson, then the International General Secretary of AIM, wrote to Entwistle encouraging RVA to take another look at the employment of national educators at the school. In replying to Dr. Anderson, Entwistle gave some indication of the complexity of the situation. First he argued that as an institution RVA's purpose was to educate the children of missionaries for a successful return to their home culture. As a result, it was important that the curriculum and the majority of the faculty be American as most of the students were. For this reason Entwistle argued that Kenyan dorm parents would likely hinder the school's mission by further confusing the children's cultural identity – not to mention creating myriad dilemmas stemming from the large cultural differences in attitudes towards discipline and the like. Concerning Kenyan faculty members Entwistle argued that this cross-cultural dilemma was further exacerbated by the need for American certification and the fear that hiring one Kenyan would create intense pressure for the school to retain an entirely national faculty, thereby eventually abandoning its mission.[61]

For Entwistle, the bottom line was that hiring a Kenyan teacher would be a difficult and upsetting process with unforeseeable, and perhaps dire, consequences; and one that was ultimately not worth the risk to the school's mission. As the school later discovered, the arguments had some merit.[62] Yet, in dismissing a search for some top-notch Kenyan teachers, RVA missed an opportunity to add exponentially to the quality of the education they provided for their students. With just one outstanding and articulate Kenyan on faculty the unintended racist message latent in the school's program could have been destroyed. But more than that, with just one intellectually and spiritually dynamic

---

[60] It is critical to remember that after independence, RVA began to admit Kenyan students, and that many of these students, through their friendships with the expatriate students, were a powerful force against the development of racist assumptions in the MKs at RVA.

[61] Letter from Entwistle to Dick Anderson, dated May 29, 1984.

[62] The school did hire a Kenyan Swahili teacher in the 1980's and by most accounts it was a failure. As it happened, he was not a good teacher and had difficulty understanding the American student's mindset. Unfortunately the school took this one example as proof that Kenyan faculty at this American school could not be a success.

Kenyan teacher the students at RVA would have had a chance to grow in their admiration and respect for the people they lived amongst in a way that a thousand encounters with the good-natured, but relatively uneducated, maintenance workers never could.

During the Entwistle years external forces were also at work, influencing the nature of the relationship RVA and its students were to have with the African culture and community surrounding it. Unfortunately, during this time those forces were primarily negative. The political corruption that had begun slowly in the Kenyatta administration was on the increase and undermined not only the country's struggling economy but its communal morale. Yet corruption only exacerbated the problems brought on by the astonishing population explosion taking place in the young nation. By the mid-eighties the signs of an economy in trouble were everywhere. For the expatriate and Kenyan communities alike, the most upsetting of those signs was the noticeable increase in armed robberies. In 1984 that trend became a reality at Kijabe as the Byler family home was broken into by a group of seven armed men. Although no one was killed during the robbery, Darwin Byler barely escaped serious injury when an ax blade aimed at his head flew off its handle just before crashing into his skull.[63]

The robbery and its violent nature had a chilling effect on the isolated community. Within months AIM mandated that iron bars be put on the windows of every missionary home at Kijabe. Nevertheless, between 1984 and 1994 the trickle of robberies turned into a flood. At its peak in 1990 alarms announcing an attempted robbery were going off every three to four nights. Male staff members had begun patrolling the station in two-hour shifts along with the school's African guards and every family went to sleep with whistles, ammonia bottles and rungus at their bedsides. In addition, five dogs were purchased to accompany the guards; and finally, a few years later, the decision was made to encircle the entire one hundred acre campus with an imposing fence, complete with ten foot high solid steel gates at each of the major entrances to the campus.[64]

Once again, under the circumstances it is difficult to criticize any of these decisions and yet, when the plague of robberies began to dissipate (most likely as a result of these measures), the imposing gated-fence

---

[63] Personal interviews with Jack Wilson Sr. at Kijabe on Dec. 19, 1997 and Dr. "Rick" Bransford at the Ashworth Estate, Seattle, WA, April 5, 2002.
[64] Personal interviews with Jack Wilson Sr., John and Elaine Barnett and personal experience.

remained, creating an unmistakable line between the Kenyan community and the American campus. The fence symbolized the complex relationship and uneasy rift that had grown up between these two communities as a result of the economic forces that were pressing in on the struggling young nation.

The country's political course mirrored its economic story. After an attempted coup against Moi's government in 1982, the Kenyan Constitution was amended in order to make Kenya a one-party state – thereby consolidating Moi's apparently weak hold on power. The stability brought by Moi in the mid-eighties was enough to give the economy a quiet rebirth, but by the late eighties corruption and population growth, coupled with a demand for greater political freedom, had again brought the nation dangerously close to a political meltdown.

While AIM continued to be officially apolitical, Moi's ascendancy to power inevitably linked the mission's fortunes to the coattails of its most famous convert. Having such a powerful advocate certainly had its advantages. AIM's now autonomous national church, AIC, grew considerably in political influence and with that AIM was able to see many of its goals accomplished without much of the usual bureaucratic red-tape. As if to cement the relationship between the current government and AIM, in the seventies Moi had sent two of his sons to RVA and in 1981 he accepted an invitation to speak at the school's seventy-fifth anniversary.[65]

Speaking at AIC Kijabe on July 12 of 1981, Moi referred to Teddy Roosevelt's book in which Roosevelt had predicted that the mission station at Kijabe would be a light to the community. Said Moi, "What has been accomplished at this complex is unbelievable".[66] Articulating the position of AIC, Moi stated his hope that the government and churches of Kenya would continue to work with the mission community in a spirit of "togetherness – working for a purpose to see lives and the country improved".[67] In these comments the community at RVA was assured that they had a powerful friend in a now largely Christian country.

Yet these remarks could cut in a variety of ways. For starters, the remarks also had to be seen as reminders to RVA and the missionary

---

[65] Official Programme for President Moi's visit commemorating the seventy-fifth anniversary of RVA at AIC, Kijabe, July 12, 1981. The Programme is available at the BGC Archives under CN81; 34-18.

[66] Handwritten notes of Moi's speech are written on the official programme found in the BGC Archives. The author of the notes is unknown.

[67] Ibid.

community that they were visitors and that their place in Kenya was not unconditional. As long as they were seen as aiding in the development of the nation they were enthusiastically welcomed. But if they came to be seen as an impediment to Kenyan advancement, the rich story of AIM and its "school in the clouds" was only an official directive away from extinction.

Even more importantly, by maintaining such a close link between AIM and the Moi government, AIM risked becoming a political player whose fortunes were every bit as vulnerable as the government from which those fortunes came. As we have already seen, one year later that vulnerability became even more pronounced when there was a significant coup attempt against the Moi government.[68] Like Moi's government, RVA and the pro-missionary status quo survived the coup. Nevertheless, the insecurities inherent in AIM's political relationships had, by this point, become a part of the school's culture.

By 1990, Kenya's increasingly corrupt and autocratic government had begun to reap its just political rewards in the form of widespread and outspoken dissent. Calls for a return to multiparty politics became deafening as university students angrily demanded change in front of the backdrop of an economy which had now slumped to its lowest growth levels since the early eighties.[69] With the next national election around the corner in 1992, it looked as if the shade cast by Moi's government over AIM and RVA would be gone, to be replaced by an uncertain future for both.

The pre-election chaos that erupted in 1990 and 1991 was rooted in the increasing tribalism that had resulted from the decline in nationalistic morale. Clashes between tribes loyal to Moi and those supporting the opposition broke out across the country. Rumors of those clashes came to Kijabe one day in 1991. Just after noon a story began spreading through the largely Kikuyu staff at RVA that several hundred Kalenjin warriors were on the way to massacre those at Kijabe. Under normal circumstances this sort of rumor would not have been given much credence, but the response at RVA and in Kijabe spoke volumes about the level of hysteria sweeping the nation. Within minutes of the rumor's arrival a meeting of African staff and RVA faculty was called at Jubilee Hall with the purpose of organizing for a fight with the alleged attackers

---

[68] Edgerton, Robert. *Mau Mau: An African Crucible*, p. 228.
[69] According to *Operation World,* by 1993 Kenya's per capita income was $380 – less than 2% of the per capita income of the USA. *Operation World*, 1993, p. 330.

at the top of the escarpment several kilometers away. Word got to acting principal Hal Cook just in time and he ordered the group back to their tasks and squelched what turned out to be a false report.[70]

Yet this false story so agitated the surrounding African communities that riots broke out in several nearby towns resulting in the deaths of three supposed Kalenjin men. In a separate incident during the pre-election tension, angry crowds began to randomly attack cars, destroying windscreens and beating those drivers and passengers that were either courageous or stupid enough to defend their property. Caught in this chaotic melee, several RVA faculty members on their way back to Kijabe retreated to the Limuru Golf Club to wait out the riot. As the rioting continued a new crisis was developing at the golf course. One of those RVA faculty members trapped at the golf course was a diabetic named Jack Wilson. With his blood sugar level moving to a critical level, Wilson got an emergency call through to the community at RVA. Those at the school were then able to contact AIM pilot and RVA graduate Scott Paulsen who made an emergency insulin drop on the Limuru golf course, perhaps saving the life of the longtime faculty member.[71]

What these politically related anecdotes illustrate is that RVA could not have hidden from the culture surrounding it, even if it had wanted to. Yet, additional external factors also helped to ensure that RVA would not become isolated from its African context. In 1996 a drought hit Kenya that was to last through the end of the century. With 70% of the nation's electricity coming from hydroelectric plants, the drought slowed the country's industries to a crawl increasing further the country's unemployment crisis.[72] Just as critically, crops were failing across the country and tens of thousands of Kenyans were threatened with starvation. In response to the crisis a group of RVA students and faculty created a food donation program for six government schools in the Rift Valley. Over the three critical months that followed the program fed 3,500 children daily. Significantly, this program's value did not stop when the worst of the famine did. Indeed, further development programs grew out of it that remain in existence to the present including

---

[70] Personal interview with Tim Cook at his Kijabe home, Dec. 20, 1997. The tape can be found at the BGC Archives, while the notes remain in the author's possession.
[71] Personal interview with Tim Cook at his Kijabe home, Dec. 20, 1997.
[72] *CIA World Fact Book* - online, 2002, "Kenya".

reforestation and water conservation projects for the surrounding communities.[73]

In short, for a variety of reasons, the American community at RVA was not the bubble culture some detractors accused it of being. The economic, political and social forces surrounding the school did not make total isolation a viable possibility. For while the school's mission was to prepare students for a return to their home culture, that preparation could never have meant a total re-creation of that home culture. Beyond the obvious truth that RVA was deeply and unavoidably linked to an inherently invasive socio-political reality that was Kenyan, the community was made up by individuals whose raison d'etre assumed intimate interaction with the Kenyan people and culture for the sake of the Christian gospel – itself a belief system based on the dignity of all humanity.

When Charles Hurlburt and the first generation of missionaries set up RVA as a way to educate their children for a return to the Anglo-American world, they attempted to create a world that approximated the cultural patterns and values of their home. When they did this, they were not thinking in the terms of the 21st Century counselor. The pioneering missionaries were not trying to remove the potential psychosocial wounds their children might bear resulting from cultural confusion because they had not fully foreseen these concerns. And, even if they had been confronted with these issues, they likely would have responded that God's calling was not to a risk-free life, but to a life of faith – in this case, faith that God would protect and provide for their children. Yet in creating an Anglo-American school within the African context what they did was create a bridge between their host and home cultures – a bridge that had the potential to be the "home" culture critical for the development in the MK of a healthy psyche. As time went on RVA, as a bridge between cultures, became a culture in and of itself. The accidental by-product of Hurlburt's attempt to prepare AIM's children for a return to the Western world was the creation of a new sort of culture – a phenomena now referred to as a "third culture".

IN THE 1950'S, sociologists John and Ruth Unseem coined the term "third culture" after observing American communities in India much like the one at RVA. What they noticed then was that expatriate

---

[73] Personal Interview with Jim Long at Kijabe, Dec. 20, 2000. Much of the same information was relayed to the author during a personal interview with John and Elaine Barnett also at Kijabe but in 1997.

communities living overseas often created a culture that was like neither their home culture nor the culture they now lived in; but instead was a unique and dynamic mix of both. As we have already seen, the third culture phenomena had existed at Kijabe from the moment Hurlburt began setting up the AIM compound in 1903. And yet, as each successive wave of history washed over the community, new cultural deposits brought both additional complexity and staying power to the third culture at RVA. Unlike the ever-changing third cultures created by the transient expatriate communities in the cosmopolitan centers of the world, RVA had begun to develop a third culture with substantial roots and history of its own.

It is undeniable that by the Entwistle era the third culture of RVA had the external appearance of being American. But the world at RVA was much more complex than that. Beyond the obvious role that Kenyan culture had had on RVA, there remained, even in the late 1990's, a strong undercurrent of Old Britannia. But during the Entwistle years the greatest change in the third culture of the school was its increasing international flavor. So significant was the international influence at RVA that the theme of the 1991 school yearbook was "the Melting Pot". In 1991 alone, 24 different nationalities representing five continents could be found within the student body.[74] In addition, not only did the third culture at RVA represent a host of nationalities, but during the three months of school holidays many of these students returned to "homes" outside of Kenya. An analysis of the 1980 yearbook found that, while over half of the student's parents worked within Kenya, the remaining students joined their parents as they worked in an additional sixteen countries spread over three continents. In short, while the typical RVA student was an American MK whose parents worked in Kenya, it was almost as likely that an RVA student would be Norwegian or English or Korean and that their parents would work in Malawi or Zambia or Chad. In other words, the pot might have been Anglo-American, and the fire Kenyan, but the contents had a flavor all its own.[75]

Although examples of the third culture at RVA are abundant, perhaps the most powerful of these has been, "RVA Shang" – the language of the third culture at RVA. While the community's language has never been what one might call "sophisticated", no one can deny that the school's students do have a language of their own and that that language is the language of a third culture. Several things stand out

[74] RVA Annual, *Kiambogo* 1991.
[75] RVA Annual, *Kiambogo* 1980.

about the language of RVA. Most obviously, RVA Shang shows the influence of several cultures. Phrases like "Titchie Swot", meaning "little school", derive from the significant British influence prior to WWII, while other terms like "weka" were taken directly from Swahili. Still others, like the sarcastic use of "lots" betray the American influence. Yet, much like the characteristics of a third culture generally, what is even more significant is the fact that very little of the Shang vocabulary has retained the pronunciation or meaning it had in the original – something new has been born.[76]

During the Entwistle years what was significant about the "third culture" concept was not its novelty – for as we have already seen a third culture had been developing at RVA from its inception. What was different was the attention that was now being given to it by missions experts, sociologists and the Anglo-American church generally. Like no other period in history, the world truly resembled a global village. As a result, what these groups of counselors and academics began to see in the MK was a new sort of person, a person who sociologist Ted Ward believed would be, "the prototype (citizen) of the 21st Century".[77]

AFTER TWENTY-TWO YEARS as the head of the Rift Valley Academy, Roy and Judy Entwistle handed over the reins of the school to long-time RVA administrator Jim Long. Five fruitful years later, Jim Long passed the baton to alumnus and former administrator Tim Cook. The tenures of Entwistle and Long did not include some of the dramatic challenges of the school's earlier eras. The once endless oceans separating Kenya from North America and Europe had shrunk. There were no world wars being fought. Epidemics rarely, if ever, threatened the school. And yet of all the periods in the school's 100-year history, the Entwistle era included, perhaps, the most profound challenges to the school's continued existence.

For one, growing political and economic instability in post-independence Kenya had created a situation in which the expatriate community was increasingly vulnerable to both violent attack and the whims of a corrupt political system. In addition, the American cultural and moral crisis of the sixties and seventies fundamentally jeopardized the earnestly Christian school culture. Yet, by far the most significant menace to the school's existence came not from external forces or

---

[76] For an in depth look at the RVA Shang please see Appendix A. This includes an introduction to the Shang, a dictionary and an exercise section.

[77] As quoted in Pollack and Van Reken, *The TCK Experience*, p. 7.

circumstances but from within the very community that had founded and supported the school throughout its long history – Anglo-American evangelicalism. During the Entwistle years, the healthy impulse to support and preserve the nuclear family that had long been near the core of Evangelicalism developed a strain that, in its most radical varieties, virtually idolized the family and thus called into question the very notion of boarding schools.

Yet in the face of these significant threats RVA did not just survive – it thrived. By the late 1980's the school reached a self-imposed cap in student population and began to turn its attention more intentionally to the development of its academic program. As a result, the school's history of turning out a disproportionally high percentage of graduates who complete graduate degrees has continued. The spiritual and moral climate also experienced renewal. A series of quiet revivals hit the school in the late 1980's that had tangible results in lives of the student population. First, by the late eighties the number of suspensions and expulsions had dropped significantly from the peak in the mid-seventies. So much so, that in the 1988-89 school year not a single student was suspended or expelled from the high school. Second, this spiritual revitalization also included a continuation of RVA's tradition of nurturing a zealous missions-minded evangelicalism in its graduates. From the class of 1988 alone at least twenty-five percent of the graduates have gone into explicitly Christian work overseas.[78] And that number does not even include the increasing number of RVA graduates who are returning to Africa as employees of Christian-friendly Non-governmental organizations (NGO's).

Just as significant as the accomplishments and stature of the school's graduates is the continuing role RVA has had in facilitating the work of the missionary parents whose children RVA has helped educate and develop. As previous chapters have made clear, without RVA, a significant number of missionary families who have devoted their lives to the development of Christianity in Africa would either not have come or would have likely left the mission field early. The class of 2001 alone represents over one hundred missionaries from twenty-two mission organizations working in over eleven countries.[79] Certainly, the unrelenting growth of Christianity in Africa as well as the countless

---

[78] There were eighty-five graduates of the class of 1988, according to the school's yearbook Kiambogo. At least twenty-one are serving, or have served, explicitly as missionaries.

[79] See Appendix B.

schools, hospitals and relief and development projects around the continent continues to testify to the significant, although not always direct, role RVA has had in the continent's development through the work of the parents of its students.[80] Yet, it may very well be that the most significant fruit of their labor will be seen in the emerging generation of African ecclesiastical and political leaders. For even as Africa continues to wrestle with the multitude of crises resulting from the trauma of accelerated modernization, HIV/AIDS, astonishing population growth, and the baggage of both its colonial past and its own traditional culture – there are hints that a new type of Christian leadership is emerging.

---

[80] Beyond the most important pieces of evidence of RVA's continuing significance in the development of Christianity in Kenya (the lives and work of the missionary parents of RVA students and the lives of the school's graduates); proof that RVA continues to hold a significant place in the spread of both Christianity and "Pax Americana" are myriad. For one the school continues to host guests of considerable international significance such as Senator Bill Frist of Tennessee who spoke in chapel on January 1998 on the role of the senate in moral reform. The school also continues to receive semi-regular attention in the Kenyan media (although not always positive). Most recently, during the time leading up to the 2002 elections, Nation TV devoted an hour to the history of the Kijabe mission station in connection to the issue of land reform – AIC still owns a considerable amount of land in and around Kijabe – including the land upon which RVA sits.

THE REMARKABLE LEGACY OF THIS "SCHOOL IN THE CLOUDS"

IN JULY OF 2006 ANOTHER GROUP OF GRADUATES WILL cross the podium, hand the superintendent the traditional shilling coin, and take their diploma signaling the conclusion of their secondary education and the end of their time at RVA. When they do this they will be joining thousands of other boys and girls who, over a century, have grown into young men and women as they made their way around the school's idyllic campus. The lightening-paced, Internet world they will walk out into will be radically different from the ox-cart and hurricane lantern world that the children of Charles Hurlburt knew in 1906. And yet, in spite of the radically different worlds that they inhabit, the students and graduates of RVA today are part of a legacy that remains fundamentally unchanged from the fledgling days of the school's first students. However, as noteworthy as the consistency of the school's legacy has been, even more startling is the unexpected significance of that legacy.

It is safe to say that even the visionary Hurlburt did not expect the legacy of RVA to have the significance it does today. Based on the school's humble beginnings and geographic isolation, assumptions of its cultural and political irrelevance were, and are, quite reasonable. Yet, from the very onset, the influence of RVA on the world around it has been anything but irrelevant. To understand the school's surprisingly significant legacy it is necessary to first briefly revisit the motives behind both RVA and the mission that started the school.

The primary motive fueling the African Inland Mission was never a secret. In the very first issue of the mission's newsletter it was spelled out in the following unambiguous terms, "the purpose of the African Inland Mission is…(to) do all that faith, and zeal, and love can do in evangelizing (Africa)."[1] To their credit, the history of AIM has provided abundant and consistent proof that they meant what they said. While other missions branched out into additional types of development work, AIM, perhaps occasionally to a fault, has remained true to its original evangelical calling. That consistency has born significant fruit, most notably in the form of the largest protestant denomination in East Africa – the African Inland Church (AIC).[2]

The complementary purpose of the Rift Valley Academy was to promote the Great Commission in Africa by providing a solution to the single greatest impediment to the missionary enterprise – the question of how missionary parents could pursue their calling without sacrificing their children's future or the health of their families. Hurlburt knew that while some potential missionaries would be willing to leave their young children in European or American boarding schools for years at a time, most would consider this a price too high to pay. Therefore he recognized that without some way of providing a healthy childhood and quality education for MKs in East Africa, the success of the missionary enterprise there would have been hamstrung from the onset.

Because the purpose of RVA has been intimately linked with the larger goal of the evangelical missionary enterprise from the beginning, it makes sense to break the school's legacy down into two complementary categories: (a) the legacy of missionaries (whose work in Africa continued in large part because of the education provided by RVA), and (b) the legacy of the students themselves.

THE LEGACY OF the missionaries can be broken down further into several categories. First, in the current era of urban missionary comfort it is easy to forget that until quite recently the average missionary was a true pioneer. RVA had not been created so that missionaries could move closer together; it existed so they could venture further apart and so bring the message of Christianity to the most isolated corners of East Africa. And spread out they did, moving further and further away from comfort, health and safety. The first generations of

---

[1] *Hearing and Doing*, "The Work", January 1896, pgs. 3&4.
[2] Placing AIC as the largest protestant denomination is based on the common classification of the Anglican Church as neither Protestant nor Catholic.

missionaries especially were risk-takers; adventurers with a purpose, and the graveyards of Africa bear painful witness to that pioneering spirit.

This heritage as self-sacrificing pioneers leads directly to the role RVA's missionary parents have had in the development of Christianity as a genuinely global faith – one not bound to the peculiar rules and dictates of a given culture. In his groundbreaking book, *Translating the Message*, African scholar Lamin Sanneh highlighted the role of translation in breaking down cultural barriers and creating in both the African converts and their missionary converters a richer and more global Christianity. Sanneh argued that the very act of translating the message of Christianity into the indigenous cultural context carried with it the assumption that the universal truths of Christianity could be applied to any given culture's set of traditions.[3] Thus, the assumed value of cultural pluralism within the context of the universal truths of Christianity drew the Christian missionary into deep contact with the beauty and strengths of the indigenous cultures.[4] One of the outcomes of this contact was often, but not always, a degree of mutual respect which encouraged both the missionary and the African convert to see faith and the world from a universal perspective. In the long run, this process has produced both controversy (as some have lost sight of the universally applicable truths of Christianity within the moral and spiritual relativism of cultural pluralism), and growth (as Christians worldwide have become more successful in separating the essential truths of the Gospel from its non-essential cultural baggage).

It is critical to point out that the process of cultural translation Sanneh described has taken generations. As a result, the role of schools like RVA in this process has been decisive. Just by existing, RVA allowed missionaries to stay in East Africa over a lifetime, and just as significantly, encouraged their children and children's children to do the same. The obvious result was that each generation could build on the lessons learned by the generation before them. That is not to say that the third and fourth generation missionaries produced by RVA have been completely immune from cultural bias. It is to say that genuine cross-cultural understanding requires longevity. RVA, by allowing missionaries to invest themselves in an individual culture over an extended period of time, has played a small but critical role in the

---

[3] Sanneh, Lamin, *Translating the Message: The Missionary Impact on Culture*, Orbis Books, Maryknoll, NY: 1989.

[4] And, of course, all missionaries are involved in cultural translation, even if not in linguistic translation.

evolution within the western worldview towards increased respect for the world's indigenous cultures. If there is any doubt of this one needs only to read samples of evangelical missionary materials from each period of RVA's history. The change in terms used to describe the African people and culture over time is striking. In 1903 we see Africans referred to as "totally uncivilized... naked black creatures ...(of) revolting filthiness... gross ignorance and indolence".[5] By the 1950's the tone was dramatically different. Generally speaking, by this point AIM's words and actions reflected a commitment to African leadership for the African Church. Finally, at the turn of the century not only the terms used, but also the assumptions behind them had changed to such a degree that it was nearly possible to argue that western culture was now the one to be pitied or scorned.[6]

The wedded legacies of cultural respect for "the other" and adherence to "essential Christianity" are closely related to another legacy resulting from the work of RVA's missionary parents – the legacy of hard questions. Beyond the multitude of tricky issues linked to the relative value of culture and cultural practices, the missionary enterprise also helped highlight the disparity of wealth between the developing and developed worlds. With the economic disparity exposed, generations of missionaries have been reluctantly forced to confront the larger questions of economic justice, the nature of Christian charity, the link between spiritual and material wealth and a host of related concerns. By forcing the Western Church to confront these issues the missionary movement has played a critical role in the continually evolving view of economic justice within Christianity.[7] Not surprisingly MKs have been at the forefront of the Church's response to questions of economic and social justice.[8]

---

[5] *A Short History of AIM* (Unpublished), pgs. 15-19. This is available at the AIM archives, Pearl River, NY. The Author is unknown.

[6] Evidence for this evolution towards equality between the missionary and the national church leadership is everywhere, but a good place to start is Mark Shaw's, *The Kingdom of God in Africa,* Baker Book House, 1996.

[7] The articles and books that illustrate a direct relationship between Christian missions and an increased awareness of, if not sensitivity to, third world poverty are legion. Ronald Sider's *Rich Christians in an Age of Hunger* is perhaps the most well known, but hundreds of others exist.

[8] One of the excellent examples of MKs addressing issues of Christian affluence in the context of missions and third world poverty is Ethiopian MK Dr. Jonathan Bonk's *Missions and Money: Affluence as a Western Missionary Problem* published by Orbis Books.

Yet the most significant portion of the legacy of RVA's missionary parents has been the startling growth of Christianity in Central and East Africa this century. If we judge the growth of Christianity in Kenya by the numbers, the story is almost unbelievable. Scholars agree that in 1900 the number of Christians in Kenya hovered around five thousand – less than 0.2% of the population. By the end of the 20th century there were over twenty-three million people in Kenya who described themselves as Christian – more than 78% of the population.[9] While the beliefs of the African indigenous religions in the region provided Africa with a philosophical foundation well-suited to take on the monotheistic message of Christianity, much of the credit for the explosive growth of the church in Kenya must be given to the Anglo-American missionary and their early African converts.[10]

At the turn of the 20th Century it was not Christianity, but its monotheistic rival Islam, that was set to conquer the continent. Relative to the insignificant and stagnant presence of Christianity in most of Africa prior to the missionary movement, Islam was strong and moving south. And yet today it is Christianity that dominates Sub-Saharan Africa. Something happened that altered the course of African religious history. That something was the missionary movement.

For better or for worse, further proof of the central influence of Anglo-American missionaries in the spread of the faith can be found in the startling resemblance East African Christianity bears to its Anglo-American forbearers. So widespread is the Anglo-American influence that the evangelical Kenyan scholar George Kinoti observed, "The denominations we belong to, the liturgies we use, the hymns we sing, the theologies which govern our beliefs and conduct, be they liberal or evangelical, are all made in the West".[11] This influence is found in the majestic English hymns that pour from the myriad stone country churches that dot the countryside. And, in the young and vibrant urban

---

[9] Barrett, David, *The Encyclopedia of World Christianity*, "Kenya", Oxford University Press, Nairobi: 1982.

[10] This book is primarily about the missionary impact on East Africa and so highlights the missionary role, but it goes without saying that that impact could not have happened without the enthusiastic and able partnership they had with many new African Christians. As Mark Shaw makes clear in *The Kingdom of God in Africa*, "Missionaries were dependent upon African evangelistic zeal and expertise in the growth of Christianity... from the ranks of these... (came) the future leaders of the African Church". p. 237.

[11] Kinoti, George, *Hope for Africa and What the Christian Can Do*, AISRED, Nairobi: 1994, pgs. 74-75.

churches, it is the American influence that is ubiquitous in the form of dramatic extemporaneous sermons and emotion-laden worship.

Yet, not all Anglo-American missionaries had ties to RVA. In fact, it was generally only the evangelical missions who relied on RVA for their children's education. Therefore, if we hope to gauge the effect of RVA on the region we must look to the relative influence of the particular brand of Christianity that originated from those missionaries tied to the school – Evangelicalism. The numbers are significant; over half the Christians in Kenya (13 million) are evangelicals – a total nearly equaling the number of evangelicals in all of Europe.[12] As expected, the hallmarks of evangelicalism – sharing one's faith (evangelism), the "born again" experience and the authority of Scripture in all issues of doctrine, spiritual life and ethics – can be found throughout Kenyan culture.[13] This is true to the extent that social introductions in Kenya often make explicit reference to the person's identity as a "born again" Christian.[14] Simply put, the influence in East Africa of the distinctively Anglo-American variety of evangelical Christianity has been massive.

But many have argued that the numbers and external trappings can be misleading – both in terms of the extent of Western influence and in terms of the depth to which Christianity has taken root in the region. On the positive side, there is evidence everywhere that the Church in Kenya has developed a degree of self-confidence that is allowing it to borrow liberally from the American Church in particular while forging out a distinctly African brand of Christianity. Indeed, Kinoti goes on to state that, "the time has come for African Christians to begin to think and do things for themselves".[15]

Less clear is the depth to which Christian beliefs have taken root in the hearts and minds of average Kenyans. In fact, many have argued that the legacy of the missionaries in Kenya is a church that is like a river "a mile wide and an inch deep". At times Christianity, while undermining much in traditional African culture, seems to have made little positive

---

[12] *Operation World*, 2001 "Kenya", p. 381.

[13] The "hallmarks" of evangelicalism are adapted from Alister McGrath's, *A Passion for Truth: The Intellectual Coherence of Evangelicalism*, IVP, Downers Grove, IL: 1996, p. 22.

[14] Casual introductions in Kenya, often follow along these lines, "Hello, I'm Jonathan Kariuki and I'm saved"; or, "Hello, my name is Jane Mutere and I love the Lord Jesus as my personal savior". In addition, on most days there are multiple evangelistic crusades taking place in Nairobi – Uhuru Park itself often has two going simultaneously.

[15] Kinoti, George, *Hope for Africa*, p 74-75.

impact on the social, moral and political economy of Kenya. Towards this end, some prominent historians have argued that by undermining traditional culture missionaries created a social and moral free-for-all and are thus responsible for many of the nation's problems.[16] And, the problems are staggering. Unemployment at the turn of the 21st century was above 40% and economic growth had stagnated, creating a rise in real poverty. Making matters worse, the immediate causes of economic stagnation seemed to be well entrenched and growing. By the 1990's Kenya regularly made the list of the top ten most corrupt nations in the world, the crippling national debt was 8.5 billion dollars and rising, and sexual promiscuity had pushed the numbers of working age Kenyans with HIV/AIDS above the two million mark.[17] Prompted by this bleak picture, Kinoti expressed the bitter irony that, "Christianity is growing faster in Africa than on any other continent. At the same time the people are rapidly becoming poorer and the moral and social fabrics of society are disintegrating fast. Christianity is clearly not making a significant difference to African nations".[18] However, Kinoti goes on to state that, in his opinion, the problem is not Christianity at all but the fact that Christianity has not truly permeated the hearts and minds of individual African Christians and the corporate perspective of the African Christian community; and that even when it has begun to affect the fundamental values of the African, it has been applied to the spiritual life only and not to the totality of life – a problem he blames on American evangelicalism's non-holistic influence.

And yet, by the turn of the century there are increasing signs that the Christian church and its message are beginning to fill the moral and cultural void left by the fragmentation of traditional African culture. Indeed, there is evidence that a distinctly African form of Christianity is starting to positively transform the social, moral and political economy of Kenya. The growth in the depth and breadth of African Christian leadership is but one example of the increasing Christianization of Africa and Africanization of Christianity. Kinoti's widely read book was itself one such sign. Besides being a prophetic critique of the Kenyan church, *Hope for Africa* was essentially a heartfelt call to authentic life-transforming faith. But Kinoti was not a lone voice crying in the wilderness. Throughout 1980's and '90's the Kenyan church became

---

[16] Basil Davidson is probably the most famous historian to make this claim, but he is just one of many. Davidson makes this claim throughout his many written works on Africa and in his video documentary series, *Africa*.

[17] *CIA World Fact Book* 2002, "Kenya".

[18] Kinoti, George, *Hope for Africa*, p. 1

increasingly outspoken against corruption and tyranny in Kenyan economic and political life. Some clergy lost their lives as a result of this struggle, while others continued to speak out in spite of ongoing physical and psychological intimidation. During this time, organizations like *Christians for a Just Society* began to come out of the woodwork, complementing the voice of the *National Council of Churches of Kenya* (NCCK) as it spoke out on issues like the politically motivated tribal clashes of the 1990's. By the turn of the Century, reform movements everywhere in Kenya seemed tied to the Church – not least of which was the call for a new national constitution.

Every bit as important as these high profile examples of Christianity's deepening influence on Kenyan society are the countless grassroots movements that have sprung up to meet the many challenges facing the nation. Notable among these has been the response of Christians within Nairobi's infamous slums to the tragically growing number of street children in the city. In the last five years alone the number of Christian organizations set up specifically to meet the needs of street children has more than doubled. What is more impressive still is the fact that while some of these have been started and run by missionaries, the vast majority are Kenyan initiatives, often organized and run on little or no budget.[19]

Movements like the one working with the street children of Nairobi give substance to perhaps the greatest sign of positive change in Kenya – the election of 2002. It may be years before any definitive verdict can be made on the results of that historic election. However, both the rhetoric and actions of the politicians during and immediately after the election have been cause for cautious optimism. Christian congregations were at the center of this peaceful revolution. Sermon after sermon before and after the election explicitly called on Kenyan Christians to apply their faith to the totality of life – taking a stand against corruption and speaking out for social justice. Notable also has been the placement of outspoken Christians to prominent positions within the new government – the Foreign Minister, the new head of the military and the nation's new Chief Justice among others. Of course, skepticism still abounds, and even the most optimistic Kenyans will concede that the battle for Kenya's cultural soul is only beginning. And yet as Kenya begins a new

---

[19] Insights on the exciting grassroots movement of Christians tackling the daunting issue of street children come from a variety of sources. Most significantly from the data collected by the Urban Ministries Serving God (UMSG) in Nairobi.

century there are good reasons for hope and many of these reasons can be traced to the deepening influence of Christianity on the public and private ethics of Kenya.

No one would argue that the missionary parents of RVA's students are exclusively responsible for this transformation. Even the spread of evangelicalism cannot be attributed solely to the American evangelicals tied to RVA. As historian Roland Oliver wrote, "the main lesson of African ecclesiastical history is that the core message tended to run far ahead of its expatriate preachers".[20] Yet it is almost as rash to argue that the role of American evangelicals has been trivial. Beyond their task of bringing the Christian message to Kenya and nurturing the growth of that faith in countless individuals over the last century, Anglo-American missionaries have been fundamental in developing the written forms of the indigenous languages that have been at the core of the growth of literacy in the nation. Anglo-American missionaries were also the pioneers of education in the country and continue to play a significant role, especially in the realm of higher education, through teaching and administration in the growing number of private Christian liberal arts colleges, universities and theological schools around the country.[21]

Evangelism, discipleship and education (theological and otherwise) have traditionally been at the core of the missionary enterprise and, without question, the parents of RVA's students have been the vanguard of each of these in Kenya. As we have seen, American style evangelicalism accounts for over half of Kenya's Christians and is growing. In addition, American Bible schools and colleges can be found throughout the country and the majority of the best Protestant seminaries were also started and run by missionaries whose children attended RVA – among these are Scott Theological Seminary (AIM), Nairobi Evangelical Graduate School of Theology (Interdenominational) and Nairobi International School of Theology (Campus Crusade for Christ – Life Ministry).

And yet over the century, the missionary parents of RVA's students have also been critical to a variety of other work around the country. Missionary initiated and run hospitals were among the first in the country – certainly the first to give quality care to the black African population – and these continue to be numbered among the best in the country (AIM's

---

[20] Oliver, Roland, *The African Experience*, Harper Collins, San Francisco: 1991, p. 204
[21] The most notable of these are Daystar University and African Nazarene University - both on the outskirts of Nairobi – but many others exist.

Kijabe and the World Gospel Mission's Tenwek hospitals are the most obvious examples here but others exist). And finally, an increasing number of RVA parents can be found in work that can be categorized as relief and development – especially in the areas of AIDS awareness, water resource management and agricultural development. This relatively recent broadening of the scope of evangelical missions to include more holistic ministries is further evidence of the role that the missionary experience in Africa has had on the worldview of the missionaries themselves, as well as the American evangelical church they represent.

In short, the legacy of RVA's missionary parents has been profound.[22] To begin with, they were among the pioneering missionaries who first brought the Christian message to East Africa. Just as significantly, RVA's missionary parents stayed in the region for long periods of time – sometimes for a lifetime. This longevity was critical to the nurturing and discipling of the many young African converts – critical because it was this group of young indigenous church leaders and evangelists who turned the region upside down. Similarly, the secular education, initiated by these same missionaries, was an essential ingredient in the strong political leadership Kenya was to enjoy as a young republic. Amidst this impressive resume it is easy to forget that RVA's missionary parents also translated a multitude of indigenous languages in the hopes of providing the Bible in the vernacular. In the process they helped bolster a sense of pride among the many ethnic groups in the region. That same zealous emphasis on the centrality of the Bible, especially notable among the mission groups tied to RVA, also provided seeds for the dramatic cultural revolution still taking place in East Africa. Finally, RVA's missionary parents have also been responsible for the creation and administration of a considerable number of first-rate universities, hospitals and agricultural projects in the region. And this is just their legacy in East Africa. Over a century, as they have wrestled with the difficult issues raised by cross-cultural interaction and third world poverty, the parents of RVA's students have also been at the forefront of the important evolution within the Anglo-American Church towards a less provincial conception of Christianity.

BUT WHAT OF the school and its students? What is their legacy to the RVA students of today? Without question, the most remarkable characteristic of the school has been its legacy as a greenhouse of future

---

[22] See Appendix B.

missionaries. As the 21st Century dawns AIM is seeing RVA MKs return as fourth generation missionaries. Significantly, this legacy of RVA has not only applied to AIM families. The new generation of American missionaries that came to East Africa during the idealistic sixties is now seeing their RVA-educated children join them on the mission field. As we have already seen, over one-fourth of the class of 1988 have gone on to serve as missionaries – some to build on the work begun by their parents, others to new support positions under African Christian leadership, and still others to begin fresh work amongst the remaining unreached people-groups of Africa. In choosing a life as an evangelical missionary, these RVA graduates have added much to the considerable legacy of their missionary parents. In this way the two-pronged legacy of RVA – the work of the school's missionary parents and the lives of the students themselves – has come full circle.

But the legacy of RVA and its students is not limited to RVA's direct role in the evangelical missionary enterprise in Africa. The school's academic heritage is both impressive and bewildering. In keeping with the pattern of other mission boarding schools around the world, RVA has for many years maintained a record of SAT scores one-hundred points above the American national average; and of sending over 90% of its students on to post-secondary education. These numbers are impressive by virtually anyone's standards. Oddly, those impressive statistics have not seemed to produce the results one might expect from such a highly educated group of alumni. Despite the school's history in the 1950's of producing an astonishing percentage of renowned writers and academics, RVA can boast very few alumni since who have gone on to considerable wealth or fame. The strange combination in the RVA alumni of significant academic success and limited public accomplishments is not entirely unexpected however when one considers motives fueling the average RVA graduate. As we have seen, a considerable proportion of RVA alumni have chosen to return overseas in service-oriented work. Choosing a life of service over the allure of wealth and fame makes sense when taking into account the values of Christian service and stewardship most alumni had been surrounded by both at home and at school. A life of service makes even more sense when we add to the values of the missionary community the RVA MKs unavoidable contact with third world poverty.

It is also not surprising that RVA graduates have, in general, not made a name for themselves in the world of academia. From the very beginning, the school has exhibited strong evidence of the anti-intellectual roots of its fundamentalist beginnings. Since WWII this anti-intellectual tendency has begun to dissipate, reflecting the influence of an increasing inclination within American evangelicalism to take the life of the mind seriously – as a spiritual duty. Nevertheless, old prejudices die hard and it may be years still before the school's graduates consistently view academia as a calling worthy of a committed Christian.

A second major category in the legacy of the school and its students is the role the school has played over the generations as a bridge between cultures. As the phenomenon of globalization has grown, the mixing of cultures that has gone into creating the Third Culture at RVA is no longer unique. And yet the results of the cultural synergy at RVA remain noteworthy – some might even say bizarre. Indeed, it is not too much to say that the school community is something of an enigma for many. The Washington Post likened it to, "a green American village... (and) a Midwestern town...".[23] Yet in this American village Rugby, a British game, is the sport of choice, Indian curry is preferred over hot dogs, and the first of July (Canada's national day) is celebrated with almost as much fervor as the fourth (America's national day). Here Kenyan students speak with American accents, Americans speak with Kenyan accents and students from more than thirty nationalities can converse in a dialect that no one outside of the school community could hope to understand. In short, RVA is an anomaly – a culture unique unto itself. It is neither American, Kenyan, British, nor any other single culture; but instead represents a dynamic and complex combination of all these cultures and traditions.

As a result of growing up in this unique third culture, for a century RVA students have brought with them wherever they have gone a distinctly broad understanding of their world. They have not always been completely understood, but when tapped this perspective has allowed the RVA MK to challenge the status quo worldviews of both the evangelical and the western worlds. In thousands of individual relationships RVA graduates have helped others see a bigger, if not always better, world. As a result, they have been at the forefront of the "global village" phenomenon. In this sense, the RVA graduate has been the "prototype of the 21st century person".[24]

But that role has not always come cheaply. Like their peers of one hundred years ago, today's RVA students have seen poverty and human suffering virtually unimaginable in the West. Many have had to wrestle with the hosts of crises linked to the trauma of social and cultural

---

[23] *Washington Post*, Feb. 2, 1993 – Susan Okie, "School in the Clouds".
[24] Ted Ward, as quoted in Pollack and Van Reken, *The TCK Experience*.

transitions. Still others have witnessed disillusioning hypocrisy from the words and actions of their missionary parents or teachers. A few have felt the loneliness and anger that they would have felt in their "home cultures" exacerbated by the boarding experience. And thus, having been deeply damaged by their TCK experience, some have floundered for a lifetime, isolated by their unique experiences from the healing experience of faith and friendship.

And yet for many, the difficult experiences of poverty, hypocrisy, separation and cross-cultural interaction have produced dynamic and emotionally healthy individuals. For these RVA alumni, the difficult experiences of the MK (because they have been experienced within the context of authentic faith and a loving family) have been a springboard from which they have leapt onto extraordinary and unique lives. In many of these lives the pioneering spirit of the early missionaries lives on. That reality is certainly reflected in the case study of the class of 1988. This class has seen its members choose lives unimaginable to the faint of heart – taking themselves and their young families to poverty-stricken Guinea Bissau, the war-torn Democratic Republic of Congo, and the strictly Islamic societies of northern Sudan and Djibouti to name only a few.

The uniqueness of the TCK experience has added to the RVA legacy at least one more significant piece. The very uniqueness that has had the potential to socially isolate RVA alumni from their Anglo-America peers has been the glue binding them to the community of MKs around the world. For generations, as the alumni of RVA have left Kijabe and spread out across the globe, they have discovered their standing membership in already existing communities of individuals who share the same heritage of cross-cultural experiences and deeply held evangelical beliefs and values. Surrounded by societies that often either ignore or misunderstand them, these individual MKs have found in each other an astonishingly deep level of understanding and community – one that in some ways exceeds the benefits of membership solely in the larger American or Commonwealth culture.

That same community principle is multiplied when applied to the mutual understanding and familial loyalty experienced wherever pockets of RVA alumni find each other. This is the case regardless of whether the individual's RVA experience was positive or negative. No one else can understand the experience of standing on Kiambogo porch as the sun sets over the Great Rift Valley. No one else has lain in their dorm bunk listening to the biting Kijabe wind tear through the surrounding forests or enjoyed the late night sprints back to the dormitory after the Saturday night video. Like membership in a family, whether it is healthy or unhealthy, emotional ties to the RVA community last a lifetime; and the individuals who make it up have the potential to understand and support each other in a way that few others can.

The test of time has proven that RVA's legacy of community is as consistent as it is profound. But has the community at RVA been a healthy one? Just as members of the same family may have very different feelings about the same set of experiences, opinions on the health of the RVA community vary significantly from one alumnus to the next. Nevertheless, the school's longevity and its large number of graduates do allow for some tentative generalizations. When considering the health of the school's community, it is critical that we do so within the context of the community's two most fundamental characteristics – an atmosphere of isolation and its fervent evangelical Christianity.

From its first days to the present, RVA has been a physically and, at times culturally, isolated community. Yet as we have seen, it is an enormous mistake to characterize that isolation as "total" or "absolute". Whether it was the outreach orientation of the school's evangelicalism, the infusion into the school by new missionaries of fresh trends in the Western worldview and culture, or the ever-intruding influence of Kenyan politics and culture – real isolation was never an option. Nevertheless, the type of community that has developed at RVA over the last century has been influenced by an awareness of isolation – both real and imagined. That sense of isolation, when combined with the evangelical Christian ethos of the community, is at the core of the school's legacy of community.

Those who have chosen to view the atmosphere of isolation negatively have easily found in RVA an ever-shrinking community, where the sense of cultural claustrophobia is only eclipsed by the feeling of forced conformity. When they have recoiled against the perceived legalistic constraints of the community, they have done so within the confines of a relational and intellectual fishbowl. As a result, they have often had to live with a feeling of self-imposed ostracism, merciless gossip and public judgment – without the hope of escape. The reality is that over its one hundred year history as an institution, RVA has permitted the growth of a culture of gossip and has had to endure more than its share of Phariseeism. Yet, to stereotype the community as something akin to the Puritans of the *Scarlet Letter* is to ignore the experience of large numbers of the school's students and graduates.

Indeed, over the years many have viewed that same atmosphere of isolation in a far more positive light. Where some have felt intrusive judgmentalism, others have found accountability and spiritual encouragement. Where some have found a community of like-minded lemmings, others have thrived and grown because of the deep sense of intimacy and mutual understanding they enjoyed within the community. Where some felt imprisoned by the consequences of defying excessively restrictive school guidelines, others have accepted the rules and been surprised by an astonishing amount of freedom. For this group, the sense of isolation at RVA only added to its rich sense of community. Indeed, while not the fault of the school, for some the irony is that that healthy experience has made the transition from RVA to their home culture all the more difficult. Said one graduate,

> I remember vividly the almost idyllic life I had there...the friends, living in the dorm, the Christian atmosphere, all contributed to the life I look back on and ...wish for again... Some of the tumult I went through in college made me cynical towards anything so ideal, so virtually pain-free. I was mad at the fact that life didn't turn out to be as I expected it would when I was at RVA.[25]

IF THE LEGACY of the Rift Valley Academy is nothing else, it is surprising. Part of the surprise concerns the extent of the school's influence. When the visionary Charles Hurlburt began the school in 1906 he did it in faith that one day the missionary movement would grow large enough that its children would fill the fifty-bed school. In the last twenty years alone, nearly two thousand MKs have graduated from the school and gone onto higher education around the world. But the unexpected significance of the school's legacy is not primarily found in the number of graduates, but in the unexpectedly large role those graduates have played in the evolution of East Africa - especially in the form of second and third generation missionaries. By conveying the message of Christianity to the most remote reaches of the East Africa, RVA parents and alumni have been critical to one of the most remarkable cultural transformations in world history. To be sure, the RVA parents and alumni were not, by themselves, responsible for this transformation. Nor were the school's graduates all exceptional individuals. Indeed, outside of their uniquely cross-cultural childhood there was little about them that could be called remarkable. They were simply obedient to the calling passed on to them by their parents and

---

[25] Letter from Heather Dunkerton to the author dated, Nov. 14, 1997. The letter remains in the possession of the author.

nurtured by the radically evangelical community at RVA. And yet, because they spoke out within a culture that was ripe for the message of Christianity, their influence has been entirely out of proportion to their abilities and their numbers.[26]

As we have just seen, parts of RVA's legacy are surprising, not because they were unexpected per se, but because they were unexpectedly large. Other parts of the school's legacy, however, are surprising in themselves. They are surprising because they were unintended. For instance, when RVA began, its goal was to provide for MKs an education suitable for their future return to North America in order that missionary parents might be at ease to continue their work in Africa. However, by pursuing this basic aim, the school allowed the MK to remain in Africa as well and in doing so, played a pioneering role in creating a new type of person – the TCK. Whether praised for their global perspective or pitied for their traumatic childhood, the missionary TCK has been at the cutting edge of the movement towards globalization. As such, RVA graduates find themselves uniquely suited for positions of leadership and influence in our brave new world.

Through their significant role in the missionary movement RVA alumni, in the form of second and third generation missionaries, have also been a part of the unexpected outcomes of the missionary movement in East Africa. For starters, it is hard to imagine a more politically and culturally conservative group than the American evangelical missionary community. In fact, AIM and other American evangelical missions have been consistently criticized by African leaders (secular and sacred a like) for their uncompromising apolitical perspective. And yet, the education provided by Anglo-American evangelicals, for the expressed purpose of creating Biblical literacy was one of the critical forces behind the explosion of revolutionary politics in East and Central Africa during the 1950s. Said one nationalist in Zimbabwe, "When Europeans took our country we fought them with our spears, but they defeated us because they had better weapons... But lo! The missionary came in time and laid explosives under colonialism. The Bible is now doing what we could not

---

[26] The important role that traditional culture played in the spread of Christianity – by acting as a foundation conducive to the Christian message – cannot be overestimated. Richard Gray has noted that, "African Christianity is not the result of brainwashing by foreign missionaries... (but rather spread because) it was seen to meet... some of the longstanding needs and demands of African societies". As quoted in Mark Shaw's *The Kingdom of God in Africa*, p. 235.

do with our spears".[27] As far back as the 1920's one British missionary in Kenya began to see the surprising political consequences of the apparently conservative missionary message saying,

> (The missionary) tells them of... a Kingdom in which all men have equal opportunity, of a Heavenly Father who has no favorites in His world-wide family, of a brotherhood that knows nothing of race or colour. Such teaching is bound to be revolutionary; it cannot be otherwise. Wherever we go, if we are true to our message, we are bound to turn the world upside down.[28]

These political implications of the Gospel were either not understood or were explicitly discouraged by American evangelicals. Yet, while American missionaries encouraged their converts to steer clear of politics, these African Christians found in the Bible a radical political message. Thus in the supreme irony, it was the influence of the most outspokenly apolitical mission – AIM – that produced the first outspokenly Christian president in the young Kenyan Republic.

The final surprise in the legacy of RVA concerns what academics have termed "agency". The initial missionary model, and the one that even many of RVA's first graduates operated under, held to the assumption that Anglo-American missionaries were the "agents" of change acting upon a passive African people. In other words, agency, or the power to act, was solely in the hands of the missionary. However, the missionary aim of conversion through persuasion quickly revealed a far more complex picture – one in which both the evangelist and the evangelized were active participants in the dynamic exchange of ideas and values. In short, in order to convert, the missionary needed to listen and in the act of listening the missionary was changed. Parents of RVA students, and later the students themselves, set out to transform a culture – and in many ways they did – but one of the unexpected legacies of the school has been the change in the perspective of the Western Church

---

[27] Ndabaningi Sithole as quoted in John Lonsdale's "Mission Christianity & Settler Colonialism in Eastern Africa" found in *Christian Missionaries & the State in the Third World*, edited by Holger Bernt Hansen and Michael Twaddle, James Currey Ltd, Oxford: 2002.

[28] Archdeacon Walter Owen as quoted in, John Lonsdale's "Mission Christianity & Settler Colonialism in Eastern Africa" found in *Christian Missionaries & the State in the Third World*, edited by Holger Bernt Hansen and Michael Twaddle, James Currey Ltd, Oxford: 2002.

seen most dramatically in the radically altered worldview of the Christian TCK.

For a relatively small, geographically isolated and culturally enigmatic school, RVA's legacy to its students and the world around it has been surprisingly significant. On an individual level, the school has been home to thousands of missionary children as they have negotiated, not only the precarious challenges of adolescence, but the additional obstacles linked to growing up in a cross-cultural context. Many times the school has succeeded admirably, developing in its students strong minds, healthy hearts and vibrant faith. These children have gone on to live remarkable lives – some by building on the work of their missionary parents and many others by acting as trailblazers of globalization.

At other times the school has been less successful. As an institution, the school has not always been able to meet the unique needs of all of its students. For some of these students, RVA has exacerbated personal problems that might have been dealt with in a healthier way elsewhere. Further, as an evangelical missionary institution, the school has also been an unconscious carrier of aspects of that movement – both positive and negative. For instance, despite the fact that evangelical missionaries were leaders in destroying racial and cultural stereotypes, the school was not immune from the prejudices predominant in Western culture, and at times did pass these on to its graduates.

Yet in the end, the influence of the Rift Valley Academy has been profoundly positive – both in terms of the lives of its graduates and its influence on the evolution of East Africa. The school has not single-handedly turned the region upside down; but it has been a central component in a movement that has done just that. Anglo-American missionaries, and more specifically the American evangelical missionaries tied to RVA, have played a critical part in changes that have fundamentally remapped the spiritual, moral and political landscape of East Africa. It is quite possible that Protestant Christianity would have succeeded in the region without RVA and the evangelical missionaries it represents. But it is certain that without this "School in the Clouds", the spiritual and political culture of the region would look significantly different.

WHAT LIES AROUND THE BEND?

OVER THE LAST CENTURY, EVANGELICAL MISSIONARIES have had an influence in Kenya well beyond their ability or numbers. However, by helping to create a new world, the evangelical missionary movement may have also jeopardized its own future and the future of all of its institutions – including RVA. In short, there may no longer be a place for RVA in the world it helped to create. Therefore, having reflected at length on the school's rich past, it is appropriate that we conclude by briefly considering what the future may hold for this "School in the Clouds".

The truth is, that even as the sun of a new century rises over the transformed African landscape, RVA's future remains as misty as the Kijabe morning air. What is clear is that three forces partially outside of its control will determine the future of the school: (a) the future of the larger Anglo-American missionary movement; (b) the nature of America's involvement in the world affairs of the 21st Century; and (c) the evolution of the political and cultural climate of Kenya.

ANY DISCUSSION OF RVA's future must begin by considering the future of the missionary movement the school supports and feeds. Simply stated, if the missionary movement becomes a thing of the past, RVA, in its present form, will also cease to exist. What, then, is the future of the missionary movement? The question itself might strike some as strange. For isn't Christianity inherently evangelistic? And if it is, doesn't it follow that the missionary movement is simply an inevitable outgrowth of the faith?

Strangely, History tells us that the modern missionary movement was not inevitable. In fact, as a mass movement of evangelical Christian outreach to the remotest corners of the globe, the missionary movement is hardly two hundred years old. That is not to say that it took Christians eighteen hundred years to discover the Great Commission, not at all. Christians throughout the ages have been aware of the need to spread the "Good News". Instead, it is to say that at most points in the history of Christianity its inherent missionary spirit has been hindered by either technological and logistical limitations or restrained by the political, cultural or economic realities of a given historical era. The modern missionary movement is something new in world history and it happened because there was a convergence of a unique set of historical circumstances that may not remain indefinitely.

The circumstances needed to produce the modern missionary movement included: (a) a society with the ample political and religious freedom necessary to allow the free association of Christian enthusiasts (political liberalism); (b) a social culture that encouraged religious zeal and the voluntary societies built around that zeal (cultural evangelicalism); (c) an economy with a surplus of capital capable of financing the international network of voluntary missionary societies bred by this politically free and religiously vibrant climate (industrial capitalism); and (d) the ability to move both the financial capital and the zealous heirs of this vibrant socio-religious culture freely around the world (geopolitical imperialism). For the first time in world history all of these were present at one time in one nation – Nineteenth Century Britain.[1]

As the 20th Century progressed, the critical components of this cultural cocktail diminished in Britain to such a degree that the once generous flow of missionaries out from its shores slowed to a trickle. Not only did the sun set on the empire that had opened up the world to "Christianity and Commerce", but the cultural and religious climate within Britain had changed dramatically – having grown increasingly suspicious of the type of faith epitomized by the voluntary societies that produced the early British missionaries. These two factors alone were

---

[1] This insight first came to my attention as a result of Andrew Wall's chapter "The American Dimension of the Missionary Movement" as found in *The Missionary Movement in Christian History*, Orbis Books, Maryknoll, NY: 1996. I have altered his categories in minor ways.

enough to stifle evangelical missions in Britain, but the relative decline in British economic strength seemed to seal the missionary movement's demise there.

The good news for the missionary movement was that during the same period a very different story was developing in America. Whether the result of its periodic nation-wide religious awakenings, the religious vitality created by the separation of Church and State, the spiritual implications of the frontier experience or some combination of these – the religious climate in America was growing increasingly vibrant. As a result of its political freedoms and religious enthusiasm, America began to produce global missionary societies late in the 19th Century. Still, it was not until the middle of the 20th Century, when the Second World War forced the country out of its self-imposed isolationism, that that dynamic religious culture combined with America's astonishing economic power to create a missionary movement in scope and size larger than anything the world had yet seen.

Those forces continue to thrive in America and from all indications will continue to do so well into the 21st Century. The spiritual climate continues to be vibrant. The percentage of evangelicals is on the rise, and has been for the last fifty years.[2] That spiritual vitality has also translated into political clout. The first American president of the 21st Century not only claims to have a deep evangelical faith but has been an active champion of evangelical causes both within America and around the globe.[3] In addition, the wealth necessary to sustain a substantial missionary movement continues to be abundant in America. At the turn of the 21st Century the American economy equaled the size of the next five largest economies in the world combined (Japan, Germany, China, France and Britain).[4] Finally, because that economic might is increasingly reliant on global forces, the once isolated nation seems to

---

[2] *Operation World* (1991 ed.), p. 435.

[3] Early in 2003 President Bush, responding to missionary pleas, proposed a fifteen billion dollar plan to fight AIDS in Africa (an amount that almost doubles Kenya's annual GDP). *Newsweek* magazine called the plan, "a favorite project of Christian missionaries who want the chance to save souls there as well as beleaguered lives". *Newsweek*, "Bush and God", March 10, 2003.

[4] According to the 2000 *World Almanac* America's GDP was 9.96 trillion dollars annually. The next five largest economies were Japan (4.8 trillion), Germany (1.9 trillion), UK (1.4 trillion), France (1.2 trillion) and China (1.1 trillion). The combined GDP of those nations is 10.4 trillion compared to the US GDP of 9.96 trillion. It is important to keep in mind that after this point the size of the following nations GDP's drops off significantly.

have embraced a new form of imperialism – albeit one characterized by political persuasion and economic influence. In short, all indications are that America will continue to produce significant numbers of evangelical missionaries.

IF THIS WERE the entire story it would seem that the future of RVA is secure. American missionaries will continue to spread out across Africa; and therefore, RVA will be needed to serve the unique needs of their children. But that is not the whole story. While it looks like America will continue to produce significant numbers of missionaries, for a number of reasons there is decreasing assurance the world will continue to accept these missionaries. In contrast to the world under the British Empire, where a colonial administration sympathetic to Anglo-American missionaries physically controlled regions, missionaries acting within the so-called American Empire have only the political persuasion and economic incentives of the American government to lean on. Thus, without a geographic empire forcing doors open for them, there are no longer guarantees that evangelical missionaries will be allowed into the independent countries of the 21st Century.

In addition, when one considers the nature of American involvement worldwide, prospects for the missionary movement grow increasingly bleak. A major advantage of the American missionary movement in the 20th Century was their status as political and cultural neutrals. Despite their cultural alliance with British values and beliefs, American missionaries were able to function within the British Empire without much of the baggage associated with being British. They were not seen as agents of British Imperialism and thus were often treated as the altruistic missionaries they believed themselves to be.

America's dominant place in the world today has destroyed the image of cultural and political neutrality once enjoyed by its missionaries. To begin with, America's military power has created an almost hysterical fear of America and inspired a reactionary Anti-Americanism that is without parallel. To put things into perspective, even at its peak the British Empire never rivaled the military power experienced by America at the turn of the 21st Century. In fact, many pundits and historians now argue that the world has never seen the type of dominance enjoyed by the United States today. Charles Krauthammer contends, "no country has been as dominant culturally, economically, technologically and militarily in the history of the world since the Roman

Empire".[5]   Yale historian Paul Kennedy goes even further in saying, "Nothing has ever existed like this disparity of power".[6]   Making matters worse is America's apparently increasing willingness to use that power – even in the face of widespread international opposition as seen in the second Gulf War of 2003.

It is likely that America's military power alone would have created hysterical Anti-American sentiment. But American capitalism and pop-culture have also added fuel to global anti-Americanism. In a way that was scarcely imaginable during the height of the British Empire, the communication and information revolutions of the late 20th Century have created a profoundly connected world; and that connected world bears the unmistakable imprint of American pop culture. Whether you walk the streets of Buenos Aires, Munich, Istanbul, Tokyo or Nairobi, teenagers sing along to the music of Busta Rhymes and Puff Daddy. In the world's movie theatres people of all ages drink Coke while watching the latest Hollywood thriller. When they finally retreat to the sanctuary of their homes, much of the globe chooses to spend their evenings with the characters of *Friends* or *West Wing*. And when they slip off to sleep it is the anchors of CNN that bid the world's population goodnight. American pop culture is ubiquitous.[7]

It is safe to say that at no time in World History has an image of a nation been as widely dispersed. For the American missionary this image might well be debilitating. For, accurate or not, Hollywood's depiction of life in America is one consumed by violence, immorality and greed. Increasingly, when people around the world see an American missionary, what they see first is not a Christian but an American and when they see an American they see these very unchristian traits. As historian Andrew Walls has remarked, "A missionary's effectiveness, or even sincerity, will sometimes be measured by the extent to which the message preached is reflected in the nation from which he or she comes; the higher the nation's visibility in the world the more likely is this measure to be used".[8]

---

[5] As quoted in the *Seattle Times*, in Emily Eakin's piece "Let American 'empire' rule, enthusiasts say", Sunday March 31, 2002
[6] Ibid.
[7] According to the World Almanac, the top 10 movies (in terms of worldwide profits) of all time are products of Hollywood.
[8] Walls, Andrew, "The American Dimension of the Missionary Movement" found in *The Missionary Movement in Christian History*, Orbis, Maryknoll, NY: 1996, p. 238.

In East Africa, where anti-Americanism exists but is moderated by the prominence of American-style evangelicalism, an additional set of issues further threaten the missionary movement and its institutions. Sadly, one of those issues is the checkered historical record of a few early missionaries. While most missionaries have been laudable examples of the Christian life, there have been some whose words and deeds have done deep and lasting harm to both the African Church and the missionary movement. And even those who acted upon motives of sincerity and service were often culturally ignorant and made their share of mistakes. The bitter taste of these mistakes still lingers in the mouths of some Kenyans and boils to the surface occasionally in blanket condemnations of "missionary imperialism" by church leaders and politicians alike. Yet generally speaking, anti-Americanism and the blemished record of missionary history are not the primary reasons for anti-missionary rhetoric in East Africa. More significant is the question of whether the Western missionary is needed any longer. Such a question has real weight in Kenya especially where there are nearly as many evangelicals as in the entire continent of Europe and where indigenous Christians have for some time provided leadership for the national church.

Because many in Kenya believe a missionary presence is no longer needed, the political establishment, long sympathetic to Christian missionaries, has begun to slowly remove the incentives and safeguards previously provided for missionaries. Most significant among these are the threatened changes in tax law which could force many less affluent mission organizations and NGOs from Kenya. In addition, while the government has traditionally been careful to preserve the sanctity of contract concerning land issues, events in neighboring Zimbabwe now act as a constant reminder to the missionary community that their properties (whether they be hospitals, colleges, national schools, homes or support institutions like RVA) are only as secure as the political and economic climate of the country. The more valuable the land, and the more that land has been developed, the greater the threat that that land will be taken from them. Late in 2002 RVA was reminded again just how vulnerable it is when one of the prominent television stations in Kenya aired a primetime documentary on Kijabe in which both the missionary controlled properties of RVA and the mission hospital were conspicuously contrasted with the relative poverty of the local community.[9]

In sum, despite American evangelicalism's continuing willingness and ability to send missionaries to East Africa, growing anti-Americanism worldwide, a spotted missionary past, and, most importantly, an apparently diminished need for outside assistance, has led many to assume that the days of the American missionary in East Africa days are numbered. It is, therefore, not surprising that for sometime missionaries and indigenous leaders have also assumed they were experiencing RVA's twilight years. And they may be right. Certainly the teacher-student relationship of the earlier missionary eras seems to be largely a thing of the past. In fact, in many instances that relationship has reversed. But a change in the relationship does not necessitate an end. Indeed, there are a number of reasons that make it likely that RVA, as a school primarily for American MKs, will continue to thrive well into the 21st Century.

TO BEGIN WITH, the very strength of the Kenyan Church that prompted criticism of foreign missionaries is also responsible for a maturing self-confidence within the Church. Because it is clear that the Kenyan Church is no longer reliant on foreign missionaries there is increasing openness within the church to a new type of partnership with Christians from outside the region in which all parties function as both teachers and students. Visionary churches like Nairobi Chapel have been global leaders in forging these new international partnerships. That same mature self-confidence in Kenya is behind the emerging conception of the Church as a genuinely global body where every part has an important role to play. As Mutava Musyemi put it, "There should always be room for a healthy... cross pollenization. It (the Church) is a family – it is a global family. It spans borders, it spans race, it spans generations... I think it is important that the Christian family sees itself as one family, prepared to receive and to give to each other in a dignified and genuine way".[10]

In this spirit there remain significant ways in which the American church can continue to support, and be supported by, the East African church. While the Kenyan Church is capable of fulfilling its mission of

---

[9] The documentary was shown on *Nation TV* during the month of December 2002.

[10] Personal interview with Mutava Musyemi on Jan. 3, 2000 at his home in Nairobi.

evangelism and discipleship alone, even in these areas there is some room for non-Kenyan assistance. For starters, efforts to evangelize the remaining unreached people groups in Kenya are often prohibitively expensive. While the Kenyan church is taking a leadership role in both the financial and spiritual support of missionaries to non-Christian Kenyans, the limited resources of the local church requires it to choose between a variety of evangelistic options. The limited number of people that can be reached by rural missionary efforts means that the church's limited resources more often go to urban or densely populated rural efforts.[11] The American Church, with its abundance of zealous evangelicals and financial capital, is more able to support efforts to reach people groups like the Daasanach and Pokot people.[12] As a result, some of the more stereotypical missionary work continues to be done by Americans.[13]

The same principle can be applied to the Kenyan Church's larger goal of developing growing disciples of Christ. This goal requires not only spiritual depth and zeal (which Kenya certainly has) but significant amounts of time, energy and finances. Time, energy and finances are what the American church in particular has in abundance and is eagerly willing to offer. Assuming that American missionaries serve under or alongside the national church, the benefits to both communities are likely to far outweigh the potential liabilities.

Thus, even in the areas of evangelism and spiritual growth within Kenya, there is likely to remain a small place for foreign missionaries partnering with the local church. Yet there are other areas where, despite

---

[11] Nairobi Chapel has already established several "sister churches" and has a goal of planting three hundred churches throughout East Africa by 2020. (Nairobi Chapel Bulletin, May 11, 2003).

[12] There is the question of why American money cannot be used to support Kenyan missionaries. This is unlikely to increase until a much deeper level of contact is established between the American churches and individual Kenyan missionaries. The Christian concept of stewardship says that money is to be used wisely and this includes how it is donated. In order for churches to give there needs to be either a substantial interpersonal relationship with the prospective missionary or accountability through a supporting sending agency they know and trust. These sorts of relationships do not exist in any significant way yet.

[13] In one of many instances of American missionaries assisting the Kenyan church by continuing to evangelize the most barren and remote of places in Kenya is the Battermann family whose home among the Daasanach people is "a day and a half drive from the nearest gas station". Conversation with Michael and Darilyn Batterman of SIM in Nairobi, in February of 2003.

its tremendous growth, the Kenyan church is likely to continue to call for external support. This is particularly true in the areas requiring people with highly specialized expertise. There are simply too few professors, engineers, linguists, doctors and nurses in Kenya to meet the needs of the population. Not only does the American church offer Christian doctors, engineers, nurses and professors, but it does so with no financial strings attached. Therefore in these highly specialized areas the Anglo-American church, with its abundance of human expertise and liquid capital, has much of value to offer in support of the local church as it seeks to display Christian love and charity in Kenya.

To this point we have been looking at the potential for a continuing positive contribution by foreign missionaries primarily to the *Kenyan Church and nation*. But the missionary families whose children have attended RVA are not only working in Kenya. Their work spreads throughout Africa into nations where the Church is not nearly as spiritually developed or materially prosperous as the Christian community in Kenya. In other words, if there is likely to be a continuing role for American missionaries in Kenya, there is an even greater likelihood of a continuing role for missionaries in the less developed nations of the continent. In fact, if the political climate liberalizes enough to allow their presence, it is possible that the numbers of American missionaries to countries like Sudan, Ethiopia, Mozambique, Somalia and the DRC will actually increase.

IT IS UNLIKELY that East and Central Africa will ever again see a flood of Christian missionaries comparable to the one that poured into the region right after independence. And yet, prophecies of an end to foreign missions in the region, and of American missions in particular, are premature to say the least. To be sure, the needs of the African church are significantly different from the needs that existed when Hurlburt arrived one hundred years ago. Thanks in part to their own effectiveness, the era of the traditional American missionary is largely a thing of the past in Kenya and parts of East Africa. Nevertheless, the basic conception of the church as a growing community of diverse aptitudes, gifts and resources remains. The challenge today, as it has always been, is how to best use those diverse talents, resources and perspectives towards the encouragement of the Christian Church universal.

For RVA to continue primarily as a school for the children of American missionaries three things will need to be true. First, American culture will need to remain politically free, economically robust and spiritually vibrant. In short, Americans will need to continue to cultivate the type of culture that produces missionaries. Second, there must be a real and felt need within the East and Central African Church for the gifts and resources that the American Church is willingly offering, as well as the self-confidence needed to receive and give in a dignified way. And third, there must be in place in the nations of the region, a political climate that will allow the presence of American missionaries. None of these criteria is assured. In fact, each leg of this three-legged stool is vulnerable. And yet, as the 21st Century begins, there are good reasons to believe that RVA's unexpectedly powerful legacy to the world will continue for some time to come.

THE LANGUAGE OF A THIRD CULTURE – "RVA SHANG"

BEFORE WE GET TO THE WORDS AND THEIR DEFINITIONS allow me to say a brief word of introduction to the slang of RVA. The first thing that stands out about "RVA Shang" is that it is a creole – a unique blend of several languages and several cultures. This should not surprise us for, as we have seen, RVA is a genuine third culture. It is not American (although some would rightly argue that it is in some ways more American than America), it is not Kenyan (despite its location, its many Kenyan staff and significant number of Kenyan students); and it is not British (although it retains many British traditions). Nor it is Korean, Canadian, Scandinavian or any other "ian". Rather, RVA is a unique and always evolving blend of all of these.

The second point worth noting is the humorous tone of the shang. The language of RVA is a self-reflective and comical commentary by the students on the cultural confusion they have grown up in. Those who speak the shang consciously or subconsciously poke fun at themselves and their bizarre mix of African and Western perspectives. Even the language's male-dominated, semi-neanderthalean preoccupation with food, girls and sports is put into a self-deprecating and whimsical form.

But the humor and cultural confusion found in RVA shang is not always whimsical. At times the language does betray the ambiguous relationship that can exist between the students and their African context. In those moments the language simultaneously identifies with, and mocks, the culture that the students have grown up within. The most dramatic example of this is the use by RVA students of the condescending colonial term "Wog". The word "Wog" was originally used in Kenya much like the word "Nigger" might have been used in the American South. Yet, in a way that is difficult to explain, many students at RVA refer to themselves as "Wogs" and use the term, regardless of to whom it is referring to, as one of admiration. To them the word describes an African perspective on life. Therefore, to the degree that they admire the highly relational values of Africa, these children have turned the meaning of the term on its head. Yet, it is not so simple. For the term is also used to criticize elements of African culture that they find objectionable. Thus, even at RVA the term has never totally escaped its original meaning and therefore when the students use it, to some degree, they identify themselves with a highly racist past.

Of course, the slang used at RVA is not the primary language of the school and so it is important not to exaggerate the insights that it can give us into the history and values of the community. However, in a small way RVA Shang does illustrate the blending of cultures, the humor and the moral and cultural ambiguity that make up this unique community's identity. For all of these reasons it is worth considering. And if not for these reasons, then simply for the fun of it because, even with all of the moral ambiguity the slang includes, it is fun.

In compiling this dictionary I am particularly indebted to the following people for their willingness to share with me the slang of their era: Tim Cook for the early seventies, "The Committee" for the mid to late eighties, "The Dry Guys" for the late eighties and early nineties, and Neil Entwistle for the terms being used at the turn of the Twenty-First Century. In most cases I have used the exact definitions and examples given to me by each of the above sources. As a result you will find multiple cases where the words in the definitions will also be unknown to the outsider and will require a further look through the dictionary. At times you will feel like an English speaker reading a French-English dictionary only to find the definitions of the French words to be in French. But it's all part of the experience. In addition, whenever possible I have given the approximate dates the term was in vogue. The spelling of the words is phonetic. Finally, like language proper, the meaning of terms do evolve over time. I have tried to make note of those changes were applicable in the definitions. Enjoy.

THE MORE OR LESS NEW AND SOMETIMES CONCISE
DICTIONARY OF RVA SHANG

abuse – Verb/ To mercilessly ridicule someone or something. Ex. (Those St. Mary's fans *abused* our fly-half hard). 1980's.

arrive – Verb/ (1) To have been given; (2) to bring into effect. Ex. (The Female arrived me with struggles last night). 2001.

baboe – Noun/ Any girl, but more often a girlfriend. Ex. (I do not have a *baboe).* 2001.

bog/boggage – Noun, Verb or Adj. (1) Stool. Ex. (Day old *bogs* left over in the toilet can reek). (2) Bad or Crusted; Struggles. Ex. (This chick issue is just *bog).* 2001.

bonyae – Noun/ The game of basketball. Ex. (ISK and Rift often bout huge in *bonyae).*

boxos – Noun/ Boxers. Ex. (Some guyos prefer *boxos,* but I prefer chupes). 2001.

cafo – Noun/ Rift's cafeteria. Ex. (The *cafo's* food on Tuesday lunches is plot because it is fries and burgers).

cause/causist – Verb or Noun/ The act of struggling for someone else; a person who constantly causes. Ex. (That chick is always *causing* for me, basically she is a huge *causist.*) *The truth is that while this term gets used with regularity no one really knows what they mean when they use it. 2001.

chafes/chaffage – Verb or Noun/ Something that bogs for you. Ex. (Variety nights *chafe* ruthlessly). 2001

changa – Verb/ To elude an opponent in sports. Ex. (Maradona *changaed* that British sonyae player). 1980's.

chapdoze – Verb/ To kiss over an extended period of time. Ex. (That couple was caught *chapdozing* on Kiambogo.) 1980's.

chew – Verb/ To eat, usually with sike. Ex. (I *chewed* like I've never *chewed* before last night). 1990's.

chillae – Noun/ A girl, usually a girlfriend. Ex. (Shema harsh *chillae).* 1970's-80's.

chill – Verb/ To melo or wait a bit. Ex. (Chicks often aren't real great at *chilling* for their boyfriends to come see them at late studees).2001.

chobose – Verb/ To put the sonyae ball between the legs of an opponent; to fake out. 1980's.

chop/chopping – Noun or Verb/ The act of being studious, or being a fundi (expert) at something. Ex. (I am *chop* at zeeing chicks). 2001.

chuck – Verb/ To ditch or to leave; also used as an order for an unwanted person. Ex. (I discreetly *chucked* right as my baboe walked through the door towards me). 2001.

chumas – Noun/ Money. Ex. (I need some *chumas* for late studee). 1980's-90's.

chupes – Noun/ Underwear, titie-whities. Ex. (I prefer *chupes* over boxos). 2001.

conch – Adj./ Something that is hard to understand or to do. Ex. (That Calculus homework was *conch*). 2001.

convos – Noun/ Conversations. Ex. (I often have dot *convos* with my friends at night down at the dorm).

crusted – Noun, Verb or Adj./ Bad or bog. (This chick ish is crusted).

DDG – Noun/ Don't Date Girls Society founded by the Bransford brothers in the early/mid eighties. The society is usually made up of those who were just broken up with by their girlfriends, although some genuine members do exist – that is, until some hated girl shows an interest in a given fraternity member. At which point she becomes the idol of one and public enemy number one for the rest.

dame – Noun/ Girl. 1980's.

deenyo – Noun/ A disco or nightclub. Ex. (That dame was caught at the Nairobi show *deenyo* when a picture of her harreeing showed up in the Daily Nation the next day). 1980's-90's.

dido – Noun/ Usually refers to a girlfriend. Ex. (DDG members are guys without *didos*). 1980's.

dot – Adj. or Verb/ Something that is meaningless, foolish or unimportant. Ex. (This boring sonyae game is *dot*). 2001.

doz – Noun/ Situation; used like "deal" in "What's the deal?" or "What's happening?" Ex. (What's the *doz* with that dido?). 1980's-90's.

D.P's – Noun/ Dorm Parents.

fethae – Noun/ Father. Ex. (Smithy's *fethae* is from Mt. Pleasant, Texas).

finyae – Verb/ To "finish" someone, or in the vocabulary of the rest of the English speaking world, to hurt someone usually by tackling them; to sambaa them. Ex. (That huge Lenana player *finyaed* me). 2001.

futhee – Noun/ A term describing hair, usually deragatory; it can also be used to insult someone more generally. Ex. (Jim, you *futhee*!) 2001.

gatathafrash – Adj./ Derived from, "I'll go to the flash", the term is used in a whimsically derogatory way to describe someone who is either ignorant or less than entirely proficient at something. Ex. (That zunyee is a real *gatathafrash*. = That white person is clueless.). 1990's.

gathogad – Verb/ To be hit by something. Ex. (I was *gathogad* by that coconut in Mombio).

graoul – Verb or Noun/ To eat something, usually in large proportions or quickly; or the thing being eaten. Sounds suspiciously like "growl". Ex. (At Senior breakfast we *graouled* hard). 1980's-present.

guyo – Noun/ Anyone of the male sex. An editor's note is appropriate here. As you might have noticed, virtually every word from any language can be understood by those at RVA if you simply add an "O" or an "AE" to the end of it.

hard/hardcore – Adj./ (1) Synonymous with "very", but used in the Swahili word order. Ex. (That guyo likes to chew *hard* = that boy likes to eat very much (or) a lot; (2) Someone or something that is admired or thinks they should be admired. Ex. (Ruge players are usually quite hard).

harree – Verb/ To dance. Ex. (That chick knows how to *harree*).

hepa – Verb/ To go, usually with speed. Ex. (Shifta *hepad* huge when the alarm went off). 1980's.

huge – Adj. or Adv./ Large or anything excessive. Ex. (That chick struggles for me *huge*).

issue – Noun/ Any situation. Abbreviated form – *Ish*. Ex. (That guyo had a chick *ish* over senior safo). 2001.

jam – Verb/ To be rejected by something or someone. Ex. (Guyo was *jammed* by his dido). 1980's.

jamaa- Noun/ Synonymous with "Guyo". 2001.

jaweze – Verb/ (1) To drink or to be drunk. Ex. (The drivo of that mathree was *jawezed*). (2) The term can also be used to question someone's credibility; as if to say, "What are you thinking?" (Are you *jawezed*?).

jive – Verb/ (1) To talk. Ex. (The *jive* sessions in Nyati A-1 regularly went on well into the night.); (2) Adj./ Something of questionable worth. Ex. (That car is *jive*).1980's-90's.

jobless – Adj./ Doing nothing or something that is stupid. Ex. (I am usually *jobless* on Saturdays). 2001.

juice/juicy – Adj./ Something that is plot or sweet. Ex. (It's *juice* that we have class off this week). 2001.

keenondu – Verb/ A more involved version of chapdoze. Ex. Those two got put on couples restriction for *keenondu*). 1980's-90's.

knock – Verb/ To hit, usually with force. Ex. (The cheaky junior higher was *knocked* by the senior). 2001.

kype – Verb/ To steal. Ex. (Shifta *kyped* my Abba Gold CD). 1980's.

lambaa – To fall. Ex. (Teeni *lambaad* hard on the steps). 1980's.

lots – Adj./ Used sarcastically to mean "nothing" or "not at all". Ex. ("Did you like writing Miss Winterberg's essay?" "*Lots* though!"). Died of overuse in the late 1980's.

mama – Adj. or Noun/ A woman, usually a substitution for Mrs. or Miss. Ex. (*Mama* Jones is hilarious). 2001.

mangaa – Verb/ (1) To eat; (2) to ruthlessly tackle someone/beat someone. Ex. (That Strathmore ruge player was *mangaad* by our prop).

mathae – Noun/ Mother.

mathree – Noun/ Matatu (or private vans used for public transportation, usually excessively crowded and less than safe).

melo ezay – Verb/ To relax; to wait; or to "take it easy". Ex. (*Melo Ezay* guy, I'm coming). 2001

mero – Noun/ An uneducated person – usually an African.

mob – Adj./ In large amounts. Ex. (People with *mob* sike for their chicks are vulnerable to struggles).

Mombio – Proper Noun/ Mombasa. Ex. (For vake we are hepaing to Mombio).

monyae – Suffix. There is no real meaning for this word. It is more or less a collection of letters put on the end of a word – usually a name – that in no way changes the meaning or tone of the word it is associated with. Ex. (Caleb*monyae* is quite plot). 2001.

mozos – Noun/ Cigarettes. Ex. (Shady teeni keeps getting demerits for sneaking *mozos* onto campus). 1990's.

mums – Noun/ Limited physical affection; kissing. Ex. (Guyos with didos think *mums* are sweet). 2001.

murassa – Noun/ Buttocks.

nast – Adj. (1) Unimpressive or lame; (2) A crust person who struggles for someone else. Ex. (The *nast* juniors did nothing on the night before senior safo). 2001.

nasted – Verb/ To knock someone ruthlessly. Ex. (In the wrestling match I *nasted* Joe). 2001.

nyab – Verb/ To grab a male in a particularly sensitive spot Ex. (In the scrum the Lenana prop *nyabbed* our hooker).

nyaf – Noun or Verb/ (1) Gases being emitted from one's person; (2) To emit those gases. Ex. (Jamaa is a real *nyaffer*). 1980's to present.

pac – Verb/ To hit with force. Ex. (Joe *pac(ed)* that pole huge). 1980's.

paca – A crude sentence introduction. Slightly above a grunt but lower than the oft-used, "Ya know what?", paca was popularized by the "misunderstood" class of 1986. Ex. (*Paca*, did you shema that wog prang his piki?).

papa- Adj. or Noun/ A substitute for Mr.

paros – Noun/ Parents.

P.C.'s – Noun/ Private Conversations, usually of the serious variety. Ex. (Guyos often go to certain chicks to have *P.C.'s* about their baboe issues).

piki – Noun/ motorcycle.

plot – Verb, Noun or Adj./ (1) To have done something (or believed yourself to have done something) worthy of praise; (2) Good. Ex. (I don't want to brag, but I have a *plot* chillae).

prang – Verb/ To crash something. Ex. (My bicycle safari ended when I *pranged* on the Nakuru road).

Rift – Proper Noun/ short for the Rift Valley Academy.

ruge – Noun/ The game of rugby. Ex. (*Ruge* is the sweetest sport at Rift).

safo – Noun/ Safari or trip. Ex. (Senior *safo* was plot).

sambaa – Verb/ See "mangaa", "finyae", "pac", etc.

scan – Verb/ To watch something closely. Ex. (That chick was *scanning* me huge last night in the gym).

sell/sellist/sold - Verb or Noun/ (1) To mess something up; (2) to be a person who made the mistake. Ex. (I *sold* on that English test) or (When it comes to making senior store donuts that class are *sellists*). 2001

shifta – Noun/ A thief. Ex. (Jamaa is a shifta).

shado – Verb/ To fake an opponent in sports, making them look foolish whenever possible. Ex. (I have never seen a guyo *shado* like that Nairobi School scrum-half). 1980's-90's.

shady – Adj./ Of questionable merit. Ex. (The cafo's graoul is shady).

shaft – Verb/ To insult. Ex. (I thought I had a sweet plan, but when I told my friends they *shafted* the idea). 2001.

shema – Verb/ To look at. Ex. (*Shema* that plot baboe). 1980's.

shika – Verb/ To steal. Ex. (Jamaa *shika(d)* my plot chick).

shrub/shrubbist – Verb or Noun/ To make a mistake, usually a large one. Ex. (I *shrubbed* on the SAT's).

sike – Verb, Noun or Adverb/ To be enthusiastic. Ex. (I try not to get immediately *siked* if a chick shows *sike* for me because she could just shaft me the next minute if she wanted to).

sonyae – Noun/ The game of soccer.

spandos/sandees – Noun/ Spandex shorts. Ex. (*Spandos* are only plot for ruge games).

speaacked – Verb/ (1) To be angry; (2) To show anger. Ex. (Teeni was *speaacked* when the mathree mangaad his deenyo). 1980's-90's.

spy – Verb/ To look at; usually of the guy to girl variety. Ex. (In ta-o I *spied* this plot chillae from ISK).

struggle – Verb/ To try hard in unpleasant circumstances. Ex. (Chick issues always *struggle* with sike). 2001.

studees – Noun/ The student center. Ex. (No one hangs out at *Studees* anymore).

swatch – Verb or Adj./ (1) To sleep. (2) To be mello/lazy on the job. Ex. (That was a *swatchist* referee).

sweet – Adj./ Good.

ta-o – Noun/ Town. Almost always referring to Nairobi.

teeni – Noun/ Any person. Originally meant any girl, but evolved over time into its current and most broad meaning.

thotch – Verb/ (1) To knock someone on the head; (2) an extremely humiliating kind of insult.

thrashist – Noun/ (1) Someone who is a rough rugby player; (2) Someone who is chop at something. Ex. (Kendi was a *thrashist* at ruge).

titchie – Noun/ A child or an elementary student.

titchie swot – Noun/ Elementary school. The exact origin of this long standing term is a mystery. 1940's, perhaps earlier.

tunage – Noun/ The act of tuning chicks, usually in an obvious, and therefore misguided, way.

tuning – Verb/ Blatant attempts to attract a particular member of the opposite sex. The word originated with the concept of needing to be "tuned" to the same "wavelength". Ex. (That guy was shamelessly *tuning* that dame). 1980's to present.

vake – Noun/ Short for vacation.

vids – Noun/ Videos. Ex. (Over vake we usually scan *vids* with sike).

vonyae – Noun/ The game of volleyball. Ex. (*Vonyae* is probably the sport that gives fans at rift the least amount of sike).

wazee – Adj./ An exclamation usually along the lines of "Nice one!". This word is also used sarcastically. Ex. (Whenever people fall in front of us, my friends and I usually say *"Wazee"* to each other to make fun of the person).

weka – Verb/ To bring or to get. Ex. (*Weka* mpira from the dorm). Swahili.

wog/woggish – Noun or Adj./ (1) To be crusted in a good way; a lifestyle or a mindset that many MKs aspire towards. Ex. (An example of a plot *wog* is John Johnson who has a huge fro and wears tire scandals and old faded shirts to college in the states). (2) a derogatory colonial term for an African. To everyone's shame, the term continues to be used in both senses.

zee/zeeist/zeed – Verb or Noun/ (1) To shaft hardcore; (2) A person who zees. Ex. (When chicks shaft guys, guys usually *zee* them back, thus resulting in a huge struggle).

zunyee – Noun or Adj./ Any person of European descent; but usually one with little knowledge of Africa and its people/worldview. Ex. (Tourists are major *zunyees*).

EXERCISE SECTION

Here is a chance for you to practice your "RVA Shang". Below are five sentences in RVA Shang and space for you to translate them into English. The correct translation for each is in small type at the bottom of the page.

1) Teeni was tuning zunyee chillae.

2) Mathae hooked me up with some plot graoul tonight.

3) Paca, the cafo chafed because bog jamaas shikad the plot graoul.

4) Guyo's dido arrived him with conch convos resulting in mob struggles.

5) Teeni was speaacked when mathree gathogad his deenyo.

ANSWER KEY: (1) That young man was making advances on that young expatriate woman. (2) My mother cooked a wonderful meal for dinner tonight. (3) You know what? The main entrees at the school's dining commons were not as good as usual, because some undesirable youths stole the best food. (4) That boy and his girlfriend had a rather distressing discussion in which the girlfriend raised some concerns that made the boy quite uncomfortable. (5) That individual was extremely angry when the overcrowded and reckless public transportation vehicle ran into his dancing club.

PROFILE OF THE CLASS OF 2001

DURING THE FINAL WEEK OF THE 2000-2001 SCHOOL YEAR English teacher Miss Constain distributed a survey to the senior class. The surveys were given out in the same manner to each of the classes. The following is a summary of that survey. Although the results speak for themselves, a couple of things are worth pointing out. Foremost is the fact that while this is a survey of just one year, it is roughly representative of senior classes at RVA over the last twenty years. The significant diversity in nationality, country of residence and denominational/organizational background of the students has been constant; as has been the size of the class. The final fact of note is the tremendous amount and diversity of work being accomplished by the parents of just this one class. Extend this abbreviated list over the history of the school and the significant influence of evangelical missions on East and Central Africa is readily apparent.

NUMBER OF STUDENTS: 82

NATIONALITIES INCLUDED IN THE CLASS: (8).
INCLUDING: American (56); Canadian (9); Kenyan (8); British (5); Korean (1); Nigerian (1); Chinese (1); South African (1).

NATIONS OF RESIDENCE FOR THE GRADUATES IN AFRICA: (11): Congo; Chad; Ethiopia; Equatorial Guinea; Kenya; Madagascar; Malawi; Mozambique; Tanzania; Uganda; Zambia.

SURVEY QUESTIONS SUMMARIES:

8) Between 1-10 (one being the lowest and ten being the highest) the chance that you will become a missionary: MEAN - 5.7.
9) Between 0-10, would you consider yourself to be a "strong Christian" (zero being, "I am not a Christian" and ten being, "I am a deeply committed Christian"): MEAN - 7.5.
10) Between 1-10 (one being the lowest and ten being the highest) would you consider yourself to be a "strong student": MEAN - 7.3.
11) Between 1-10 (one being the lowest and ten being the highest) rate your overall experience at RVA: MEAN - 8.0.

COLLEGES AND UNIVERSITIES TO BE ATTENDED:

University of Arkansas; Asbury College*; Bethany Bible College; Biola University*; Bruzasport University; Brown University; CIU; Cedarville College; Central Bible College; Circleville Bible College; University of Connecticut; University of Delaware; Furman University; Houghton College; University of Illinois at Urbana; Illinois State University; Indiana Wesleyan University; Judson College; James Madison University; John Brown University*; Lawrence Technical College; Louisiana State University; Memorial University (Canada); Messiah College; Michigan State University; University of Mississippi; Oral Roberts University; Palm Beach Atlantic College; Prairie Bible College (Canada); Queens University (Canada); State University of New York; Taylor University*; Temple University; Trinity University (IL); Trinity Western University* (Canada); Union College*; Valparaiso College; Wake Forest University; Washington College (VA); Washington State University; Waterloo University (Canada); Wheaton College (IL)*.

Several students indicated they would take a year off before entering college.

The "*" identifies colleges where more than one graduate will be attending.

A LIST OF THE MISSION ORGANIZATIONS THE PARENTS OF THE GRADUATES REPRESENT:

African Inland Mission (31); Assemblies of God; Baptist Bible Fellowship International; Bible Fellowship International; CMML (2); Cornerstone Mission; Evangelical Alliance Mission; Friends; Global Mission Society; Independent Missionaries (2); Master's Mission; Mennonite Central Committee; Nairobi Evangelical Graduate School of Theology; Pentecostal Assemblies of Canada; Presbyterian Church of America; Reformed Church of America (2); Scripture Gift Mission; Southern Baptist Convention (6); Sudan Interior Mission (now Society of International Ministries) (SIM) (5); Wesleyan Mission of Zambia; World Gospel Mission(5); Youth With A Mission (YWAM).

A LIST OF THE GRADUATE'S PARENT'S OCCUPATIONS:

The following is a brief summary of occupations served by the parents of the 2001 graduates. Following the occupation I have also listed in abbreviated form their country of residence. An "*" is added for each additional person who fits a given description. It is important to note that I have included only one of the often several tasks that each missionary parent is involved in. For obvious reasons I have, therefore, listed only the principal work of each missionary. Finally, for those few parents who are not involved in missionary work I have explicitly said so by placing (Non Missions) after the stated occupation.

Academic Registrar – Bible College (KEN)
Academic Secretary – Bible College (KEN)
Academic Dean – Bible College (KEN)
Accountant for Mission (KEN)
Agricultural Development (TZ)
Agricultural Development (KEN)*
Agricultural Development (ZAM)
AIDS Awareness Program Leader (KEN)
AIM-AIR Technical Support (KEN)
Banker (Non Missions) (KEN)*
Bible College Teacher (ZAM)

Bible College Teacher (MOZ)
Bible School Teacher (MAD)
Bible College Teacher (UG)
Bible College Founder (KEN)**
Bible College Finance & Records (KEN)
Bible College Principal (ETH)
Bible College Principal (KEN)****
Bible College Administrator (KEN)*
Bible Study Leader and Coordinator (KEN)
Bible Study Fellowship Country Leader (UG)
Bible Translator (KEN)
Bingham Academy Station Manager (ETH)
Bingham Academy Operations Manager (ETH)
Business and Finance Head at RVA (KEN)
Business (Flower Exporting – Non Missions) (KEN)
Business & Manufacturing (Non Missions) (KEN)
Children's Bible Clubs Supervisor (TZ)
Children's Ministries Leader (CHA)
Church Builder – Construction (KEN)*
Church Builder – Construction (CON)
Church Builder – Construction (MAD)
Church Builder – Construction (TZ)
Church Planter (KEN)*
Church Planter (TZ)***
Church Planter (CON)
Church Planter (CHA)
Church Planter (MAD)
Church Planter (ZAM)
Church Strategy Facilitator (TZ)
Counselor (TZ)
Counselor (KEN)
Country Representative MCC (UG)
Development Facilitator (KEN)
ESL Teacher (KEN)
ESL Teacher (UG)
Economist (Non Missions)
English Teacher (ETH)
Energy Resources Developer (ETH)
Field Treasurer (KEN)
Field Representative/Church Planter (EQU)
Financial Advisor (Non Missions)

Head Supervisor for Assembly of God Primary Schools (EQU)
Headmistress of a Pre-School (TZ)
Headmistress of a Secondary School (TZ)
Home School Coordinator (KEN)
Hospital Developer & Administrator (UG)
Islam Expert for AIM (KEN)
Language Translator (MOZ)
Leadership (Church) Development (UG)
Librarian International School of Kampala (UG)
Mechanic for SIM (ZAM)
Ministry to Asian-Africans (KEN)
Mission Director (KEN)
Mission Administrator (KEN)*
Missionary Facilitator (KEN)
Missionary Services Officer (KEN)
Missionary Kid Care Coordinator (ETH)
Missionary Guest House Manager (ZAM)
Missionary Pilot (ZAM)
Music Teacher (KEN)
New Missionary Transition Care Coordinator (KEN)
Nurse and Clinic Administrator (ETH)
Nurse and Teacher of Nursing (KEN)
Nurse (CON)
Nurse (ETH)
Nurse (KEN)
Nurse (TZ)
Physician (KEN)***
Pilot (Non Missions)
Pilot AIM-AIR (UG)
Professor – Nairobi Evangelical Graduate School of Theology (KEN)
Professor of Agriculture Makarere University (UG)
Publisher of Christian Children's Books (KEN)
Refugee Worker – Developing Education Programs (ETH)
Relief and Development Consultant (MAL)
Rural Development Facilitator (KEN)
RVA Chaplain (KEN)
RVA Dean of Students (KEN)
RVA Dorm Parents (KEN)
RVA Academic Principal (KEN)
RVA Music Department Head & Choir Director (KEN)
RVA French Teacher (KEN)

RVA O-Level Teacher for British Students (KEN)
RVA Swahili Teacher (KEN)
RVA Teacher (KEN)*
Street Children Ministry (UG)
Street Children Ministry (KEN)**
Surgeon (KEN)
Surgeon – Orthopedic (KEN)
Teacher (Non Missions) (KEN)
Textiles Teacher (KEN)
Theological Education by Extension Facilitator (UG)
Women's Bible Study Leader (KEN)
Women's Bible Study Leader (ETH)
Women's Bible Study Leader (TZ)
Women's Bible Study Leader (ZAM)
Worship Team Leader (ETH)
Volunteer Missions Coordinator (ZAM)
Volunteer Missions Coordinator for AIM Africa (KEN)
Volunteer Missions Coordinator for AIM Kenya (KEN)
Volunteer Missions Coordinator for AIM Uganda (UGA)
Youth Camp Manager (ETH).

The activities of the missionary parents of the class of 2000-2001 can be broken down roughly into seven categories: Aviation (2); Church Planting (34); Education (20); Medicine (13); Missionary Administration (19); Relief and Development (14); and Theological Education (20)

ROLL CALL:
A LIST OF RVA GRADUATE

1949
Paul Smith

1950
Gayle Downing
Harold LaFont
Gloria Kitts
Esther Shaffer

1951
Harold Amstutz
Don Kirkpatrick
Gerald Morrison

1952
Charles Barnett
Glenn Downing
Grace Manning

1953
David Kellum
Mary Lichty
Eleanor Morrison
Paul Teasdale
Elwin Wines

1954
Joyce Baker
Joel Guldseth
Paul Skoda
John Stauffacher
Dick Woll

1955
Willy Danielson
Daphne Downing
Eddie Downing
Elizabeth Guldseth
Lois Teasdale

1956
Ruth Glock
Grace Lyon
David Morrow
Judi Retherford

1957
Herb Andersen
Charlotte Bisset
Dick Boda
Bill Butler
Herb Cook
Tim Davis
Lois Hollenbeck
Gerald May
Helga May
Jon Morris
Martha Morrow
Sam Wagner
Martha Woll
Mildred Woll

1958
Willard Andersen
John Barnett
Paul Barnett
Martha Belknap
Betty Bisset
Grace Capen
Van Davis
Helen Devitt
Herb Lyon
Lila Propst
David Rawson
Benny Schwieger
Rodney Udd

1959
Ron Cook
Dave Downing
Charlotte Felton
Ruth Skoda
Jewel Udd

1960
Howard Andersen
Art Davis
Ruth Ann Downing
Anita Francis
Don Hoover
Faith Lyon
Mike Malloy
Alice Propst
Marcia Propst
Kathy Schwieger
John Skoda
Mary Ann
Stauffacher
Joy Williams

1961
Maxine Boda
Dottie Downing
Gwen Friesen
Elizabeth Hoover
Jess Lynn
Dottie Machamer
George McQuarrie
Chris Nelson
Marlyce Pedersen
Irvin Renner
Trum Simmons
Tom Smith
Steve Van Nattan

1962
Sharon Barlow
Helen Barnett
Martha Brown
Norman Dilworth
Linda Felton
Irene Hutchinson
Deborah Johnson
Janice Lynn
Helen Malloy
John Morrow
Willa Rae Schwieger
Phil Skoda
Sharon Stam
Bill Stauffacher
Brigitte Walter
Richard Weiss

1963
Elizabeth Barnett
Bill Barnett
Winnie Brown
Sandy Campbell
Lynne Davis
Alan Hahn
David Lincoln
Steve Lyons
Donald Mattson
Jeannie Nelson
Sheila Propst
Bill Renner
Joanne Schellenberg
Carol Schuit
Marion Williams

1964
Jon Arensen
Hal Boone
David Campell
Malcolm Collins
Ray Davis
Dianne Dilworth
Daniel Hahn
Mike Hall
Bob Hollenbeck
Linnea Johnson
Jon Machamer
Pat Marsh
Wilfred May
David Philips
Bob Robinson
Jonathan Salseth
Ruth Schuit
Tim Udd

1965
Stanley Armes
Cathy Boone
Jim Camp
Valerie Clark
Harold Felton
Josepth Friberg
Jim Gaunt
John Hendry
Janet Johnson
Judy Machamer
Ann Pearson
Norman Smuck
Richard Stauffacher
Charles Trout
Martin Vonderheyden
Susanne Walter
Priscilla Wegmueller

1966
Lanny Arensen
Ted Barnett
Barry Beatty
Ralph Bethea
Linda Carlson
Joylene Correll
Paul Crumley
Martha Ebeling
Tim Epp
Oddvar Espegren
Mark Faust
Faye Hinkel
Linda Hull
Carol Johnson
Georgia Kevorkian
Tom Lindquist
Paul Lyons
Rosie May
Frederick Malloy
Freddie Miller
David Ness
Luella Peterson
Andrea Propst
Barb Propst
Cynthia Salseth
Chris Schmalgemeier
Sara Stauffacher
John Woll

1967
Carolyn Barnett
Susan Boone
Beverly Borden
Timothy Buyse
Phyllis Dilworth
Lee Downing
William Ebeling
Philip Fox

1967 Cont…
Beth Glock
Virginia Harris
Jim Hoover
Kirsten Hunter
Joel Jackson
Dean Jackson
Mary Johnson
Dave Lyons
Steve Machamer
Mark Monson
Duane Palm
Rachel Peterson
Christof Puttfarken
Brent Robinson
David Salseth
Jim Schuit
Daniel Shaffer
Edith Trout
Suzanne Knapp
Dorothy Phillips
Grace Philpot
Nancy Pinkerton
Helen Stough
Steve Wilson

1968
Liz Allen
Cammy Arensen
Laura Armes
Eileen Barnett
Pat Barnett
Vic Downing
Ann Faust
Bill Gaunt
Dave Gottneid
Patricia Green
Esther Hulbert
Harry Johnson
Arlene Kindel
Jim Lee

1968 Cont…
John Lofgren
Harold MacDowell
Ruth MacDowell
Susie MacLin
Beatrice Palm
Pearl Philips
Jim Propst
Joy Sanford
Mary Saunders
Dave Schaefer
Dan Swenson
Norman Tonnissen
Cynthia Tope
Marianne Vail

1969
Bill Bisset
Joanne Camp
Dave Carlson
Dan Cook
Bill Cox
Bob Eames
Becky Felton
Mary Friberg
Susan Gottneid
Ruth Harrison
Norman Henderson
Wanda Hinkel
Ray Hull
Beth Jackson
Deanne Jacobson
Eric Johnson
David Kaskela
Steve Kellogg
Paul Kline
Cathy MacLin
David Mallory
Dave McMillan
Judi Martin

1969 Cont…
Ozzie Mensah
Dave Mshila
Julian Murage
David Okken
John Pelletier
Dave Peterson
Brenda Robinson
Dave Schuit
Marshall Smalling
Becky St.John
Bonnie Stoudt
Phil Thornberg
Steve Wolfe

1970
Doug Atkins
Max Albright
Martin Amoke
Esther Armes
Meryl Bainbridge
Carol Barnett
Barbara Beatty
Betty Borden
Becky Brown
Kay Carlson
John Cullen
Allan Davis
Jim Dorsch
Karen Dunkerton
Mark Edstrom
Loren Fast
Linda Faust
Dan Fox
Paul Frew
Carolyn Gaunt
Chris Ghrist
Esther Glock
Linda Harris
Stephen Harris
Gail Hincks

1970 Cont...
Elleta Hull
Kim Jackson
Marilyn Kaskela
Vesa Kusmin
Colleen Lewton
Judy Lindquist
David Lofgren
Jill Lynn
Kathy Lyons
Margie MacDowell
Bill McAllister
John McMillan
Carl Monson
Lewie Morris
Allen Muchmore
Jon Orcutt
Jim Philpot
David Pinkerton
John Propst
Darlene Robinson
Paul Robinson
Dani Sanford
Susan Saunders
Dan Scheel
Don Schuit
Herman Siebert
Tom Schumaker
Mark Smalling
Bob Snyder
Bill Stoudt
Randy Thornburg
Ruth Tonnissen
Marjorie Trout
Don Vanderploeg
Kristine Ward
Dorothy Williams
Susan Williams
Ruth Wilson
Phillip Woll

1971
Carolyn Alexander
David Askey
Martha Barnett
Carl Becker
Dale Beverly
Cathy Bickers
Barbara Bisset
Dan Boone
Steve Brashler
Howard Brown
Peter Crossman
Martin Downing
Karen Folk
Judy Deyoung
Kathy Dunkerton
Susan Eschtruth
Nancy Fox
Steve Harrell
Rick Hendrix
Doug Jones
Susan Jones
Mark Kile
Bryan Kingsriter
Ken Lewton
Charles Mallory
Steve McMillan
Christy Montgomery
Betty Morris
Ben Mshila
Eugene Palm
Steve Pelletier
Mosella Perry
Marilyn Petersen
Pam Phillips
John Pinkerton
Rick Rineer
John Saunders
Miriam Scheel
Steve Simonsen

1971 Cont...
Bob Spurlock
Tom Storhaug
Curtis Teasdale
Bill Wester

1972
Judi Adkins
Rod Albright
Debbie Amstutz
Matt Bainbridge
Bernard Banzhaf
David Baugh
Jim Bedenbaugh
Cindy Bickers
Liz Conely
Steve Cook
Jim Cornelius
Joceyln Deyoung
Ela Diefenthall
Sue Evans
Chuck Fennig
Jim Frew
Pete Friberg
Mary Beth Genet
Rich Hightower
Becky Kellogg
Judd Kile
John MacDowell
Angela Mattock
Janet McCleny
Joan McCleny
Bert Mensah
Mim Monson
Lynn Moss
David Muchmore
Stuart Northwood
Becky Nyblade
Tim Okken
Wesley Peacock
Kat Perry

1972 Cont...
Becky Petersen
Bobbie Petersen
Kathy Pienarr
Ron Pontier
Keith Robinson
Jon Robitschek
Cindy Smalling
Steve Snyder
Sherry Spurlock
Heather Stevenson
Larry Strong
Dan Ward
Larry Ward
Esther Wester
Karen Wilcke
Ralph Wolfe

1973
Zelda Anderson
Beth Baker
Peggy Becker
Lynn Butler
Ruth Campbell
Ron Cole
Karen Coon
Kathy Crumley
Anita Denmark
Jon Donner
Shirley Dorsch
Jon Douglin
Martha Eschtruth
Leanne Fennig
Carol Folk
Jennifer Frew
Libby Gibbon
Debbie Harris
Glenn Harris
Cheryl Highfield
Doug Hincks
Becky Holloway

1973 Cont...
Alice Hull
Paul Hull
Kenny Johnson
Garnet Kindel
Jim Kreutter
Sharon Lister
Bill MacKenzie
Paul Marsh
Suzi Martin
Linda Miller
Eucled Moore
Wilson Morris
Issac Munyua
Phillip Northwood
Steve Okken
Dan Olsen
Roger Orner
Sheri Pearce
Jim Pinkerton
Don Rineer
Wendy Salseth
Pat Sharp
Cindy Simmonds
Naomi Simonson
Mike Smalling
Connie Strong
Lori Telke
Sherrie Watson
Pam Welch
Doug Wilhite
Sheila Williams
Esther Wilson

1974
Mike Adkins
Mark Allison
David Amstutz
Shelly Arensen
Kathy Armes
Margeret Askey

1974 Cont...
Jan Barney
Paul Barney
Barbara Baugh
Robin Bedenbaugh
Lynda Bowler
Dorothy Brown
Lorraine Butler
Donna Clark
Carolyn Conley
Marilyn Conley
Tim Cook
Murray Cornelius
David Crossman
Cathy Cummins
Al Dobra
David Doughlin
James Dunkerton
Mary Edstrom
Marit Espegren
Debbie Flood
Nancy Folkerts
Cindy Fonseca
John Ford
Trevor Fossum
Terrie Foulkes
Steve Friberg
Mark Holloway
Marilyn Jacobson
Richard Knapp
Linda Lister
Kerry Little
Ruth Lofgren
Jan MacDougall
Rick Marrow
Charlene Martin
Tim Morris
Sam Karanja
John Murage
Nathan Mwaura

1974 Cont...
John Nelson
Janice Qwens
Ron Peters
Thad Peterson
Becky Phillips
Don Pierce
Judy Riley
Andy Robitschek
Dave Rogers
Nina Saunders
Tim Schlehr
Ted Simmonds
Nate Simonson
Cindy Steury
Marita Sundin
Peggy Teasdale
Pal Tidenberg
Noelle Tope
Bill Vinton
Kathy Ward
Ken Ward
David Whelchel
Mark Whelchel
Mike Whitson
Joan Williams
Karen Wood
Louis Zanos

1975
Ray Albright
Bernice Banzhaf
Jay Barnett
Dina Bateman
Chris Bowler
Larry Buyse
Lois Coombs
Tammy Coon
Mike Coursey
Diane Cunningham

1975 Cont...
Jon Davis
Denny Denmark
Judy Doggett
Dave Entwistle
Caroline Eschtruth
Kathleen Evans
Joe Fennig
Sandy Fonseca
Burt Garvin
Doug Ghrist
Bev Harrell
Dee Dee Hooten
Mona Houser
Martha Jackson
Paul Kaskela
Kirk Kingsley
Mark Licklider
Glenn Little
Margie MacKenzie
Tom McMillan
Cindy Moore
Suzanne Moss
Barry Nagle
Cindy Newman
Walter Nyblade
Karen Olsen
Marsha Orner
Judy Robitschek
Arden Schellert
Nancy Smith
Dan Snyder
Lydia Snyder
Vic Sommer
Debi Spahr
Jim Teasdale
Dan Tyler
Jenni Welch
Keren Whitson
Tim Wilson

1976
Janet Armes
John Becker
John Benson
Ricky Blakely
James Boone
Betsy Booth
Jan Bray
Corinne Chiarelli
Louise Clark
Pam Cooley
Mim Coombs
Jim Davis
Ross Duncalfe
Alan Duncan
Eileen Enright
Brad Fast
Ken Gaunt
David Gibbon
Craig Hincks
Colleen Hoffman
Davey Hooten
Bev Horrill
Terry Horrill
Bryan Houser
Debbie Jackson
Jill Jackson
Kris Johnson
Asle Jossang
Nancy Kairo
Debbie Kato
Keith Kennedy
Rebecca Kennedy
Mark Kinzer
Georgia Lindsey
Tim Lofgren
Heidi Madsen
Gary McLain
Melodie McMillan
John Moi
David Muraya

1976 Cont…
Evelyn Ncharo
Vangi Newberry
Debbie Norton
Russ Nyblade
Carol Olson
Ruth Owens
Marlene Petroskey
John Phillips
Joan Pierce
Janice Poe
Eileen Reeves
Cheryl Rosenau
Debbie Seaboyer
Becky Simonson
Gloria Smethers
Jedi Solitei
Gordie Spahr
Rick Spurlock
Tim Stevenson
Billy Teasdale
Debbie Vinton
Krissy Welling

1977
Gary Allen
Ann Armes
Beth Baker
Keith Baker
Debbie Barnett
Eunie Barney
David Bates
Susan Baugh
Becky Borman
Debbie Bunch
Tim Carroll
Jon Cook
Laura Coursey
Patty Cunningham
Cindy Davis
Ralph Davis

1977 Cont…
Doug Dealy
Paula Denmark
Kent Dixon
Joy Dorsch
Dan Entwistle
Jane Fast
Rhonda Ford
Gwennie Foulkes
Terry Fretz
John Friberg
Tamra Garvin
Lynnae Hagberg
Sandi Hall
Ruth Holloway
Sally Jones
Chuck Kauffman
Doug Kingma
Karen Klebe
Nathan Kreutter
Tim Laffoon
Steve Lister
Annie MacDowell
Jeanette Marrow
Maureen McBride
Julie Mosman
Estar Murage
Jim Muir
Mary Myers
Doug Orner
Will Partain
Scott Paulson
David Rae
David Ramey
Nancy Rhea
Jeff Riemenschneider
Esther Roberts
Anne Robinson
Karen Schlehr
Gwenda Scott
Randy Senter

1977 Cont…
Dan Shani
Lois Smethers
Rhea Synder
Shelly Steward
Beth Welling

1978
Tara Bateman
Chris Batterman
Todd Benson
Lesley Brand
Pete Brown
Phil Buyse
Steve Davis
Janelle Deally
David Dix
Barb Fennig
Dan Gottneid
Fay Green
Ralph Hendrickson
Wendy Hennigh
Lori Ipema
Debbie Jealouse
Kathy Kaskela
Debbie Kellum
Keith Kingsley
Mark Labrentz
Carl Madsen
Brenda Moore
Mark Norton
Andy Nyblade
Pete Ondeng
Mike Peterson
Mahau Pheko
Russ Radach
Alf Rhea
Becky Rineer
David Robitschek
Paul Rosenau

1978 Cont...
Betsy Shaffer
Tim Solitei
Sheila Somaia
Kerri Spain
Sandra Spurlock
Jon Stilwell
Bobbi Teasdale
Jim Tidenberg
Tim Tidenberg
Dan Walker
Anne Warnock
Becky Wenninger

1979
Brian Arensen
David Arthur
Celene Barnes
Linda Barnett
Tim Bascom
Manny Belete
Mandy Blakely
Mike Borman
Phil Bowler
Kim Brand
Karen Brooks
Tracy Brown
Suellen Butler
Stan Cannata
Ken Cherogony
Dan Coleman
Paul Cooley
Ruth Ann Copeland
Lois Crossman
Ruth Cumbers
Mary Cunningham
Janice Duncalfe
Kenny Duncan
Mary Dye
Doug Eaton
Dean Ferguson

1979 Cont...
Ken Garvin
Rochelle Hagberg
Esther Herring
Lorrie Horton
Mark Hulbert
Tom Jones
Kevin Kingma
Clark Lasse
Bryan MacDougall
Brian MacKenzie
David Marrow
Joe McElroy
Karen McLain
Debbie McMillan
Leonard Mpoke
Becky Muir
Liz Mull
Becky Norton
Cindy Oliphint
Bjorg Olsen
Mike Olsen
Debra Owens
Peter Phillips
Bev Radach
Diane Rae
David Reeves
Becky Reimer
Ruth Roberts
Bel Senter
Karen Shenk
Rhilda Smith
Martha Stewart
Greg Stough
Brian Thomas
Leanne Thomas
Sharon Thomas
Robert Tipis
Caroline Walker
David Walsh
Alice Waweru

1979 Cont..
Mary Wester
David Willet

1980
Scott Amstutz
John Armes
Jon Bainbridge
Janice Baker
Esther Batterman
Joel Bedenbaugh
Gregg Beggs
Cindy Beverly
Doug Blakely
Steve Bowler
Becky Boyd
Debbie Brown
Judy Camp
Bill Cole
Scott Coursey
Debbie Dix
Faith Edstrom
Carole Ennis
Paul Erickson
Allan Erion
Lynda Fargher
Dwight Ferguson
Tammy Fraley
Peter Franz
Monte Gann
Dan Gibbon
Stephanie Hagemeier
Laura Hampton
Grace Harris
David Hennigh
Steve Holloway
Dan Jealouse
Andy Jones
Sherri Kocsis
Julie Koop

1980 Cont...
Dawn Kurtz
Linnea Lee
Julie Lindholm
Bruce Linquist
Karin Lowenberg
Nancy Maillefer
Elvin Marangu
Dee Moore
Marie Moore
Norman Muraya
Steve Neumann
Melanie Phifer
Betty Ann Rhea
Markus Schwartz
Ginny Shaffer
Mark Sharp
Joyce Shenk
Roy Small
Charity Solitei
Nila Somaia
Jon Steury
Beth Stewart
Mike Sturkie
Janet Swafford
Heidi Ward
Suzanne Watts
Darla Welling
Drew Whitson
Steve Williams

1981
Rodges Ankrah
Mertie Armes
Donna Baker
Rajeev Bhalla
Gilbert Bomett
Valarie Bowler
Lyn Burman
Sandy Clayton
Matt Cooch

1981 Cont...
Mim Cooch
Russ Copeland
Cindy Crumley
Paul Cumbers
Dee Dee Dison
Clark Dixon
Mark Dye
Roxie Eaton
Charles Evans
Sue Fennig
Dawn Ferguson
Mark Franz
Gertrud Franz
Sam Harrell
Karen Hershberger
Larry Hinkel
Kjersti Holmedahl
Marian Hunter
Suzaane Hurlburt
Marguerite Joseph
Reuben Kamwathi
Bruce Kinzer
Margie Kirkpatrick
Jon Konnerup
Carolyn Linquist
Vic Madsen
Renee Maillefer
Wayne Martin
Gideon Mburu
Sara McCallum
Rob McNeely
Roland Moore
Andy Mull
Luis Munoz
Steve Musen
Todd Myatt
Jim Myers
Kim Newmann
Cheryl Norton
Abigael Odanga

1981 Cont...
Linda Olsen
Bob Orner
Jay Piercy
Lee Robitschek
Steve Seaboyer
Pam Sentman
Robin Smith
Agatha Solitei
Mina Somaia
Kathy Steeves
Tim Stough
Ruth Teasdale
Debbie Voetmann
David Welling

1982
Andy Adams
Yasmin Adhiambo
Valerie Allen
Karen Angel
John Bakke
Roger Batlle
Hugh Beck
Ruth Belete
Paul Bliese
May Bomett
Lisa Borman
Calvin Brain
Janice Camp
Cathy Cannata
Melody Carroll
Shaleen Cunningham
Steve Cunningham
Yvonne Cunningham
Serena Denmark
Allan Dickens
Dawn Dison
Sharon Dix
Kathy Dye
Rick Ely

1982 Cont...
Bruce Erickson
Rhonda Erion
Pete Fahnestock
Janice Fargher
Jesusa Figueroa
Jackie Foulkes
Eleni Gabre-Madhin
Seble Gabre-Madhin
Earl Gardner
Debbie Garvin
Jon Gibbon
Lene Gjerding
Peter Grafe
Janette Green
Melody Hagemeier
Byron Hall
Jay Horton
Scott Houser
Jon Huston
Esther Keefer
Leroy Kellum
Tami Kocsis
Janelda Koehn
Charity Lantey
Kim Lasse
Steve Lindholm
Jon Marrow
Twyla McPherson
Paul Mifflin
Reade Mitchell
Margie Muiruri
Sheri Myatt
Marcia Neil
Frances Ngumbi
Rose Nthiwa
Bunny Pattison
Kent Paulson
Randal Pearce

1982 Cont...
Mamello Pheko
Ricky Phillips
Mick Rineer
Rachel Roberts
Mary Lou Robinson
Dave Rosenau
Andrea Russell
Ingrid Sagsletten
Paul Scott
Paula Senter
Sam Sibley
Cathy Smith
Nate Steury
Jon Stewart
Brian Sturkie
Pam Swafford
Adrian Thomas
Roger Thomas
Ruth Thomas
Sheri Van Wyk
Diane Voetmann
Kathy Walberg
Cherrie Walker
Tammy Ward
Walter Waweru
Karen Wehrenberg
Scott Whitson
Flo Woodhams
Linda Woods
Paul Woods

1983
Aba Ankrah
Mark Baker
Mark Bally
Peggy Bannister
David Batlle
Jeff Baumann
Gideon Berhanu
Jeff Bodenhamer

1983 Cont...
Kathy Borman
Marika Bosse
Irene Bugimbi
Victoria Bugimbi
Greg Butler
Derek Byler
Kristin Carlson
Jan Cook
Phil Cooley
Greg Cunningham
Doryce Douglin
Denise Dretke
Don Dunkerton
Karen Ennis
Sharon Ennis
Elinda Enright
Sue Ferguson
Carmina Figueroa
Charisa Figueroa
Fred Gardner
Julia Garner
Bonnie Ghrist
Kelly Green
Mark Groom
Kennedy Kamwathi
Sarah Keefer
Nduku Kiiti
Kikwai Kiprono
Danny Koech
Mary Komen
Bryan Lane
Linda Lasse
Jusline Lempaka
David List
Wilson Mburu
Nkrumah Mngola
Keith Mueller
Patrick Munga
Maria Munoz
Madaliso Murharika

1983 Cont...
Curtis Myers
John Myers
Muthue Ngumbi
Faye Nicolaison
Charles Phifer
Ruth Ricker
Donna Sipe
Mike Steeves
Dawit Tekye
Sallie Waddill
Bobby Webb
Joan White
Ken White
Kathy Wood

1984
Jim Abendroth
Bruce Allen
David Alloway
Peggy Amstutz
Allen Balisky
James Bardwell
Mark Bardwell
Rajpal Brar
Franco Brescia
Perry Brinkeback
Carol Burrow
Jeff Butler
Patricia Carlson
Heather Charity
Jackie Charity
Marlene Cook
Jennifer Dement
David Dixon
Jack Ellison
Ralph England
Laurie Erickson
Glenn Erion
Diane Fargher
Scott Ferguson

1984 Cont...
Greg Forman
Nadine Frew
Patricia Fulbright
Phil Grose
Lisa Hampton
Megan Hunter
Jennifer Huss
Lynn Hutchins
Jennifer Jacobsen
Joanna Jones
Ajit Joseph
Ndunge Kiiti
Karon Kingsley
Paul Koning
Peter Lewis
Lillian Lister
Tim Locken
Charles Mburu
Bonar McCallum
Barb McClure
Wes McNeely
Edith Miller
Andrew Mitchell
Brenda Mngola
Rebecca Moore
Robin Moore
Dwight Mueller
Darren Mullenix
Don Musen
Mike Ness
Mulei Ngumbi
Mark Parker
Prashula Patel
Tammie Rape
Solofo Razafinarivo
Ruth Rhea
Elizabeth Ricker
Michael Robert
Mary Rowe
Christine Schaaf

1984 Cont...
Tseday Sirak
Scott Smith
Kirk Spain
Tim Stevens
Sandy Stobbe
Pam Thomas
Steve Turner
Colleen Walker
Carrie Watson
David Watts
Dawn Wesche
Christalene Weyrick
Debbie Willner
Mark Woodhams
Susan Young

1985
Dave Abendroth
John Adams
Kip Anderson
Peter Anderson
Sharon Barnett
Sheila Barrow
Fred Beam
Gideon Belete
Enock Belete
Nina Bosse
Bob Bowers
Leslie Brant
Robin Brown
Mitch Brown
Pam Brubeck
Barb Bunch
Sean Canady
Becky Cass
Kristi Chapman
Lina Cherogony
Peta Cooley
Edward Densham

1985 Cont...	1985 Cont...	1986 Cont...
Steve Dickens	Erika Olsen	Grace Broomes
Dawn Downing	Rachel Phifer	Russ Buchwalter
Dona Elliston	Daren Phillips	Karen Carlson
Sara Jo Entz	Mark Phillips	Kelly Chapman
Jace Fahnestock	Rhonda Posein	Ellen Chege
Barbie Fast	Heather Primrose	Scott Cousens
Lars Fjose	Glenn Quanbeck	Julie Crandall
Brent Foreman	Donna Rae	Ted Davis
Chris Franz	Janice Redekopp	Karen Desjardine
Mark Frew	Denise Robert	Ashiana Dhillon
Joe Garner	Danny Rowe	Debbie Dolifka
Judy Grafe	Janne Sannesmoen	Shelley Downing
Brian Grennell	Ken Schoemaker	Steve Faustino
Joelle Grooms	Debbie Steury	Dan Franz
Elleni Hailu	Melissa Stewart	Ralph Granados
Karen Harding	Rachel Stough	Scott Hampton
Tim Hodges	Sylvia Suganadam	Sarah Harris
Richard Homeier	Teresa Swafford	Rob Heuer
Kelly Hopkins	Tim Tyner	Darryl Hollingsworth
Diane Hurlburt	Jeff Walberg	Vegard Holmedahl
Steven Judd	Jeff Willner	Ian Hunter
Brenda Kauffman	Andy Wolford	David Huston
Cara Kirkpatrick	Phil Workman	Anil Joseph
Hanne Kristiansen	Vickie Young	Steve Kaufman
Susan Lacy		Andy Kilpatrick
Derek Lane	1986	Andrea Kitchen
Timo Lantey	Andy Andersen	Shannon Koop
Renee Lasse	Carolyn Andersen	Soili Kurkola
Lloyd Lepage	Robb Andersen	Robert Lapka
Sabrina Lo	Tammy Andersen	Kelly Lasse
Sharalyn Lyon	Jean Andersen	Craig Linquist
Roger Maillefer	Ashild Austgulen	Tom Lo
Tim Mechem	Kevin Barnes	Lynda Locken
Molly Mitchell	Karen Barnett	Ruth Lohnes
Chris Moore	Russ Baumann	Andy Lyon
Phillip Ngezayo	Bill Bergman	Thomas Mahinda
Curtis Nissly	Michael Bossler	Trevor Maxwell
Bruce Noden	Chris Bransford	Jon McCallum
Noella Akwiri	Debbie Brogden	Javan Mngola
Raposhi Ole Sein		

1986 Continued...
Lori Morrison
Trevor Nandi
Darrin Nicolle
Wayne Nissly
Sandi Norton
Suzi Norton
Nancy Otto
Lora Piercey
Tim Rape
Jim Ryckman
Emmanuel Sentanda
Dan Shewmaker
Arne Solbakken
Craig Sorley
Oddbjorn Stangeland
Cedric Steffens
Anne-Marie Steinkuller
Karen Strong
Praveen Suganandam
Philip Ward
Brian Wells
Annette Zacho

1987
Jackie Anderson
Damon Auer
Charmaine Arthur
Karin Austin
Greg Bakke
Loren Balisky
Jennifer Ball
Susan Baumann
Cathy Bomett
Peter Bowers
Beth Brown
Bruce Buckwalter
Tonya Clair
Adam Clements
Dan Cochrane
Beth Densham

1987 Cont...
Leona Devries
Mike Dickens
Dan Dixon
Jenny Doggett
Lisa Erickson
Scott Fredricks
Greg Freshour
Renatta Gastineau
Sheryl Hansen
Brent Hanson
Dan Harding
Ted Harkema
Joe Henderson
David Hodges
Rebekah Homeier
Tammy Hopkins
Winston Joffrion
David Karumuna
Christine Kaufman
Jim Keefer
Ron Lapka
Becky Logan
Jon Long
Christine Loveday
Sheryl Lund
Gordie MacGowen
Scott Martin
Jason Maxwell
Aric Meyer
Judy McCallum
Donia McCully
Todd McPherson
Karen Miller
Keith Miller
Renita Miller
Gena Moore
Rick Morse
Kevin Mullenix
Nomusa Mzimela
Angela Ndemange

1987 Cont...
Liza Nelson
Chris Ness
Nyoli Nicolle
Cindy Quanbeck
Amber Rhodes
Staci Ross
Marcus Shewmaker
Alicia Sibley
Kristin Synder
Caryn Sorley
Maryann Spahr
Cheryl Stough
Brian Strong
Graham Swinfen
Craig Turner
Jim Turner
Tim Wetzel
Deborah Workman
Chaeran Yoo
Andrew York

1988
Heather Andersen
Tadd Andersen
Joy Anstice
Kerri Armstrong
Tim Austin
Kevin Balisky
David Bardwell
Glenn Barnett
Sharon Barrow
Denicia Bass
Tim Bliss
Andy Bossler
Andy Bowen
Sara Bowers
Richard Bransford
Harpreet Brar
Richard F. Brogden
Jolene Byler

1988 Cont...
Matt Canady
Eric Church
Cathy Clements
Rachel Clements
Robert Cousins
Heather Daub
Caroline Davis
Kristin Davis
Trevor Demille
Peter Dirkson
Darryl Dison
Philip E. Dow
Susie Entwistle
Todd Everden
David Fannin
Hudson Fahnestock
Steve Farag
Tony Fuller
Rebecca Garvin
Kristin Hales
Sharon Hales
Duane Hall
Scott Hanson
Heather Harkema
Myra Harris
Diethelm Hartmann
Andy Heuer
Becky Huston
Eric Kamau
Kendell Kauffeldt
Ben Kilpatrick
Kyle D. Kirkpatrick
Silja Kurkola
Melody Lyon
Dorothy Maingi
Mumbua Makau
Jondo Malafa
Karen Martin
Phil Matthewson
Jennifer McCollough

1988 Cont...
Brian McKenzie
Bart McNeely
Ron Miller
Sandra Mueller
Troy "Choo" Neuenberg
Chris Oldford
Charlie Orange
Steve Piercey
Debra Pollard
Chris Richardson
Guy Roabaugh
Scott Rowland
Claude Shabantu
Gayle Shewmaker
D. Kevin Smith
David Stevens
Graham Strong
Rich Todd
Terry Toso
Altaz Valani
Mark Wardley
Matt Weaver
Debbie Wenninger
Eddie Weyrick
Jack H. Wilson II
Heather Wilton
Suzanne York

1989
Jeff Allison
Kara Austin
Steve Barnes
Jeff Barnett
Kristin Barnett
Richard Batlle
Mary Beth
Bergman
Janey Berry
James Biel

1989 Cont...
Marit Brandsma
Mohanjeet Brar
Beckie Brogden
Winston Broomes
Tim Brown
Dan Brubeck
Rob Burrow
Melanie Bustrum
Arnold Carlson
Mirium Chege
Evan Church
Bob Clements
Jeni Daub
John Davis
Karen Davis
Davis Dillard
John Dilworth
Melanie Dolifka
Heather Dunkerton
Gerry Dyer
Tina Falk
Mark Fredricks
Jeff Freshour
Robyn Gastineau
Kristan Grennell
Ricky Hasse
Tanya Hales
Brenda Harding
Martin Hartmann
Phil Hodges
Mark Hollingsworth
Allison Hope
Bill Houser
Jon Hovingh
Gina Hulin
Libby Inlow
Paul Kaufman
Justin Kelly
Samantha Koehn

1989 Cont…	1990 Cont…	1990 Cont…
Tina Konnerup	Scott Canady	David Kuguru
Ken Kratzer	Noel Carpenter	Burleigh Law
Eric Kurtz	Michelle Chandler	Julie Lout
Tracy Kurtz	Lori Chapman	Doug Lund
Stephanie Law	May Cherogony	Evans M'Narodi
Jennifer Long	Heather Corbitt	Mutwiri M'Narobi
Carrie Loveday	Norma Dakowah	Lynda Macgowan
Allan MacGowan	Sherrie Dickens	Zeb Mengistu
Andrea Mayer	Christy Dow	Wes Minor
Dori McCulley	Nichole Dyer	Hope Mitchell
Jared Miller	Steve Eaton	Brad Moreland
Neil Miller	Steve Entwistle	Bret Moreland
Amy Mitchell	Berit Eirckson	Mike Morrison
Monica Morris	David Erickson	Esther Muigai
Holly Musen	Rachal Erickson	Kris Oliver
Christina Pedersen	Kristen Evernden	Ryan Oliver
Hans Olav Raen	Ruben Falk	Shep Owen
Susie Randall	Damian Fannin	Jim Parker
Jon Ricker	B. A. Florian	Melanie Parker
Tanvir Sidhu	Katrina Garrison	Kirk Phifer
Lakelie Simoneaux	Nathan Gehman	Andres Pollard
Kristi Spain	Rebekah Good	Luke Prentice
Michelle Stevens	Jessica Greenlee	Lilli Quanbeck
Michel Stringfield	Kristina Hansen	Vicki Quanbeck
Walter Walberg	Mark Harman	Matt Rhodes
Pam Ward	Sharon Harris	Mike Schimming
Charles Wilson	Peter Hartmann	Brian Seiler
Gina Wilson	Desta Haspels	Phil Shuart
	Monica Hauxwell	Kent Smith
1990	Mike Henshaw	Bryan Snyder
David Anonby	Carrie Hess	Esther Stewart
Sharon Beck	Jennifer Hoffmaster	David Stillman
Paul Besole	Marny Hopkins	Bruce Strong
Nathan Belete	Moira Hunter	Angela Swafford
Laura Berkely	Rachal Jongeward	Maria Takkunen
Sherrie Bontrager	Irene Kamau	Kiri Tan
Steve Bossler	Kelvin Kauffeldt	Michelle Warner
Amy Brown	Tim Kirinda	Lisa Weaver
Laura Brown	Vija Krishnan	Elizabether Werlinder
Jonathan Buth	Lisa Krohn	Elissa Weston

1990 Cont...
Jeff Wilson
Bruce Wilton
David Yohannes

1991
Christopher Adala
Kathryn Allison
Caroline Andrew
Kristine Arensen
Cindy Armstrong
Ruthann Baker
Kathryn Bardwell
Melissa Barnett
Andrew Barr
Artin Barzgar
Karen Beam
Russell Berry III
Lisa Bontrager
Bethany Bransford
Aaron Brent
Julie Brubacher
Wendi Buboltz
Amanda Byllesby
Jason Carpenter
Grant Casady
Lillian Chege
Andrew Clarke
Stephen Cochrane
Michel Colen
Timothy Colen
Sharon Cook
Heathcliff Costabir
Natasha Costabir
William DeLaughter
Gillian Densham
Richard Dilworth
Timothy Dixon
David Downing
Krisy Eppy

1991 Cont...
William Fuller
Brian Garrison
Rene Gastineau
Mark Grafe
Maury Hayashida
Benjamin Hekman
Nathaniel Hekman
Brandon Hoult
Jason Hovingh
Shelah Hubbard
Allan Josiah
Diana Kile
Tania Mahinda
Anna Mattson
Tanya Maxwell
Rosemary McCullough
John Molyneux
Elizabeth Morse
Nathalya Ngezayo
Nereah Okanga
Eva Rapold
Catherine Rhodes
Genevieve Rhodes
Jeffrey Rhodes
Renae Ross
Paul Saoshiro
Jeremy Scales
Merilee Shattenberg
Janna Stroup
Emily Van Fleet
Jonathan Walker
Joseph Weaver
Todd Whitmer
Soo Me Yoo

1992
Maria Backstrom
Rachel Baird
Karolyn Bardwell

1992 Cont...
Michael Barnett
Phil Bedsole
Holly Berkley
Debbie Bowers
Amanda Boyle
Kenna Braddock
Muno Brar
Laura Brubaker
Clint Brubeck
Joy Bustrum
Rachel Buth
Abigail Clements
Lori Clements
Zach Corbitt
Beckie Daub
Jeff Davis
Jon Day
Jesus De la Torre
Shelly Dick
Steve Dunham
Mark Dunkerton
Meagan Erickson
Alyssa Fader
Daniel Garner
Jonathan Grebe
William Hasse
Yohannes Hailu
Chuck Haspels
Cora Hegler
Anne Henderson
Andrew Herrod
Pam Hersman
James Hess
Jordan Hodges
Christina Hoffmaster
Ruth Imende
Suzanne Jeffers
Mirjam Jensen
Faith Jongeward

1992 Cont...
Angela Joseph
Amy Kerich
Hyun-Ji Kim
Kim Kirkeeide
Kevin Krohn
Scott Lout
Mumbi M'Narobi
Debbie Malumbe
Tom Mboya
Mara Miller
Oddvar Naustvik
Erik Ness
Heidi Newbery
David Njoroge
Moses Osiru
Julie Otto
Carol Ouko
Rosemary Owino
Outi Palmu
Jonathan Partelow
Shannon Petersen
Kathryn Roach
Rebecca Rowse
Charlotte Savage
Andrew Scudder
James Scudder
Andre Shabantu
Lynn Sillavan
Amy Sivage
Scott Stelck
Pamela Strong
Billy Stroup
Nalini Suganandam
Rehma Suleman
Vernon Swanepoel
Markus Takkunen
Ezekial Tan
Kenya Thompson
Beth Turner
Angela Waddill

1992 Cont...
Lavinia Wasawo
Rachel Watters
Aaron Wenger
Silas West
Jonathan Wilton
John Yates

1993
Fikerte Abede
Jennifer Akins
Philip Andersen
Lisa Arensen
Rebecca Barnes
Jeremy Barr
Jared Barrow
Charity Bishop
Deborah Brown
Mark Brubacher
Joseph Burchel
Lucas Casady
Sanjit Chadha
Paul Chandler
Sophie Chinchen
Vila Cobb
Foluke Cole
Christy Davis
Timothy Day
Kathleen Eaton
Gitte Falk
Naomi Gabler
Rebecca Hasse
Douglas Hanna
Heather Harman
Alysia Hawkins
Elizabeth Henderson
Erik Hersman
Jon Hildebrandt
Christian Holmedahl

1993 Cont...
Kendrica Jackson
Victoria Kiambi
Carmen Koetz
Esther Langford
Raymond Lapka
Daniel Lins
Eric Mbuu
Rebecca Minor
Margaret Muigai
Noel Mwangi
Evalyna Ngezago
Coriena Nicolle
Asante Nsilo-Swai
Lora Oliver
Amy Owen
Lauri Palmu
Jennifer Randolph
Timothy Ricker
Philip Rowse
Ian Rowsell
Robinson Rupp
Tomoko Saoshiro
Elizabeth Scudder
Kari Shattenberg
Timothy Shuart
Genevieve Shultz
Pekka Soderlund
Grant Swanepoel
Sam Talala
Gladys Tan
Bethany Tapp
Cerissa Thompson
Beth Tippett
Jessica Van Fleet
Kathryn Watson
Jill Wilson
Robin Young

1994
Stephen Aim
James Albright
Martha Allison
James Baker
Jonathan Ball
Cheryl Barr
Peter Bedsole
Kayla Braddock
Richard Brooks
Sara Brubaker
Sharon Buth
Brian Casady
Eunice Chege
Sandy Chilcote
Jennifer Christian
Christopher Clair
Chad Coats
Chandra Coleman
Shawn Collins
Heidi Conrad
Peter Cowles
Emily Creson
Patricia Leigh Davis
Jedidjah De Waal
Andeep Dhillon
Melody Dick
Brandon Dillard
Sonya Dilworth
Kent Dunham
Christopher Earedensohn
Taletha Enoch
Dwayne Eppy
Nathan Gabler
Anthony Garrison
Angie Garvin
Michael Graber
Elizabeth Gray
Hannele Gutt
Steven Harding
Heather Herrod

1994 Cont...
Esther Herron
Jeanette Holcomb
Joyellen Hovingh
Markus Ilomaki
Elizabeth Imende
Timothy Jeske
John Kratzer
Kenny Kuguru
Kimmo Kuosmanen
Peter LeBlanc
Chinyelu Lee
Meredith Lee
Naomi Leonard
Jorn Lillebo
Marita Lillebo
Monica Lo Russo
Mesay Lulsegged
Daniel Lund
Makoyo Makoyo
Oloo Makoyo
Cheryl Martin
Isabel Matwawana
Amanuel Mengistu
Jonathan Miller
Sharon Morad
Constance Mosha
Kari-Pekka Murtonen
George Njiiri
Edna Ogada
Patricia Owino
James Peterson Jr.
Ashley Plett
Adrian Roach
Suzanne Rorabaugh
Jeremy Rupp
John Savage
Jamie Scheer
Joy Seiler
Joy Stillman
Mark Thompson

1994 Cont...
Elizabeth Turman
Crystal Velasquez
Wendy Wetzel
Sandra Wilton
Paul Yoo

1995
Kimberly Akins
Katherine Arensen
Andrew Baumann
Nathanael Bennet
Ralph Boyle
Jonathan Bransford
Susan Bransford
Carrie Brock
Sarah Brooks
Johanna Buck
John Cady
Jason Carroll
Stephanie Caulley
Jennifer Clements
Cheryl Cornett
Brenton Correll
Hannah Dainty
Shawn Deal
Carrie Doty
Alisha Dyck
Cameron Epp
Jason Fader
Sara Farnsworth
Samuel Ferguson
Karyn Gardner
Joy Gehman
Hannah Gillihan
Richard Hanna
John Haspels
Timothy Hawkins
Malia Hayashida
Shannon Hodges
Elaine Kerich

1995 Cont…	1996	1996 Cont…
Esther Kile	Heather Adkins	Samuli Kivimaki
Leigh Kirkeeide	Seung Ahn	Brian Klotz
Mumbe Kithakye	Elizabeth Albright	Nathan Langford
Rachael Komant	Edward Andersen	James Langston
Nathan Laity	Sarah Ball	Lori LeBlanc
Laura Lins	Premo Brar	Sarah Leonard
Brian Mbuu	Lillian Brubaker	Amanda Madden
Clancey McNeal	Catrin Bryne	Andre Madsen
Heidi Michael	Dan Carpenter	Kathleen Messer
Jacob Mills	Saranjit Chadha	Nina Miettinen
Jonathan Mirich	Venessa Chandler	Natalee Miller
Stephan Morad	Amanda Christian	Amanda Mooney
Mikewa Ogada	Brian Collier	Kivunzi Musili
Vivian Ojal	Erin Dainty	Thomas Mwarabu
Sandy Olenik	Ana Rosa de la Torre	April Ness
Benjamin Oliver	Nathan Dodson	Sharon Ngok
Andrew Ouko	Josh Dyck	Hak-Chul Park
Mirium Pedersen	Nathan Engebretson	Christine Penny
Michelle Persons	Phillip Enoch	Gayle Pollard
Chad Pumpelly	Trevor Epp	Courtney Pugh
Mirium Rasmussen	Scott Evans	Lisa Pumpelly
Melody Ricker	Jeremy Feser	Rochelle Raybuck
Douglas Rutten	Amy Gardner	Teresa Rutten
Samara Sanchez	Matthew Gordon	Malaika Scudder
Uta Saoshiro	Stephen Graham	Christopher Sheach
Brian Schaad	Hannu Gutt	Keri Sivage
Nathaniel Schmidt	Caroline Haafkens	Elizabeth Stuebing
James Shattenberg	Michael Hamline	Jonathan Sugimoto
Rachel Skinner	Andrew Harding	Laura Talley
Peter Strenstrom	Katherine Hardy	Christopher Teasdale
Joel Takala	Chad Harrington	Cherie Turner
Andrew Tapp	Daniel Herron	Nathan Vanderhoof
James Tatum	Paul Hildebrandt	Daniel Walker
Hannah Tippett	Esther Im	Joshua Washburn
Willem van Steenbergen	Esther Imende	Alice Williams
Annette West	Nathaniel Jeffers	Markus Ylenius
Kelly Whitmer	Dorrit Jensen	
Rachel Williaume	Elijah Johnson	
Karen Wilton	Malaika Johnson	
Kristen Wright	Elizabeth Kiambi	

1997	1997 Cont...	1998
Heath Arensen	Sarah Middleton	Bryan Adkins
Bryan Brock	Bethlehem Mills	Nicole Allison
Amy Buck	Suzanne Morad	Jeffrey Arensen
Ruth Campbell	Luke Morrison	Reid Arensen
Joy Clark	Sussan Munoru	Mark Barany
Gregory Collins	Philip Mwarabu	Jacquelyn Beckett
Timothy Cowles	Elicia Nicolle	Ryan Beckett
Robert Cullen	Valerie Njiiri	Austin Bell
Benjamin Dainty	Bonnie Olenik	Adam Bennett
Daniel Davis	Mark Oliver	Keely Brandon
Heidi DeJong	Charles Ouko	Emily Brandon
David DeLaughter	Gi-Hoon Park	Jasmeer Brar
Andrew Eernisse	Simon Pedersen	Heather Brock
Margaret Farnsworth	Andrew Peed	Jennette Brubacher
Kara Gillihan	Elise Perkins	Keri Carpenter
Brian Gray	Karen Powdrill	Angela Canfield
Mark Hales	Christy Prins	Jared Christensen
Heather Hamilton	Luke Raymond	Ryan Critser
Johannah Hegler	Brianne Riley	Aimee Crowl
Jeffrey Herrmann	Bryce Riley	Sara Cunningham
Peter Herron	Christa Ring	James Douglass
Jesse Howard	Frank Rorabaugh	Robert Duncan
Timothy Hudson	Kathryn Ryder	Andrew Engebretson
Kylea Jackson	Timothy Ryon	Timothy Enoch
Jesse Johnson	Anna Scudder	Nadine Feser
Sanna Kivimaki	Shelley Shattenberg	John Fletcher
Jeffery Komant	Lisa Shaw	Rachel Gilbertson
Daniel Law	Siana Sheldrick	Joseph Grant Jr.
Stacy Law	Anastacia Sibley	Bethany Greene
Hyon-Chol Lee	James Skinner	Sarah Hamilton
Andre LeLeu	Peter Slayton	Ryan Harding
Joshua Lewis	Philip Sugimoto	Rebecca Head
Sarah Lins	Russell Tatum	Ruth Hegler
Jennifer Linton	Christopher Toews	Philip Hendersen
William Long	Christine Van Wagenen	Jane Hoover
Mutugi M'Nairobi	Hannah Van Wagenen	Christina Johnson
Iain Mackie	Jacob Washburn	Timothy Jones
Thomas Madden	Cynthia Wasonga	Kavuli Kithakye
Joshua Mann	Leah Williams	Anne Koetz
Simeon McKay		John Lorusso Jr.

1998 Cont...	1999 Cont...	1999 Cont...
Megan Lunberry	James Barfoot	Daniel Long
Mise Kakoyo	Nigel Barham	Sarah Mann
Louise Madsen	Kari Beighle	Derick Mattern
Lora Marston	Ryan Beverly	Belinda Mbuu
Matthew McDonald	Jasmeet Brar	Matthew McCall
Mueni Musili	Jawad Braye	Kristie McKay
Jung-Hoon Park	Sarah Byrne	Keeley McNeal
Bethany Pevey	Daniel Chung	Azariah Mengistu
Jonathan Price	David Collier	Michelle Mitchell
Cara Robbins	Michelle Collins	Kathleen Morrison
Sachin Rupani	Charlie Combs	Michael Munoru
Jody Rupp	Thomas Crane	Minna Murtonen
Cameron Russell	Carrie Critser	Maina Njuguna
Darla Rutten	Jessica Cunningham	Tina Okken
David Sampson	Brian DeJong	Maria Pedersen
Simeon Sanchez	Melissa Dilworth	Bradford Penner
Matthew Scheer	Sarah Dobra	Andrew Persons
Katherine Schuit	Elizabeth Downing	David Poidevin
Andew Sheldrick	Ryan Entwistle	Stephen Poidevin
Kimbra Smith	Eli Fader	Daniel Propst
Katrina Stanton	Shawna Fannin	Krista Propst
Andrea Stirewalt	Rachel Farmer	Elijah Reid
Joan Strong	Erin Gardner	Derek Reimer
Andrea Swanepoel	Jacqueline Gichinga	Amy Roach
Matthew Talley	Letha Gillihan	Nathan Sawatzky
Richard Taylor	Sarah Gordon	Amy Scheel
Timothy Teasdale	Emily Gray	Amy Schoof
Danealle Thompson	Robert Hargrave	Elizabeth Schoof
Sarah Vanderhoof	Patricia Henry	Danielle Shaw
Francis Wanjai	Merrilee Heyer	Heike Skaggs
Jeremy Williams	Heather Jacobson	Joshua Skaggs
	Joshua Jones	Heidi Slayton
1999	Jonelle Judy	Daisy Soderlund
Michelle Adkins	Nathan Kelty	Bethany Sorensen
Jun Hyung Ahn	Anton Kinaiyia	Cara Strauss
Heather Akins	Amy LeBlanc	David Stuebing
Kieran Allen	Kelly LeBlanc	Kimiko Sugimoto
Rebecca Anderson	Yo Sup Lee	Leah Swart
Beth Anstey	Chad Lewis	Andrew Thompson
	Kyle Little	Mark Toews

1999 Cont...
Rachel Tolan
David VanYperen
James Veitch
Christopher Wade
Andrew Warren
Hannah Warren

2000
Bethany Ackerman
Blake Arensen
Michael Arensen
Julia Baker
Krista Baker
Christina Barany
Katherine Brandon
Rachel Brooks
Chrystalene Buhler
Bethany Burk
Rebecca Chinchen
Ayo Cole
Elisa Cook
Matthew Cromer
Jennifer Duerksen
Brent Duncan
Emukule Ekirapa
Steven Enoch
Maggie Evans
Lydia Farmer
Rachel Fletcher
Rodrigo de la Torre
Joshua Ghrist
Daniel Grant
Philip Greene
Kara Harding
Deborah Head
David Henderson
Luke Herron
Sammy Imende
Luke Johnson
Antje Kamminga

2000 Cont...
Sara Kawira
Caleb Kim
Julie Kim
Samuel Kim
Angela Kioko
Amy Kirkland
Rachel Konnerup
Paul Kwon
Issac Lee
Rebecca Linton
Corrie Madden
Elizabeth Madsen
Bethany Mathias
Daniel Mazara
Sophie Mbugua
Charles McCordic
Matthew Mitchell
Stephanie Morad
Michelle Muthiani
Benjamin Neill
Allan Olweny
Hak Park
Hilary Payton
Sarah Pennington
Amber Persons
Miriam Powdrill
Jill Rebert
Nicole Ryan
Michelle Ryon
Rebecca Sanchez
Annie Schuit
Melissa Shaffer
Jonathan Shaw
Krista Smith
Fiona Sortor
Jennelle Speichinger
Marci Stirewalt
Van Thompson
Kipkios Tubei
Sander Verduijn

2000 Cont...
Lisa Wasonga
Rose Williams
Abigail Wolcott
Andrew Wollman
Rachel Wright

2001
Jonathan Adkins
Stephen Anstey
Emily Ardill
Emily Beachy
Amy Broers
Philip Buck
Daniel Byrne
Allison Carroll
Katrina Christian
Nathan Chu
Stephen Chu
Jenifer Cobbs
Jonathan Cobbs
Tunde, Cole
Daniel Collins
David Collins
Rebecca Cook
Rebekah Cornelius
Nathan Cromer
Brett Deal
Jason DeSmidt
Lisa Douglass
Timothy Downing
Brian Engebretson
Neil Entwistle
Caleb Fader
Andrea Fast
Heidi Gillihan
Joshua Hamilton
Amanda Hamline
Virginia Hargrave
Robert Henry
Jeremiah Herrmann

2001 Cont...
Rebecca Hodel
Ann Howard
Tabitha Howard
Joshua Jeffers
Emmanuel Johnson
Jamie Jones
Jeremy Jones
Trixie Kioko
Aleda Klassen
Kindel Kramer
Eric Kreutter
Yo El Lee
Trent Lunberry
Joseph Madden
Aaron Mathias
Luke McAuley
Colin McCordic
Rebecca Mead
Kalkidan Mekuria
Miriam Miller
John Mills
Talisi Mwai
Timothy Neill
Mimi Ng'ok
Magana Njuguna
Jared Olander
Joy Peck
Janine Penner
John Poidevin
Rebekah Poidevin
Heidi Propst
Julie Propst
Sean Reimer
Kirsty Rothery
Cristen Russell
Andrew Ruturi
Andera Scheel
Gwendolyn Shaw
Kevin Shaw
Caleb Slayton

2001 Cont...
Joshua Smith
Audrey Sorensen
Mark Strauss
Caleb Swart
Janet Talley
Michelle Taylor
Ryan Thomas
Johnathon Tidenberg
Jelagat Tubei
Jeremy Turley
Daniel Veitch
Abraham Wanjai

2002
Aaron Adkins
Lian Allen
Christopher Allison
Daniel Anderson Jr.
Luke Ardill
Christina Barham
Caleb Bell
Jordan Belton
Aaron Beverly
Josiah Boehlke
Emily Bouchard
Jeffrey Brown
Maria Bruen
Bonnie Byerly
Alicia Collier
William Cornelius
Randall Cullen
Julie Douglass
Saralee Epp
Hannah Farmer
Allissa Gardner
Ian Ghrist
Joel Ghrist
Faith Githua
Kristen Harding

2002 Cont...
Rachel Head
Jeremy Hoover
Abigail Jarnet
Annette Johnson
Enbi Kim
Lydia Kim
Kristi Kirkland
Aimee Komant
Dawn Kuguru
Eun Hye Kwon
David Leber
Jung-Han Lee
Christopher Lewis
John Lyu
Malene Madsen
Domitila Mashiku
Jakin Mattern
Timothy McDonald
Emily Meredith
Rebekka Mischnick
Michael Mitchell
Timothy Moor
Peter Morrison
Fiona Ngaruro
Colleen Obino
John Okken
Steven Orner
Kevin Panicker
Jin Hun Park
Soo Min Park
Christopher Paulson
Michelle Pierce
Walter Ruigu
Alicia Sawatsky
Amy Schuit
Nathaniel Smith
Jason Speichinger
Erin Sprunger
Kristal Streit
Ruth Techand

2002 Cont...
Heather Thomas
Silas Tolan
John Turley
Paige Witmer
Daniel Wright

2003
Danny Adkins
Josh Bell
Brock Bersgalio
Peter Blosser
Laura Bouchard
Daniel Brobst
Laura Buhler
Jeremy Burk
Nathan Carpenter
Nathan Carter
Elizabeth Cheluget
Hye-Yeon Cho
Ryan Dahlman
Jared Duersen
Julia Farmer
Tim Fosythe
Junior Guimaraes
Janis Hamilton
Becky Hargrave
Kim Harris
Heather Haspels
Lydia Herron
Benji Hodel
Joshua Hoffman
Kati Hoffman
David Hunziker
Cliff Johnson
Sheri Jones
Hanna Kammensjo
Esther Kelty
Young Kim
Kara Klassen
Cheri Kramer

2003 Cont...
Dana Lunberry
Wagaka Makoyo
Tobey Mann
Elsie Mbuguah
Matthew McAuley
Cameron McCordic
Kristen McGinley
Ben Mead
Josephine Muthengi
Nicholaus Mwai
Carolyne Njihia
Wanjiku Njunguna
Ashley Paulson
Michelle Perret
Donnie Price
Sam Ray
Joshua Rothery
Andrew Scheer
Candice Selph
Bethany Shaw
Neville Sheldrick
Micah Slayton
Laura Smith
Jamie Soderland
Ellim Song
Hyng Sup Song
Shelah Swart
Kyle Talley
Philip Techand
Libby Tedder
Jonathan Teusink
Laura Tidenberg
Ashley Tocco
Rachel Vinton
Michael Williams
Luke Witmer
Aaron Wolcott

APPENDIX D

AN ANALYSIS OF POLLOCK AND VAN REKEN'S CONCLUSIONS REGARDING THE ISSUE OF SEPARATION AND THE TCK

THE ISSUE OF SEPARATION IS ABSOLUTELY CENTRAL TO any discussion of MK education and MK emotional and psychological health. If separation is inherently harmful to those who experience it, then evangelical churches and organizations worldwide have a moral obligation to rethink, if not fundamentally restructure, their missions programs. It is important to remember that most of the research seems to argue that separation, in and of itself, is neutral. And yet the study by Pollock and Van Reken deserves a closer look because of its size (it was one of the largest done to that point –1986); and because of who conducted the study (for years Pollock and Van Reken have been two of the most well-respected authorities in the field of MK/TCK issues).

As I mentioned in the main body of this book, in *The TCK Experience* Pollock and Van Reken produced research that they believed proved that the cycles of separation experienced by the boarder had a significantly negative impact on at least 40% of third culture kids (TCKs).[1] They contended that the chronic cycles of separation created in

---

[1] Pollock, Dave and Ruth Van Reken, *The Third Culture Kid Experience: Growing Up among Worlds*, Intercultural Press, Maine: 1999, p. 302. TCKs include all children growing up in a culture other than their own, but Pollack and

TCK's "a fear of intimacy because of a fear of loss".[2]   Yet this significant and well-respected study was far from definitive.   Indeed, some of their own research contradicts this conclusion.

If, as Pollock and Van Reken claimed, the cycles of separation were the primary cause of this fear of intimacy in the TCK boarder, then the percentage of those who identified with this fear must necessarily remain essentially the same over time.   Pollock and Van Reken came to the conclusion that this was the case by dividing the TCKs they studied into two broad categories – those born before World War II and those born after it.   They then averaged the sentiments of each group.   When they did this the percentage of respondents who believed the cycles of separation had been harmful was almost equal between the groups (40.1% and 39.2% respectively).[3]   Quite reasonably, from this broad aggregate average they concluded that because the percentages of respondents had remained relatively constant over time, the separation itself must be independently responsible for the pain of these Adult Third Culture Kids (ATCKs).

Yet when we look at their own graphs, the percentages of those who saw separation as a negative factor in their lives varies considerably from one period to the next – strongly implying that other variables do matter. For instance, the group of ATCKs surveyed who were born around 1930 present the largest gap between those who said the separation was positive and those who said it was negative.   Barely 10% of this group believed the cycles of separation had been healthy, while over 40% believed the separation had harmed their ability to experience intimacy and live otherwise healthy emotional lives.[4]

At this point it is absolutely critical to note that this group also represented the peak of those "Separated from parents for longer than one year at a time before the age of 18".   Over 80% of this group fell within that category.[5]   Noteworthy also is the fact that over 30% of this

---

Van Reken deal mainly with the North American children of missionaries – although they are increasingly addressing the concerns of the children of international business people and military personnel as well.   International business families tend to be in major cities with American schools nearby. Military children also have Department of Defense schools, allowing them to live at home.   Therefore when dealing with TCKs and separation due to boarding, they are referring primarily to MKs such as those at RVA.

[2] Ibid.

[3] Ibid.

[4] Pollock and Van Reken, *The Third Culture Kid Experience*, Graph 7, p. 301.

[5] Pollock and Van Reken, *The Third Culture Kid Experience*, Graph 5, p. 299.

group lost a family member to death before the age of 18. Only those born between 1931 and 1935 had a greater chance of losing a family member before they turned 18, at approximately 40%.[6] Finally, this same group of TCKs (those born around 1930) experienced separation from their parents for an average of four years at a time.[7] Before we take a look at a second group, remember that this group of TCKs were among the most likely to say that the cycles of multiple separations had been harmful (40%) and by far the least likely to say the separation had been healthy (10%).

NOW CONSIDER THE group born after 1961. The numbers are almost reversed. Over 35% believed that the cycles of separation had been primarily positive, allowing them to be "more empathetic, independent, etc."; and only 10% believed the separations to have been negative.[8] This group also had no one in it that had lost a family member before they had reached eighteen (compared with 30% in the first group).[9] They also averaged being apart from their parents for less than six months at a time (compared with four years in the first group).[10] Now remember that, for the multiple cycles of separation to be responsible for the fear of intimacy, as Pollock and Van Reken claim, there should be little, if any, variation over time in the perspective of ATCKs towards the experience of separation. But there is variation – significant variation in fact! And what is more, that variation appears to be tied to other variables. This begs the question – what else, beyond separation in and of itself, could be responsible for the significant variation in the TCK's perception of separation?

What was going on during the adolescence of the first group – those born between 1925 and 1930? That's right – WWII! Not only did parents and children experience prolonged and forced separation when the war erupted, but contact between parent and child dried up almost completely. Mail was lost in the chaos of war or it was destroyed as boats carrying it were regularly torpedoed and sunk.[11] Like no other

---

[6] Pollock and Van Reken, *The Third Culture Kid Experience*, Graph 3, p. 296.

[7] Pollock and Van Reken, *The Third Culture Kid Experience*, Graph 4, p. 297.

[8] Pollock and Van Reken, *The Third Culture Kid Experience*, Graph 7, p. 301.

[9] Pollock and Van Reken, *The Third Culture Kid Experience*, Graph 3, p. 296.

[10] Pollock and Van Reken, *The Third Culture Kid Experience*, Graph 4, p. 297.

[11] It should also be noted here that most of those who experienced this separation were separated by the Atlantic Ocean. Because RVA did not have the faculty or facilities to educate high school students prior to WWII most of its students went to the America or England for the remainder of their education.

group before or after it, this group of children was cut off from contact with their parents; but it gets worse. The war (and the disease, famine and violence that it brought) created a scenario in which it was quite likely that these children would lose a parent. Indeed thirty percent lost a loved family member – thirty percent! And even those who did not lose a family member had to live not knowing whether they would see their parents again. Is it any wonder that so many of them grew up with a "fear of intimacy because of a fear of loss"? Simply put, emotionally they could not afford to believe that the separation would not be permanent. They could not afford to trust the relationship and who could blame them.

Contrast their experience with those TCKs born after 1961. By this time RVA, and schools like it, had offered a full college preparatory program, allowing missionary children to remain in Africa until college. The school term was now only three months, giving them regular contact with parents who could, and did, fly in by plane. Further, during the shorter periods of separation, families were more able to communicate regularly by phone or an infinitely faster postal system. For these children, every call and every term ending brought renewed proof that the separation was not permanent and that the relationship was, likewise, permanent. Assuming that the parents had worked to develop a significant bond with their child, that child could put her weight on the promise that their relationship was safe. As a result, when she returned to school, she went with confidence that her parents' love did not end when their presence did. This freed her up to develop that healthy sense of independence and empathy that this group reported experiencing. Remember, over 35% of this group saw the "chronic cycles of separation" as healthy and only 10% viewed it as harmful. This leaves us with 90% who saw the separation inherent in boarding, in and of itself, as either positive or neutral. The point is simply this – radically different circumstances created radically different perspectives on separation among these adult TCKs. Or said differently – separation, in and of itself, was not the issue.

In other words, it was the lack of a fully functioning boarding school, and not its existence, that exacerbated this separation.